THE RATTLER

Writer
Jason McNamara

Artist
Greg Hinkle

Editor
Joel Enos

The Rattler created by
McNamara/Hinkle

INSPIRED BY TRUE EVENTS

IMAGE COMICS, INC.
Robert Kirkman · Chief Operating Officer
Erik Larsen · Chief Financial Officer
Todd McFarlane · President
Marc Silvestri · Chief Executive Officer
Jim Valentino · Vice-President
Eric Stephenson · Publisher
Corey Murphy · Director of Sales
Jeff Boison · Director of Publishing Planning & Book Trade Sales
Jeremy Sullivan · Director of Digital Sales
Kat Salazar · Director of PR & Marketing
Emily Miller · Director of Operations
Branwyn Bigglestone · Senior Accounts Manager
Sarah Mello · Accounts Manager
Drew Gill · Art Director
Jonathan Chan · Production Manager
Meredith Wallace · Print Manager
Briah Skelly · Publicity Assistant
Sasha Head · Sales & Marketing Production Designer
Randy Okamura · Digital Production Designer
David Brothers · Branding Manager
Ally Power · Content Manager
Addison Duke · Production Artist
Vincent Kukua · Production Artist
Tricia Ramos · Production Artist
Jeff Stang · Direct Market Sales Representative
Emilio Bautista · Digital Sales Associate
Leanna Caunter · Accounting Assistant
Chloe Ramos-Peterson · Administrative Assistant
IMAGECOMICS.COM

THE RATTLER OGN
ISBN: 978-1-63215-655-6
FIRST PRINTING. MARCH 2016.

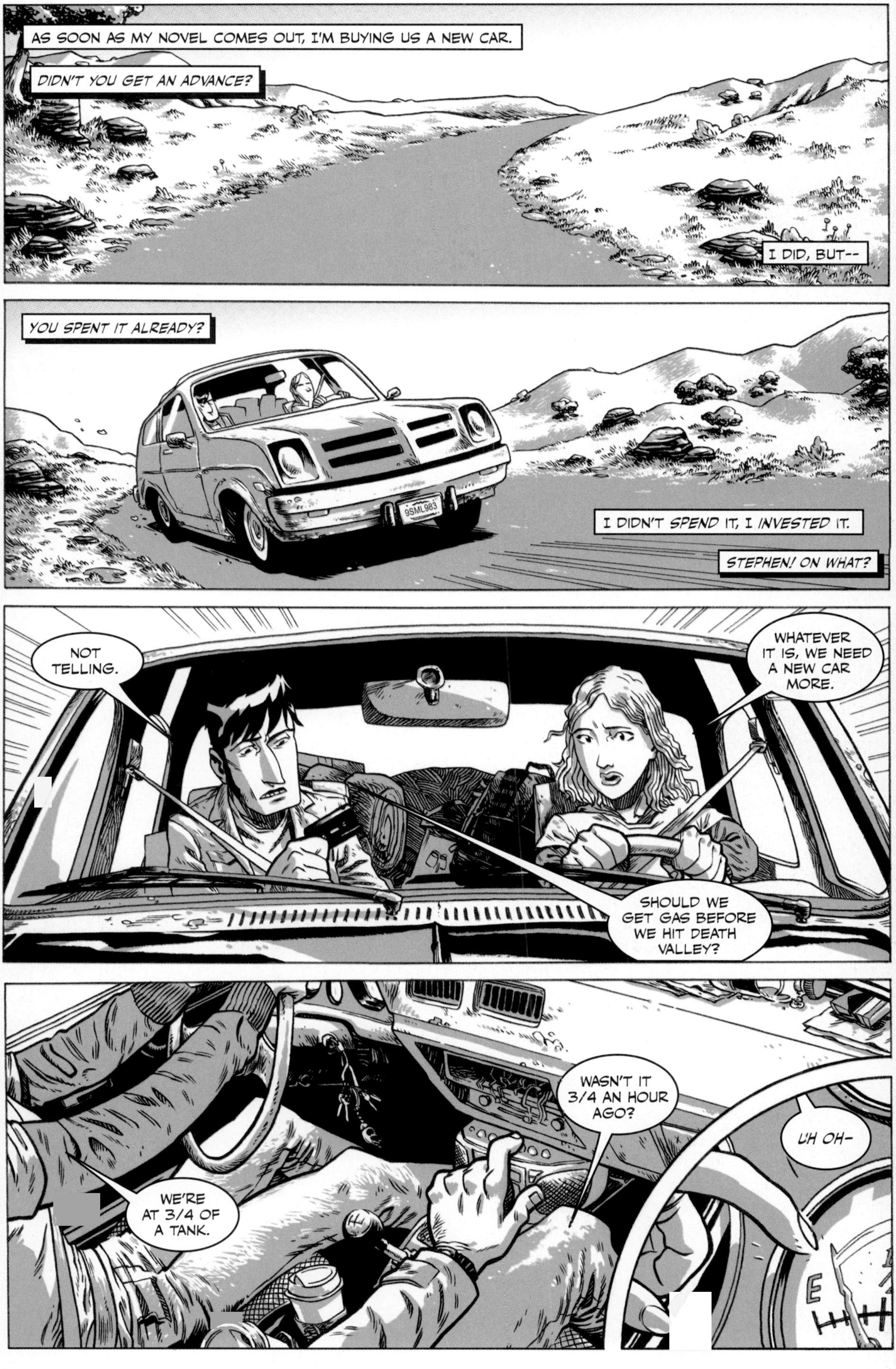
AS SOON AS MY NOVEL COMES OUT, I'M BUYING US A NEW CAR.
DIDN'T YOU GET AN ADVANCE?
I DID, BUT--
YOU SPENT IT ALREADY?
9SML983
I DIDN'T SPEND IT, I INVESTED IT.
STEPHEN! ON WHAT?
NOT TELLING.
WHATEVER IT IS, WE NEED A NEW CAR MORE.
SHOULD WE GET GAS BEFORE WE HIT DEATH VALLEY?
WE'RE AT 3/4 OF A TANK.
WASN'T IT 3/4 AN HOUR AGO?
UH OH-

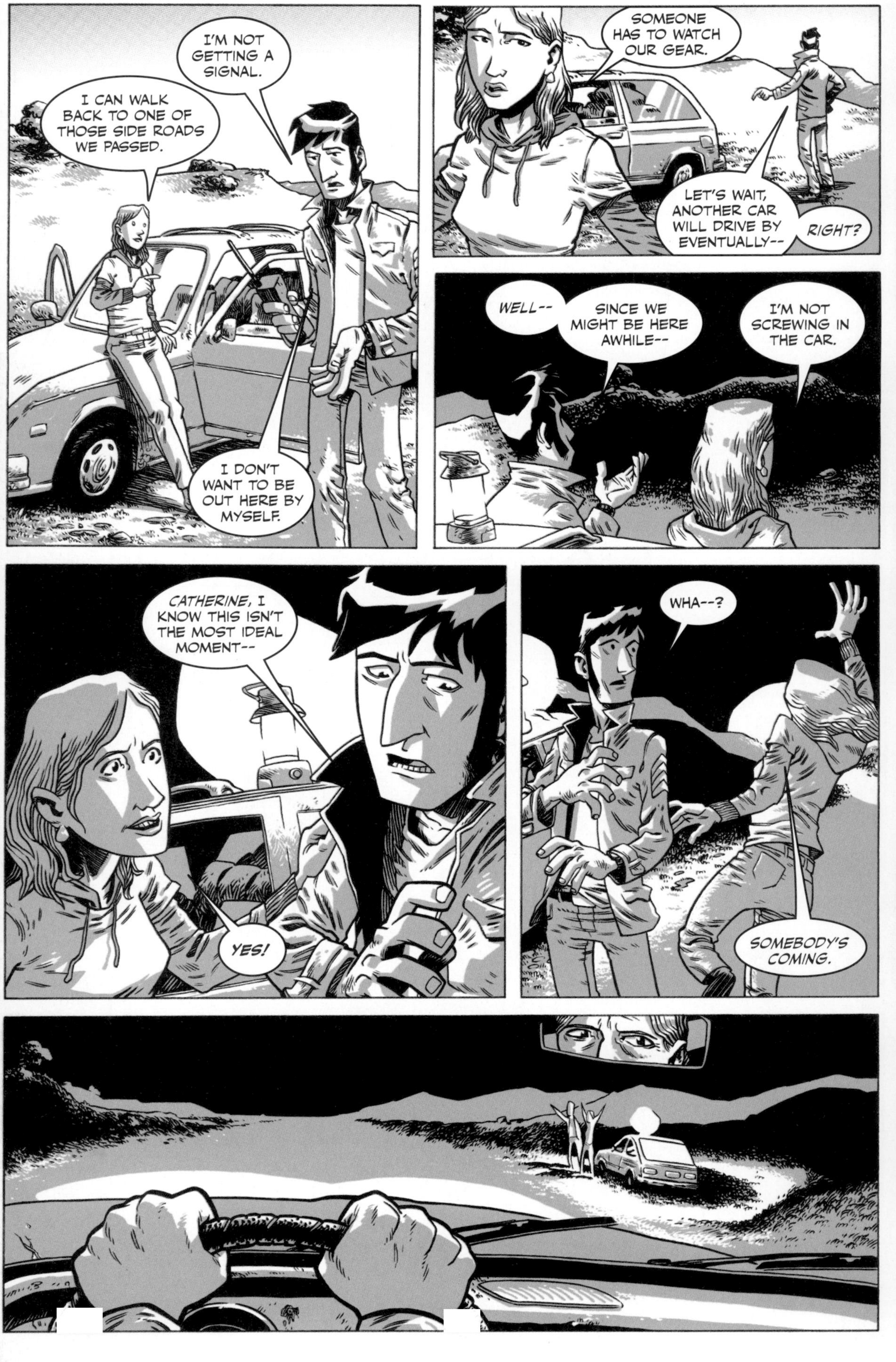
I CAN WALK BACK TO ONE OF THOSE SIDE ROADS WE PASSED.
I'M NOT GETTING A SIGNAL.
I DON'T WANT TO BE OUT HERE BY MYSELF.
SOMEONE HAS TO WATCH OUR GEAR.
LET'S WAIT, ANOTHER CAR WILL DRIVE BY EVENTUALLY--
RIGHT?
WELL--
SINCE WE MIGHT BE HERE AWHILE--
I'M NOT SCREWING IN THE CAR.
CATHERINE, I KNOW THIS ISN'T THE MOST IDEAL MOMENT--
YES!
WHA--?
SOMEBODY'S COMING.

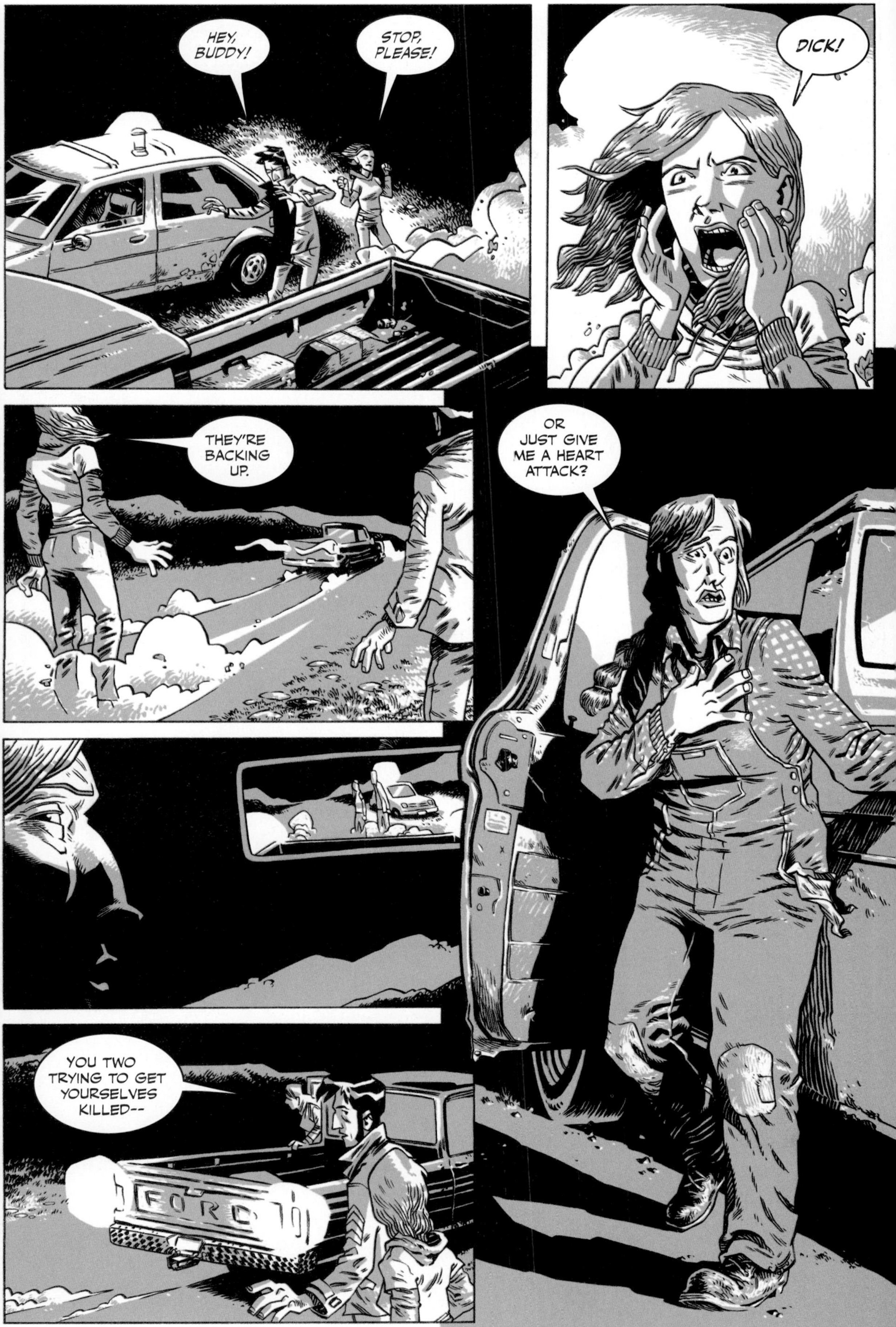
HEY, BUDDY!
STOP, PLEASE!
DICK!
THEY'RE BACKING UP.
OR JUST GIVE ME A HEART ATTACK?
YOU TWO TRYING TO GET YOURSELVES KILLED--
FORD

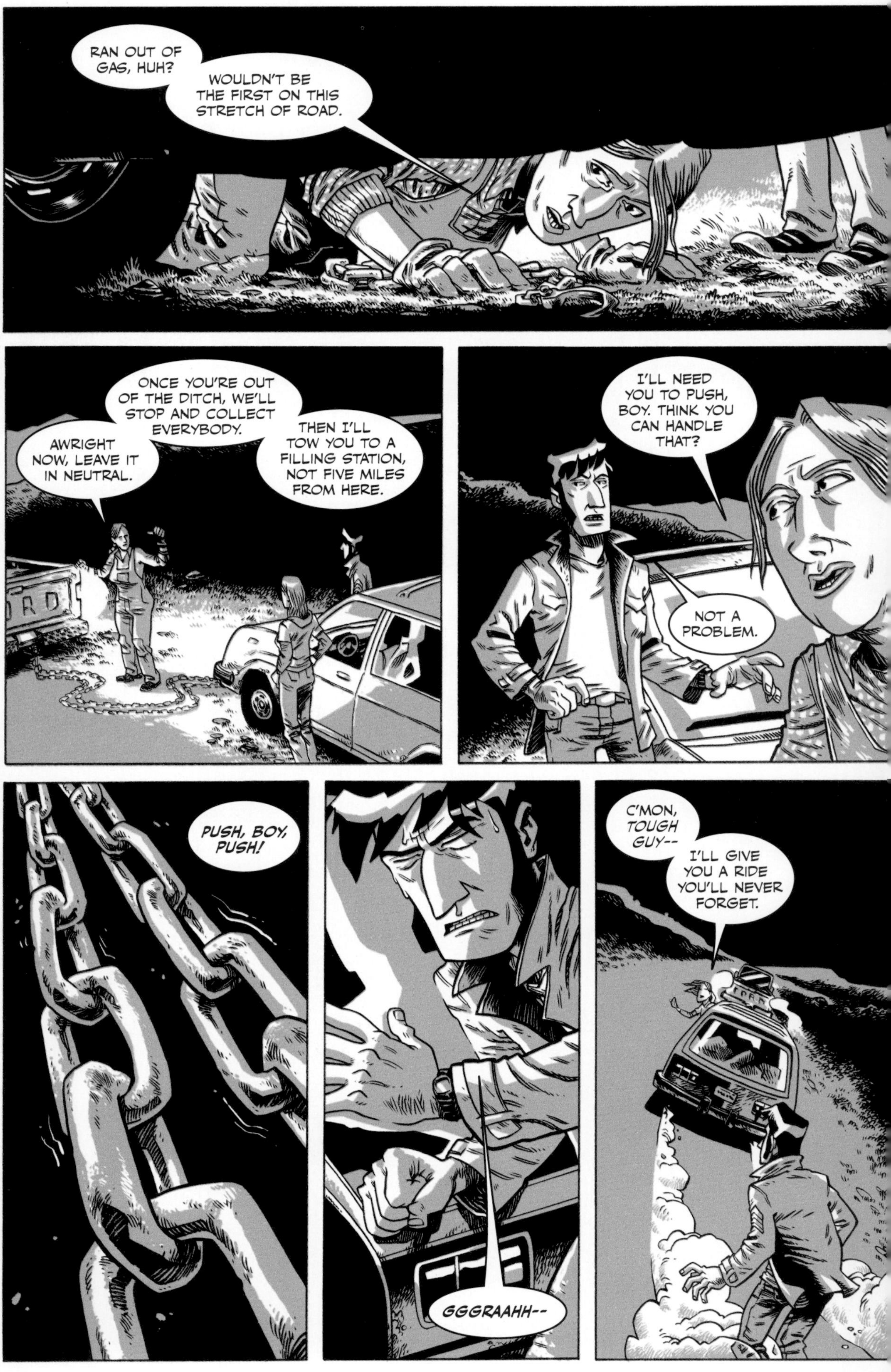
RAN OUT OF GAS, HUH?
WOULDN'T BE THE FIRST ON THIS STRETCH OF ROAD.
AWRIGHT NOW, LEAVE IT IN NEUTRAL.
ONCE YOU'RE OUT OF THE DITCH, WE'LL STOP AND COLLECT EVERYBODY.
THEN I'LL TOW YOU TO A FILLING STATION, NOT FIVE MILES FROM HERE.
I'LL NEED YOU TO PUSH, BOY. THINK YOU CAN HANDLE THAT?
NOT A PROBLEM.
PUSH, BOY, PUSH!
GGGRAAHH--
C'MON, TOUGH GUY--
I'LL GIVE YOU A RIDE YOU'LL NEVER FORGET.

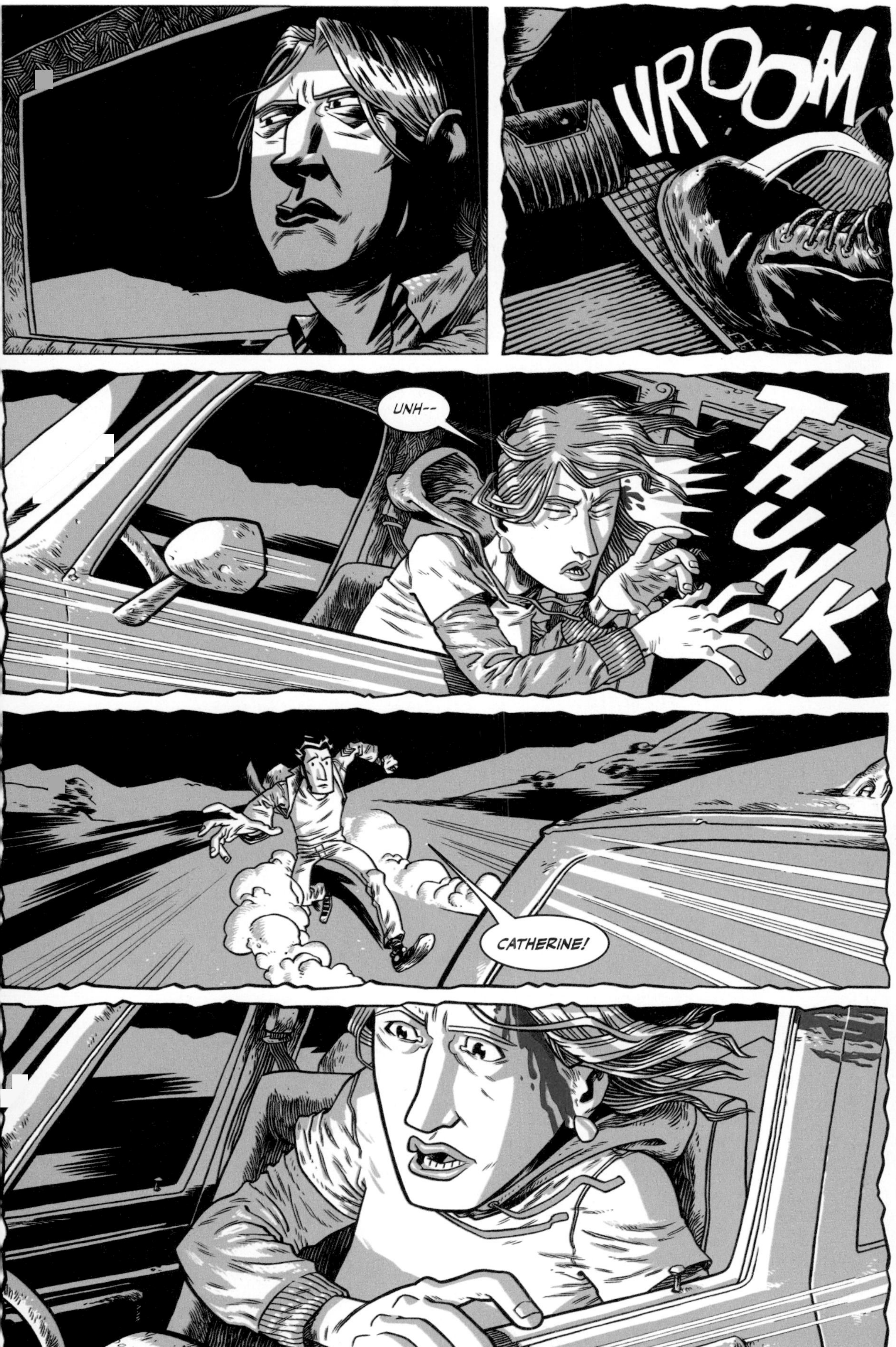
VROOM
UNH--
THUNK
CATHERINE!

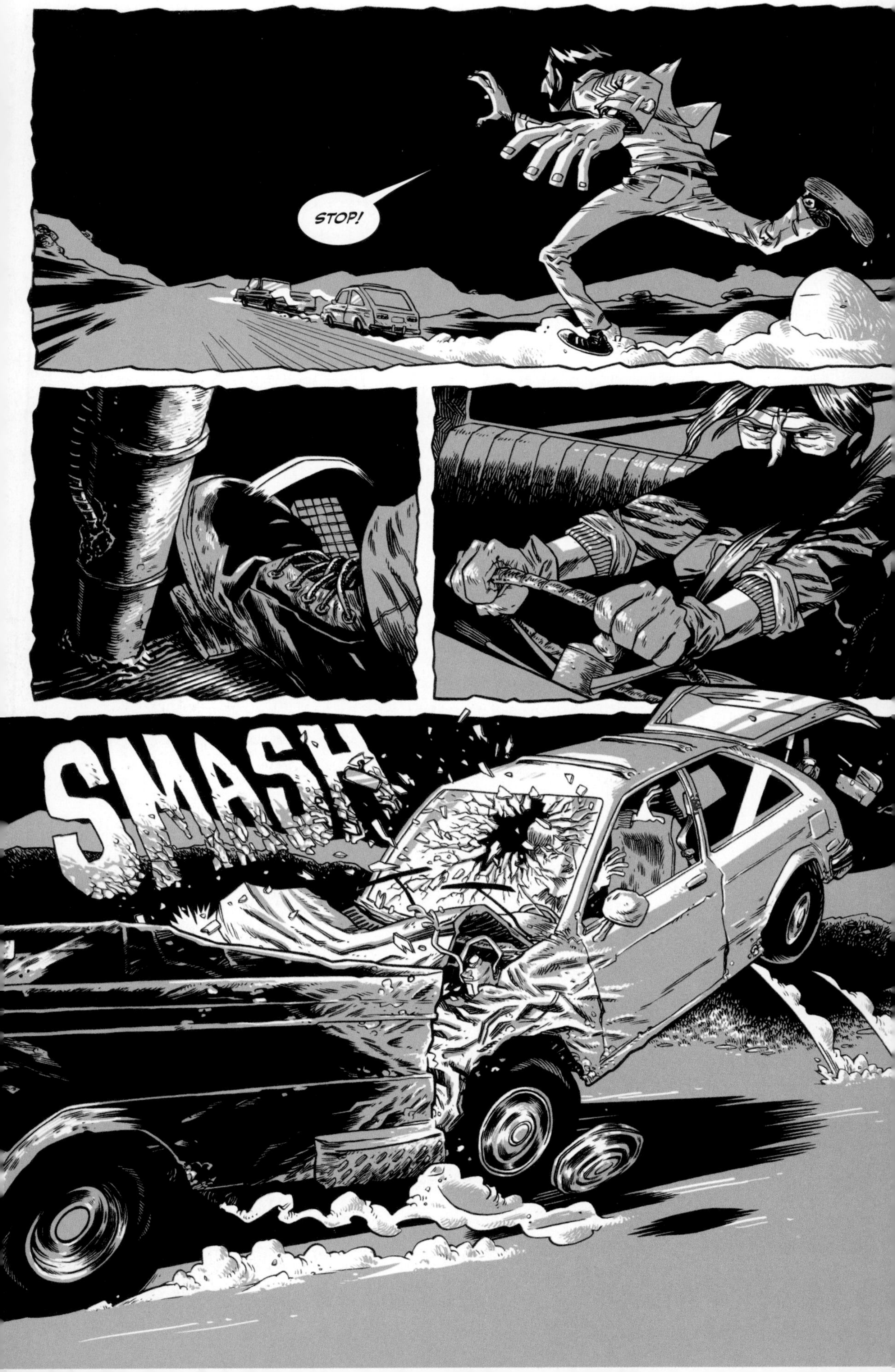
STOP!
SMASH

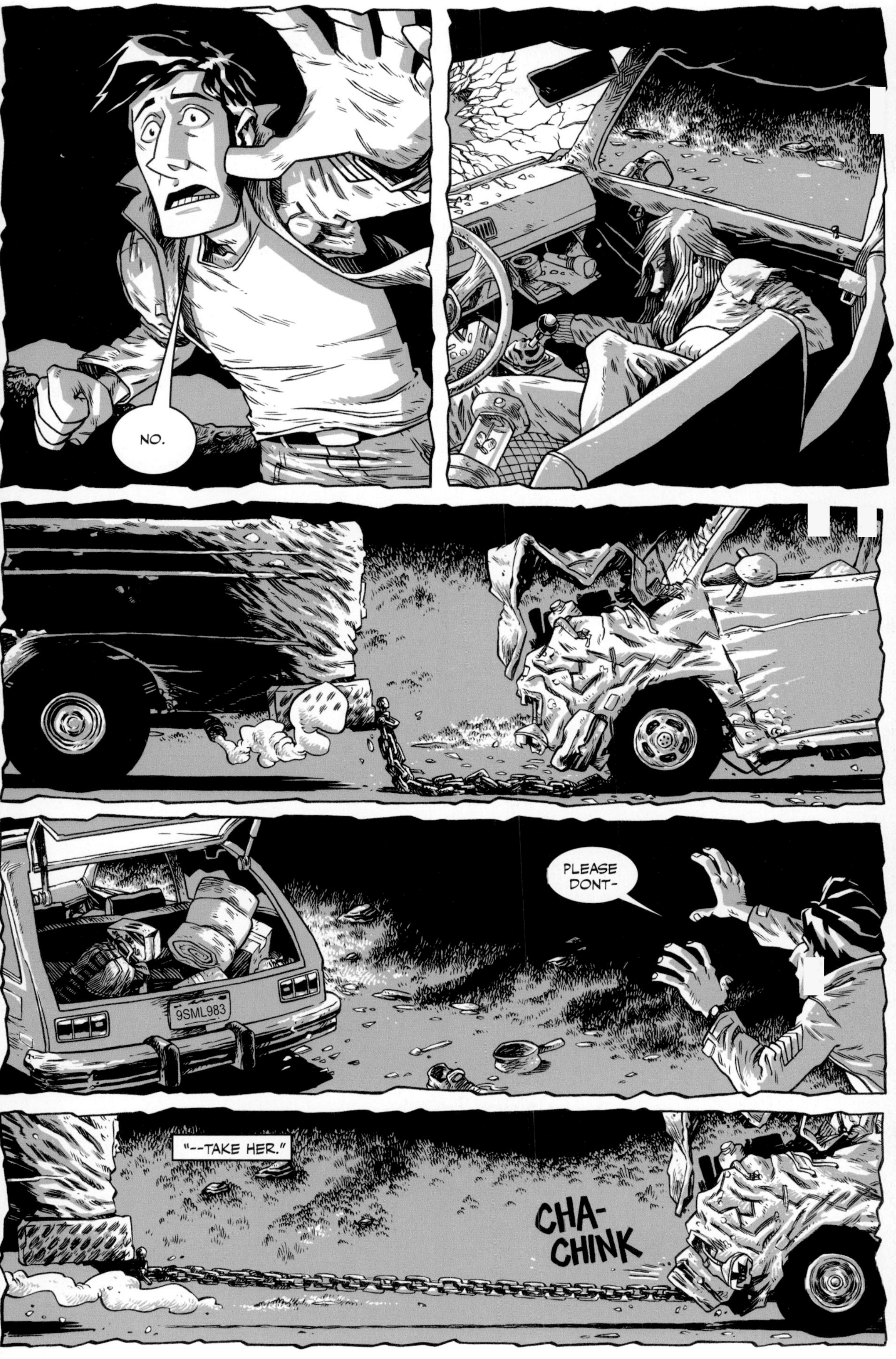
NO.
PLEASE DONT-
9SML983
"--TAKE HER."
CHA-CHINK

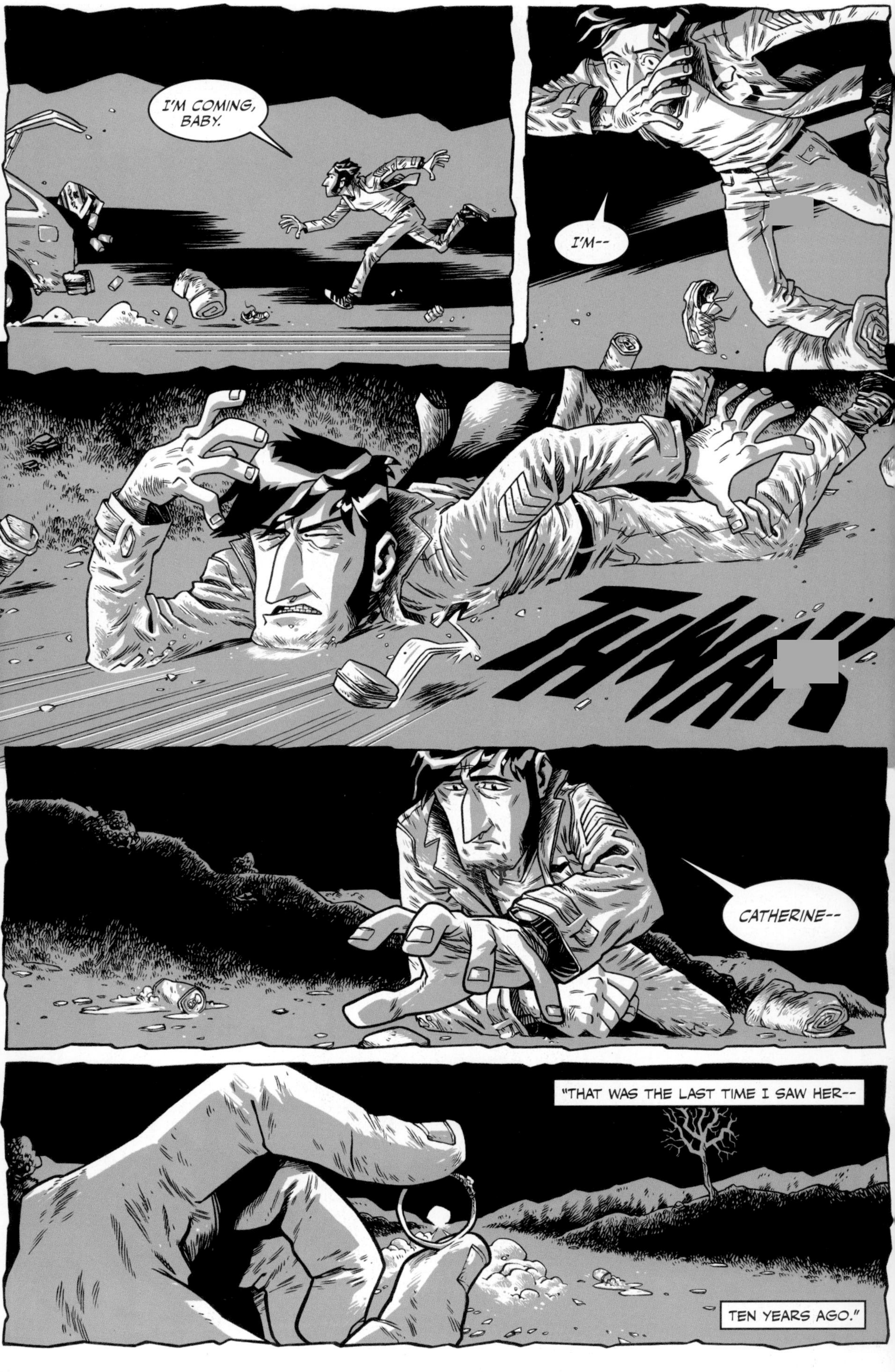
I'M COMING, BABY.
I'M--
CATHERINE--
"THAT WAS THE LAST TIME I SAW HER--
TEN YEARS AGO."

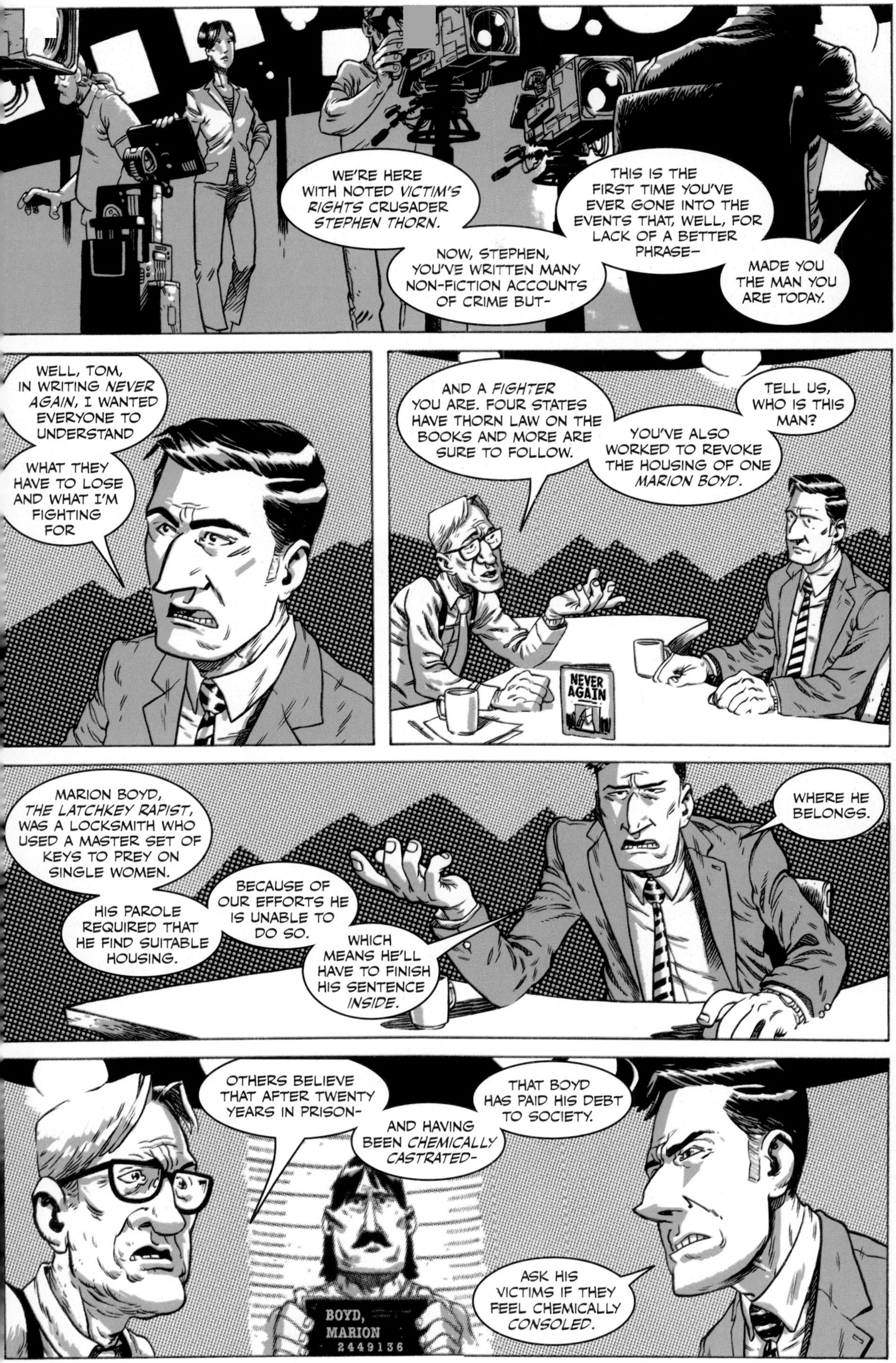
WE'RE HERE WITH NOTED *VICTIM'S RIGHTS* CRUSADER *STEPHEN THORN.*
NOW, STEPHEN, YOU'VE WRITTEN MANY NON-FICTION ACCOUNTS OF CRIME BUT-
THIS IS THE FIRST TIME YOU'VE EVER GONE INTO THE EVENTS THAT, WELL, FOR LACK OF A BETTER PHRASE-
MADE YOU THE MAN YOU ARE TODAY.
WELL, TOM, IN WRITING *NEVER AGAIN*, I WANTED EVERYONE TO UNDERSTAND
WHAT THEY HAVE TO LOSE AND WHAT I'M FIGHTING FOR
AND A *FIGHTER* YOU ARE. FOUR STATES HAVE THORN LAW ON THE BOOKS AND MORE ARE SURE TO FOLLOW.
YOU'VE ALSO WORKED TO REVOKE THE HOUSING OF ONE *MARION BOYD.*
TELL US, WHO IS THIS MAN?
NEVER AGAIN
MARION BOYD, *THE LATCHKEY RAPIST*, WAS A LOCKSMITH WHO USED A MASTER SET OF KEYS TO PREY ON SINGLE WOMEN.
HIS PAROLE REQUIRED THAT HE FIND SUITABLE HOUSING.
BECAUSE OF OUR EFFORTS HE IS UNABLE TO DO SO.
WHICH MEANS HE'LL HAVE TO FINISH HIS SENTENCE *INSIDE*.
WHERE HE BELONGS.
OTHERS BELIEVE THAT AFTER TWENTY YEARS IN PRISON-
AND HAVING BEEN *CHEMICALLY CASTRATED*-
THAT BOYD HAS PAID HIS DEBT TO SOCIETY.
BOYD, MARION 2449136
ASK HIS VICTIMS IF THEY FEEL CHEMICALLY *CONSOLED*.

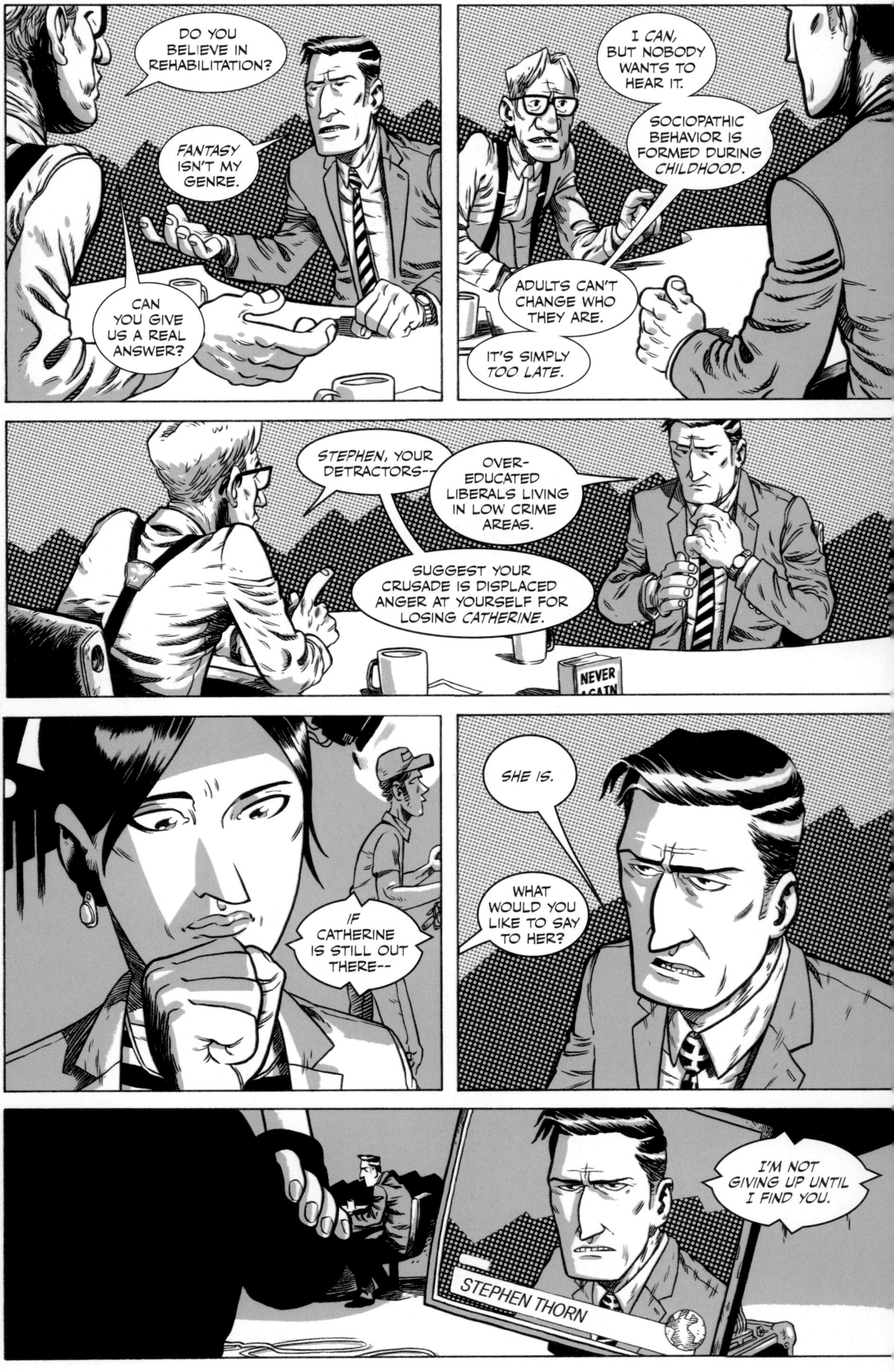
DO YOU BELIEVE IN REHABILITATION?
FANTASY ISN'T MY GENRE.
CAN YOU GIVE US A REAL ANSWER?
I *CAN*, BUT NOBODY WANTS TO HEAR IT.
SOCIOPATHIC BEHAVIOR IS FORMED DURING *CHILDHOOD*.
ADULTS CAN'T CHANGE WHO THEY ARE.
IT'S SIMPLY *TOO LATE*.
STEPHEN, YOUR DETRACTORS--
OVER-EDUCATED LIBERALS LIVING IN LOW CRIME AREAS.
SUGGEST YOUR CRUSADE IS DISPLACED ANGER AT YOURSELF FOR LOSING *CATHERINE*.
NEVER
IF CATHERINE IS STILL OUT THERE--
SHE IS.
WHAT WOULD YOU LIKE TO SAY TO HER?
I'M NOT GIVING UP UNTIL I FIND YOU.
STEPHEN THORN

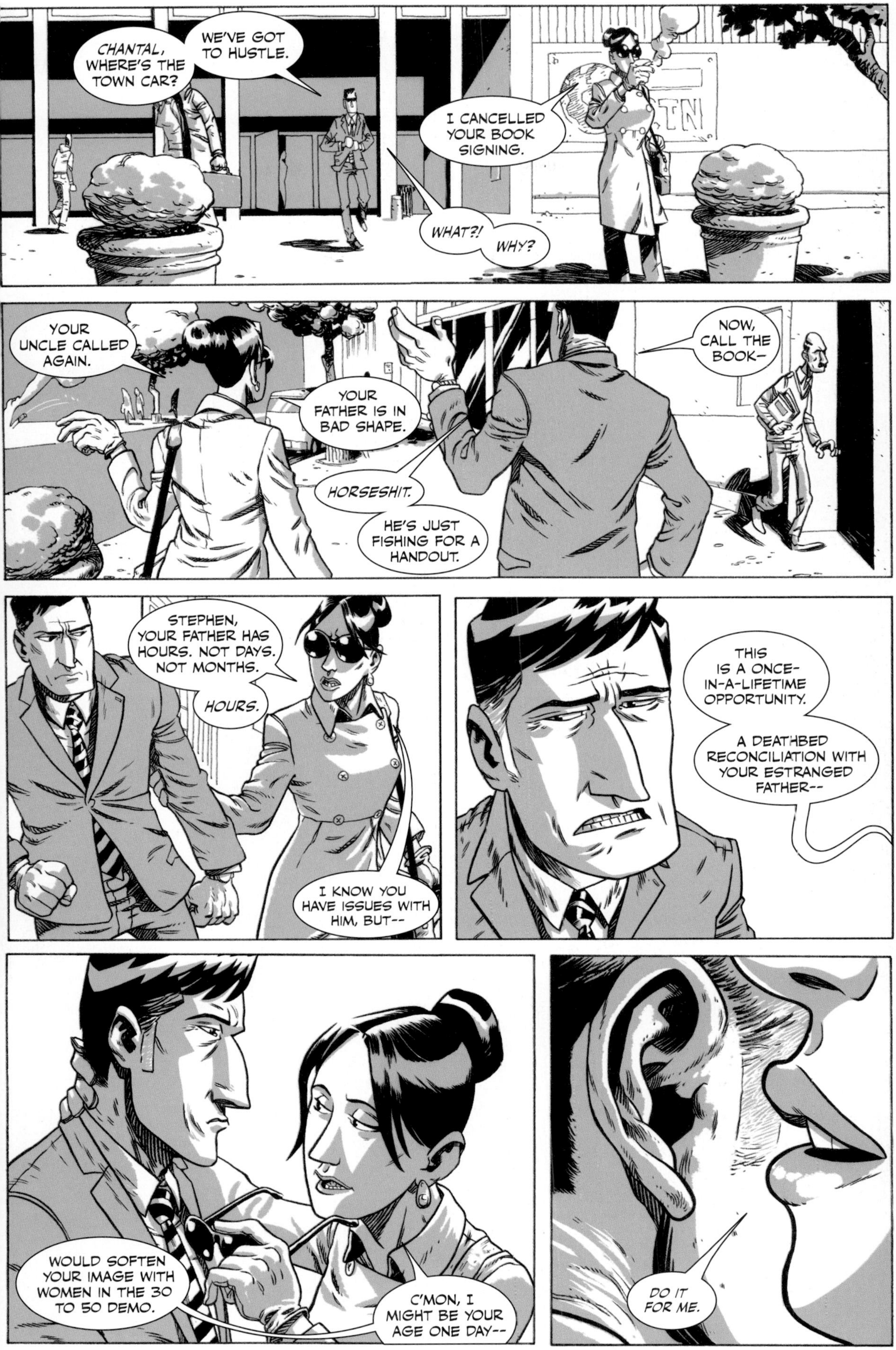
CHANTAL, WHERE'S THE TOWN CAR?
WE'VE GOT TO HUSTLE.
I CANCELLED YOUR BOOK SIGNING.
WHAT?!
WHY?
YOUR UNCLE CALLED AGAIN.
YOUR FATHER IS IN BAD SHAPE.
HORSESHIT.
HE'S JUST FISHING FOR A HANDOUT.
NOW, CALL THE BOOK—
STEPHEN, YOUR FATHER HAS HOURS. NOT DAYS. NOT MONTHS.
HOURS.
I KNOW YOU HAVE ISSUES WITH HIM, BUT--
THIS IS A ONCE-IN-A-LIFETIME OPPORTUNITY.
A DEATHBED RECONCILIATION WITH YOUR ESTRANGED FATHER--
WOULD SOFTEN YOUR IMAGE WITH WOMEN IN THE 30 TO 50 DEMO.
C'MON, I MIGHT BE YOUR AGE ONE DAY--
DO IT FOR ME.

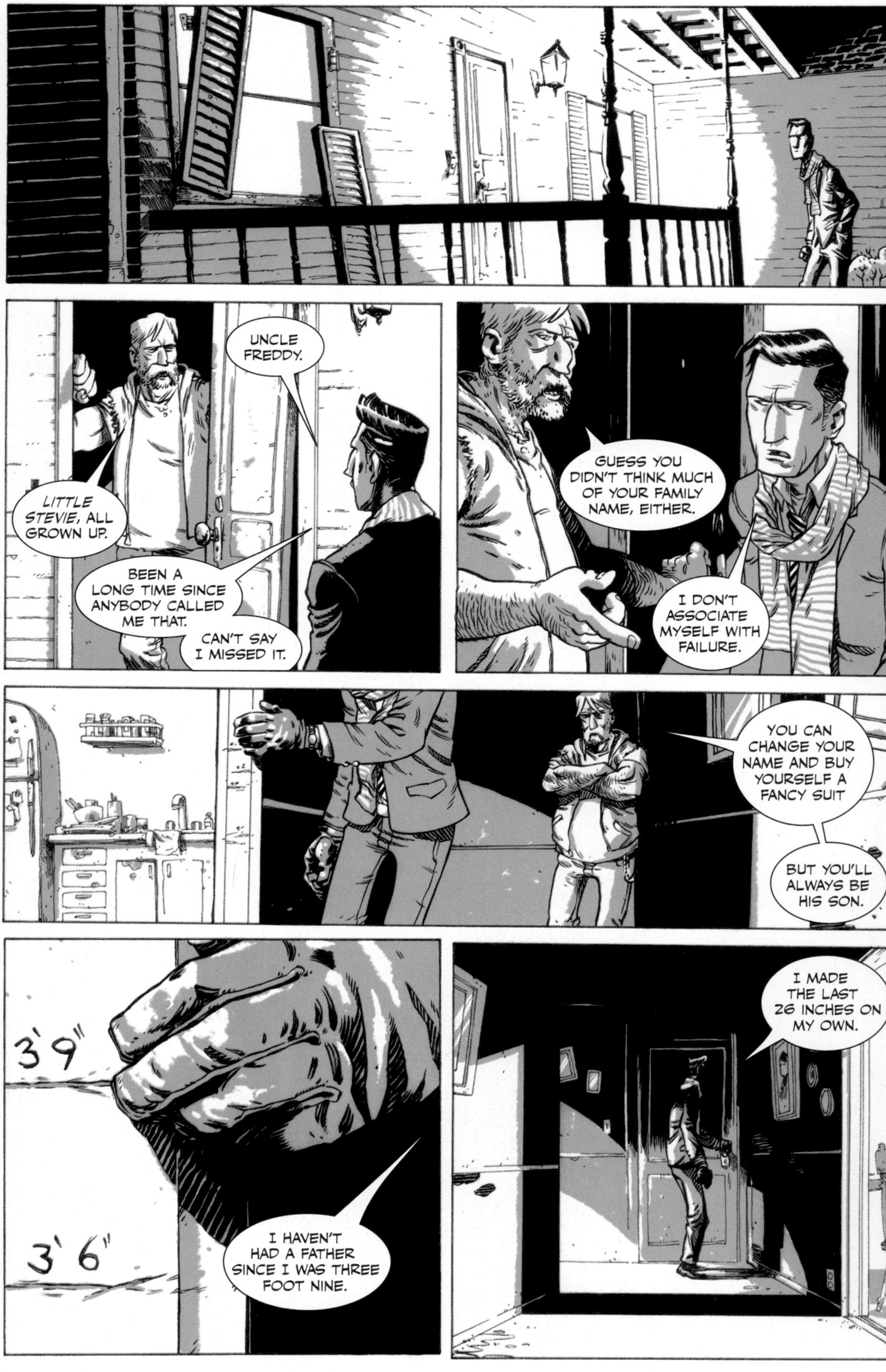
UNCLE FREDDY.
LITTLE STEVIE, ALL GROWN UP.
BEEN A LONG TIME SINCE ANYBODY CALLED ME THAT.
CAN'T SAY I MISSED IT.
GUESS YOU DIDN'T THINK MUCH OF YOUR FAMILY NAME, EITHER.
I DON'T ASSOCIATE MYSELF WITH FAILURE.
YOU CAN CHANGE YOUR NAME AND BUY YOURSELF A FANCY SUIT
BUT YOU'LL ALWAYS BE HIS SON.
3'9"
3'6"
I HAVEN'T HAD A FATHER SINCE I WAS THREE FOOT NINE.
I MADE THE LAST 26 INCHES ON MY OWN.

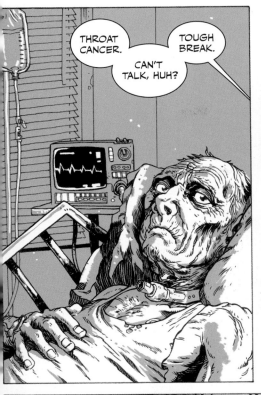

THROAT CANCER.

TOUGH BREAK.

CAN'T TALK, HUH?

SHE ALWAYS WANTED YOU TO QUIT.

BUT YOU COULDN'T DRINK WITHOUT SMOKING

OR SMOKE WITHOUT DRINKING.

IT TOOK YOU A WEEK TO EVEN REALIZE SHE WAS GONE.

I USED TO SIT ON THE PORCH AND WATCH THE CARS DRIVE BY.

WAITING FOR HER TO COME BACK FOR ME.

BUT NO CAR EVER STOPPED.

INSTEAD I LIVED HERE *ALONE.* WITH *YOU.*

I CONVINCED MYSELF THAT IF I EVER FOUND SOMEONE SPECIAL--

I'D HOLD ONTO THEM FOREVER.

BUT, AS IT TURNS OUT

WE'RE NOT SO DIFFERENT.

I HOPE YOU KNOW THAT-- I--

JESUS.

YOU LOOK TERRIBLE, POP.

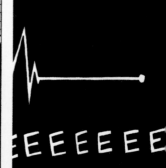

EEEEEEEE

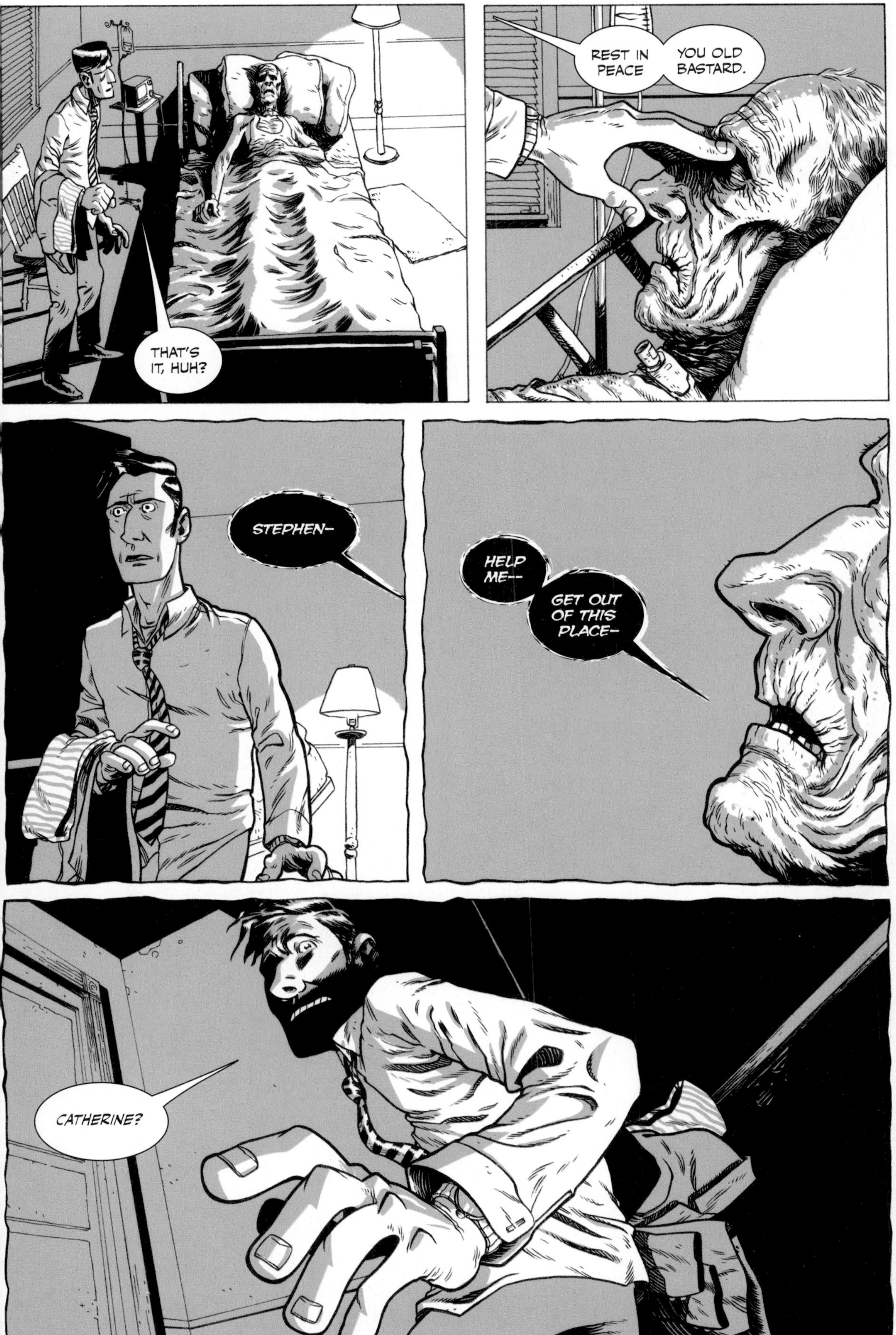
THAT'S IT, HUH?
REST IN PEACE
YOU OLD BASTARD.
STEPHEN-
HELP ME--
GET OUT OF THIS PLACE-
CATHERINE?

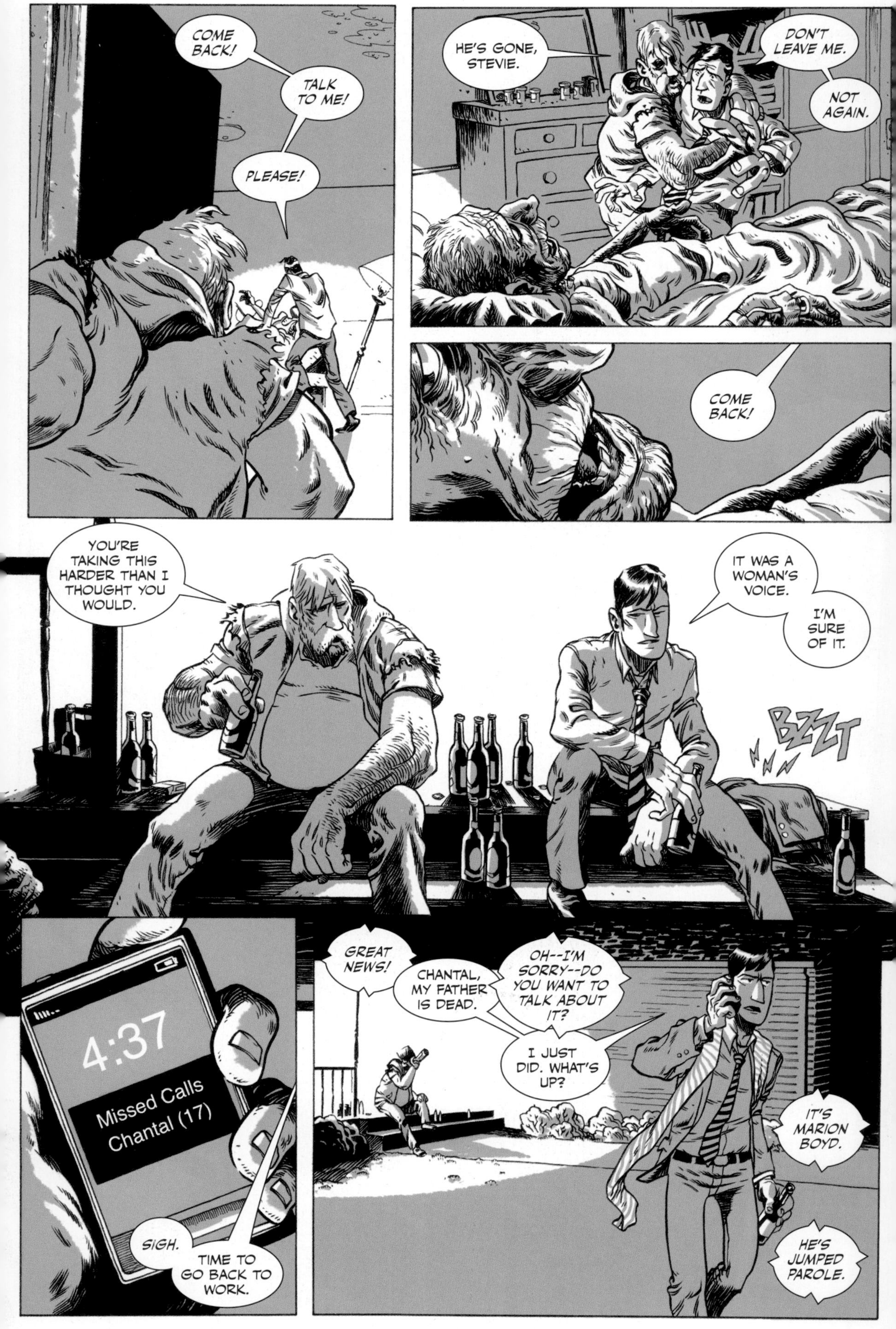
COME BACK!
TALK TO ME!
PLEASE!
HE'S GONE, STEVIE.
DON'T LEAVE ME.
NOT AGAIN.
COME BACK!
YOU'RE TAKING THIS HARDER THAN I THOUGHT YOU WOULD.
IT WAS A WOMAN'S VOICE.
I'M SURE OF IT.
BZZZT
4:37
Missed Calls
Chantal (17)
SIGH.
TIME TO GO BACK TO WORK.
GREAT NEWS!
CHANTAL, MY FATHER IS DEAD.
OH--I'M SORRY--DO YOU WANT TO TALK ABOUT IT?
I JUST DID. WHAT'S UP?
IT'S MARION BOYD.
HE'S JUMPED PAROLE.

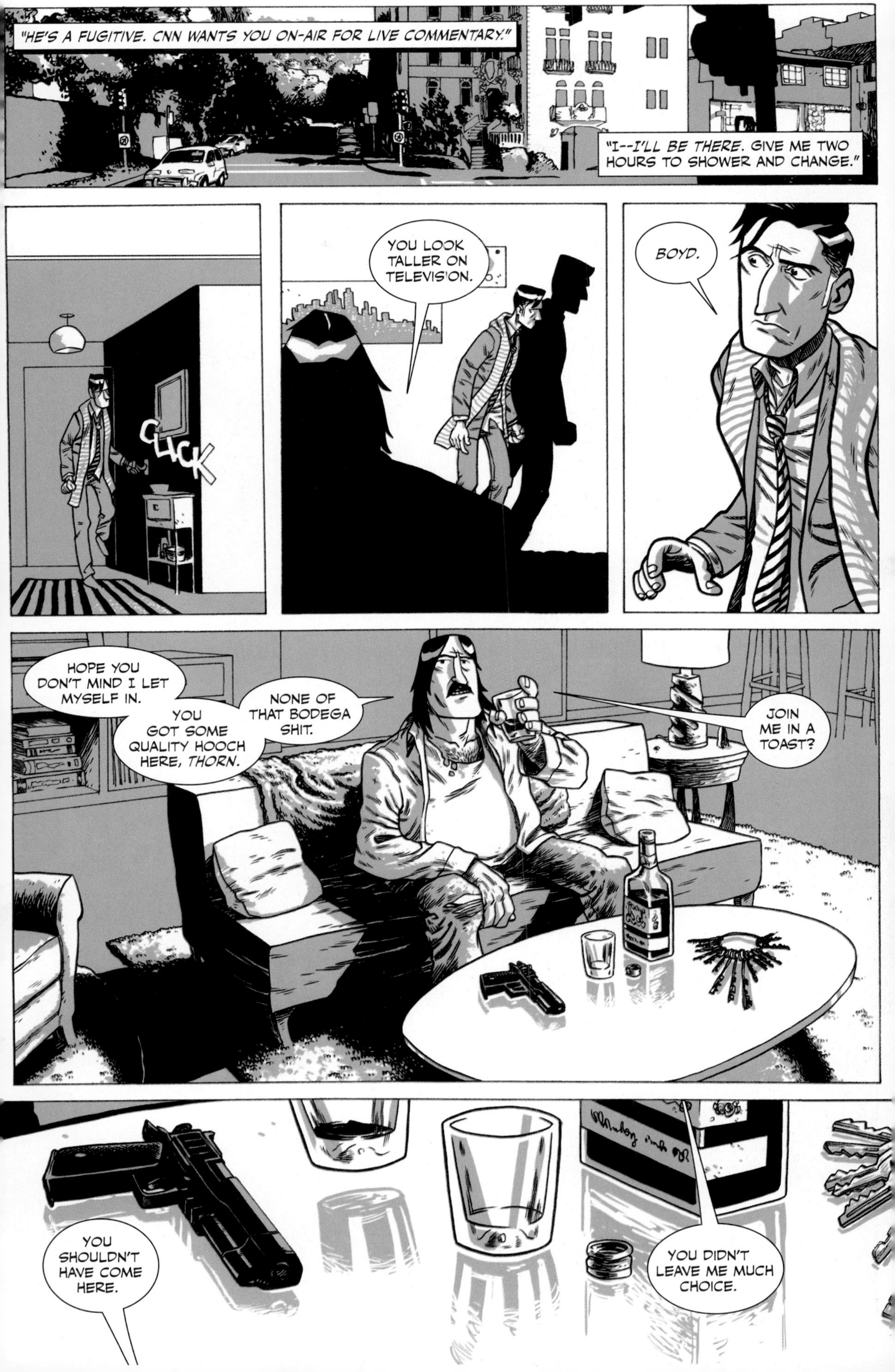
"HE'S A FUGITIVE. CNN WANTS YOU ON-AIR FOR LIVE COMMENTARY."
"I--I'LL BE THERE. GIVE ME TWO HOURS TO SHOWER AND CHANGE."
CLICK
YOU LOOK TALLER ON TELEVISION.
BOYD.
HOPE YOU DON'T MIND I LET MYSELF IN.
YOU GOT SOME QUALITY HOOCH HERE, THORN.
NONE OF THAT BODEGA SHIT.
JOIN ME IN A TOAST?
YOU SHOULDN'T HAVE COME HERE.
YOU DIDN'T LEAVE ME MUCH CHOICE.

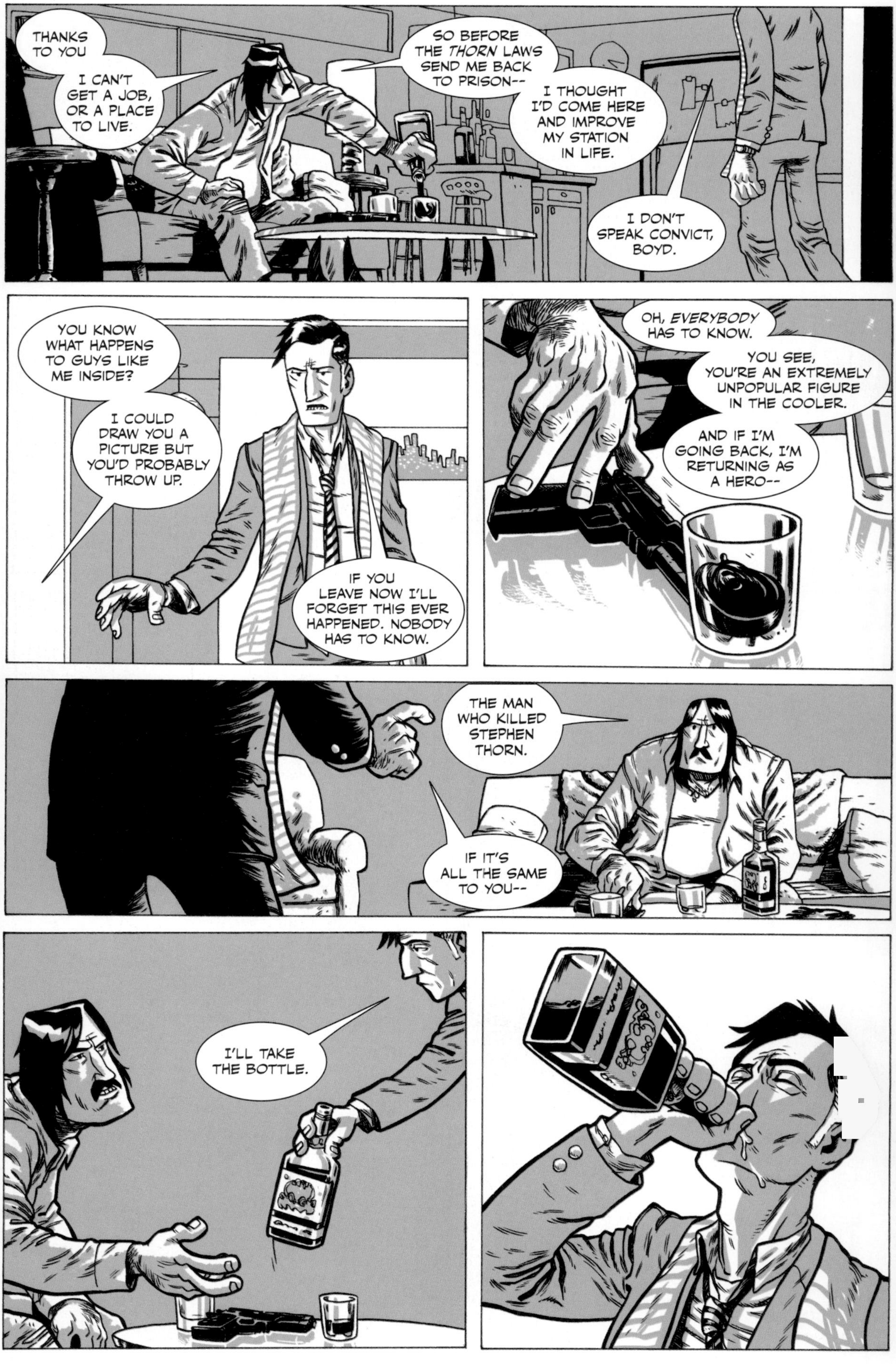
THANKS TO YOU
I CAN'T GET A JOB, OR A PLACE TO LIVE.
SO BEFORE THE *THORN* LAWS SEND ME BACK TO PRISON--
I THOUGHT I'D COME HERE AND IMPROVE MY STATION IN LIFE.
I DON'T SPEAK CONVICT, BOYD.
YOU KNOW WHAT HAPPENS TO GUYS LIKE ME INSIDE?
I COULD DRAW YOU A PICTURE BUT YOU'D PROBABLY THROW UP.
IF YOU LEAVE NOW I'LL FORGET THIS EVER HAPPENED. NOBODY HAS TO KNOW.
OH, *EVERYBODY* HAS TO KNOW.
YOU SEE, YOU'RE AN EXTREMELY UNPOPULAR FIGURE IN THE COOLER.
AND IF I'M GOING BACK, I'M RETURNING AS A HERO--
THE MAN WHO KILLED STEPHEN THORN.
IF IT'S ALL THE SAME TO YOU--
I'LL TAKE THE BOTTLE.

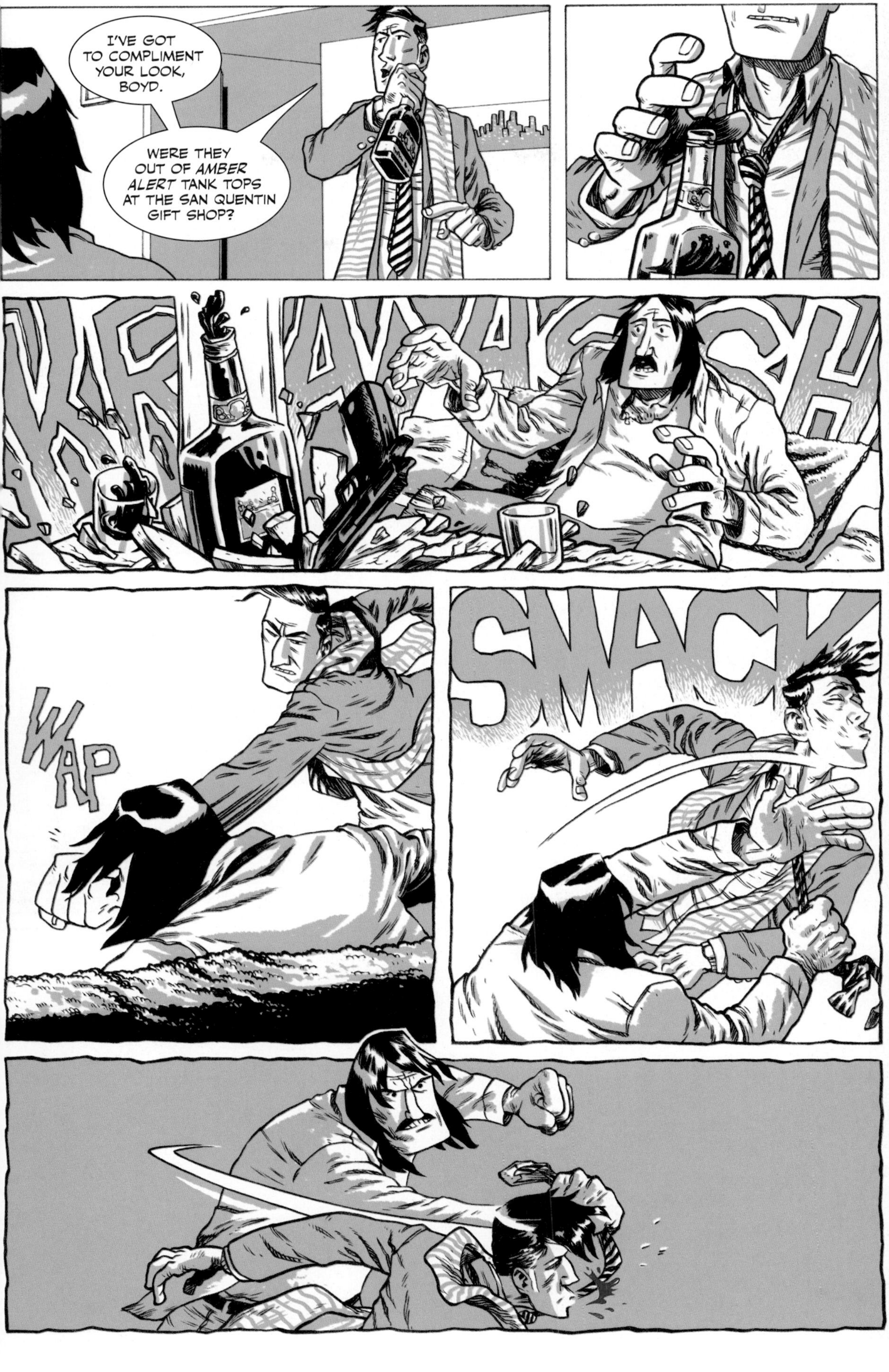
I'VE GOT TO COMPLIMENT YOUR LOOK, BOYD.
WERE THEY OUT OF *AMBER ALERT* TANK TOPS AT THE SAN QUENTIN GIFT SHOP?
WAP
SMACK

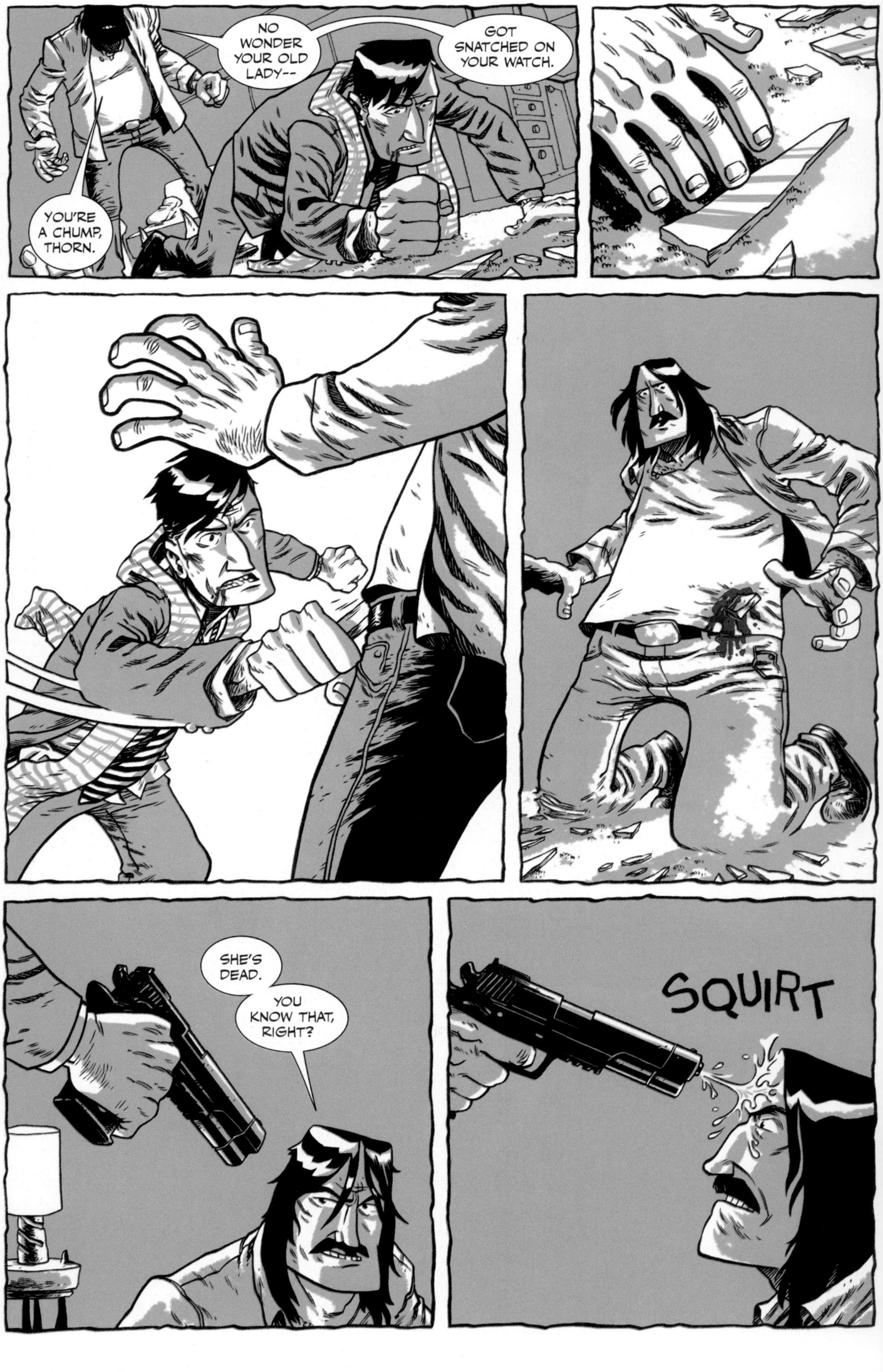
NO WONDER YOUR OLD LADY--
GOT SNATCHED ON YOUR WATCH.
YOU'RE A CHUMP, THORN.
SHE'S DEAD.
YOU KNOW THAT, RIGHT?
SQUIRT

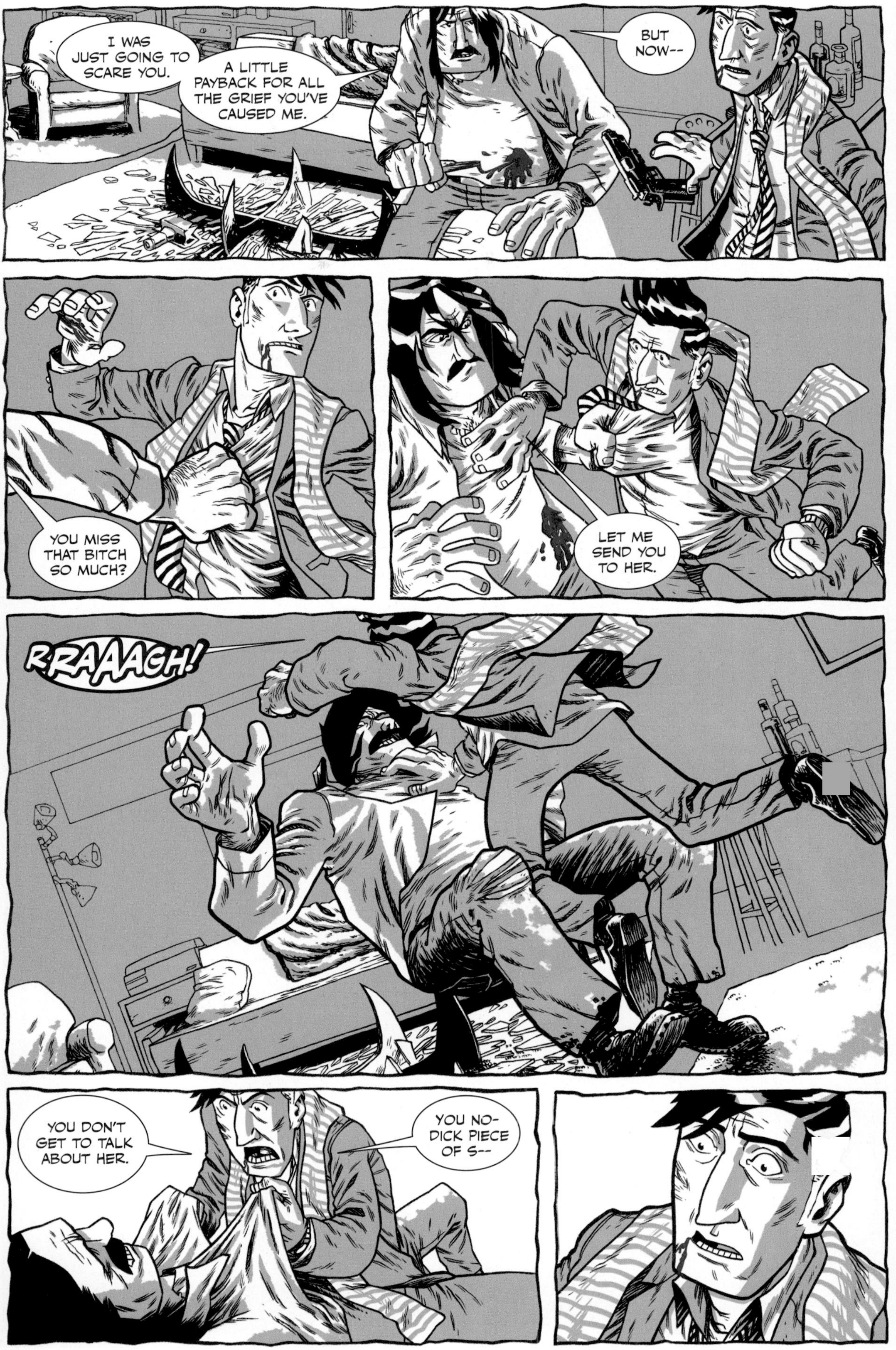
I WAS JUST GOING TO SCARE YOU.
A LITTLE PAYBACK FOR ALL THE GRIEF YOU'VE CAUSED ME.
BUT NOW--
YOU MISS THAT BITCH SO MUCH?
LET ME SEND YOU TO HER.
RRAAAGH!
YOU DON'T GET TO TALK ABOUT HER.
YOU NO-DICK PIECE OF S--

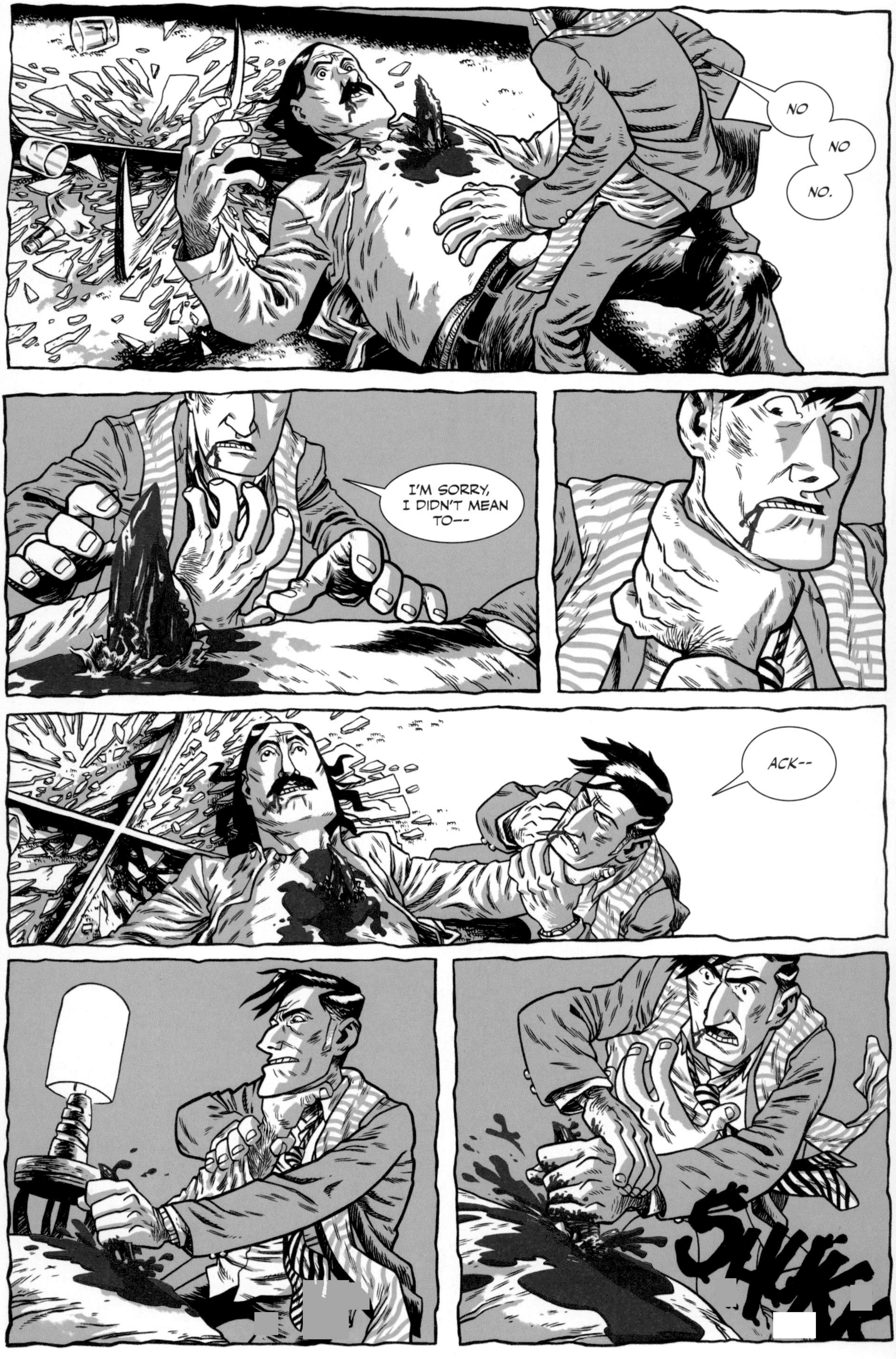
NO
NO
NO.
I'M SORRY, I DIDN'T MEAN TO--
ACK--

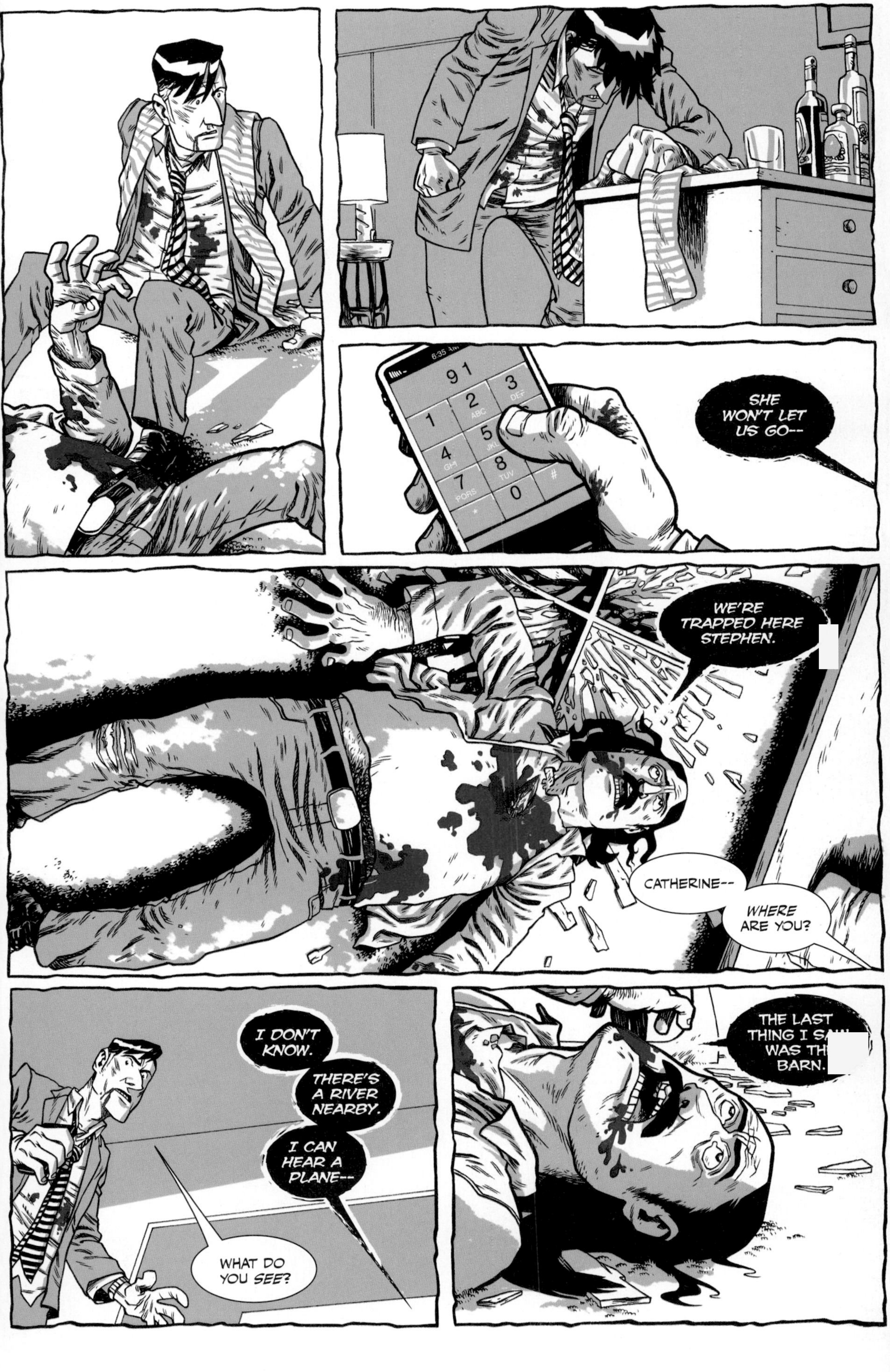
SHE WON'T LET US GO--
WE'RE TRAPPED HERE STEPHEN.
CATHERINE--
WHERE ARE YOU?
I DON'T KNOW.
THERE'S A RIVER NEARBY.
I CAN HEAR A PLANE--
WHAT DO YOU SEE?
THE LAST THING I SA
WAS TH
BARN.

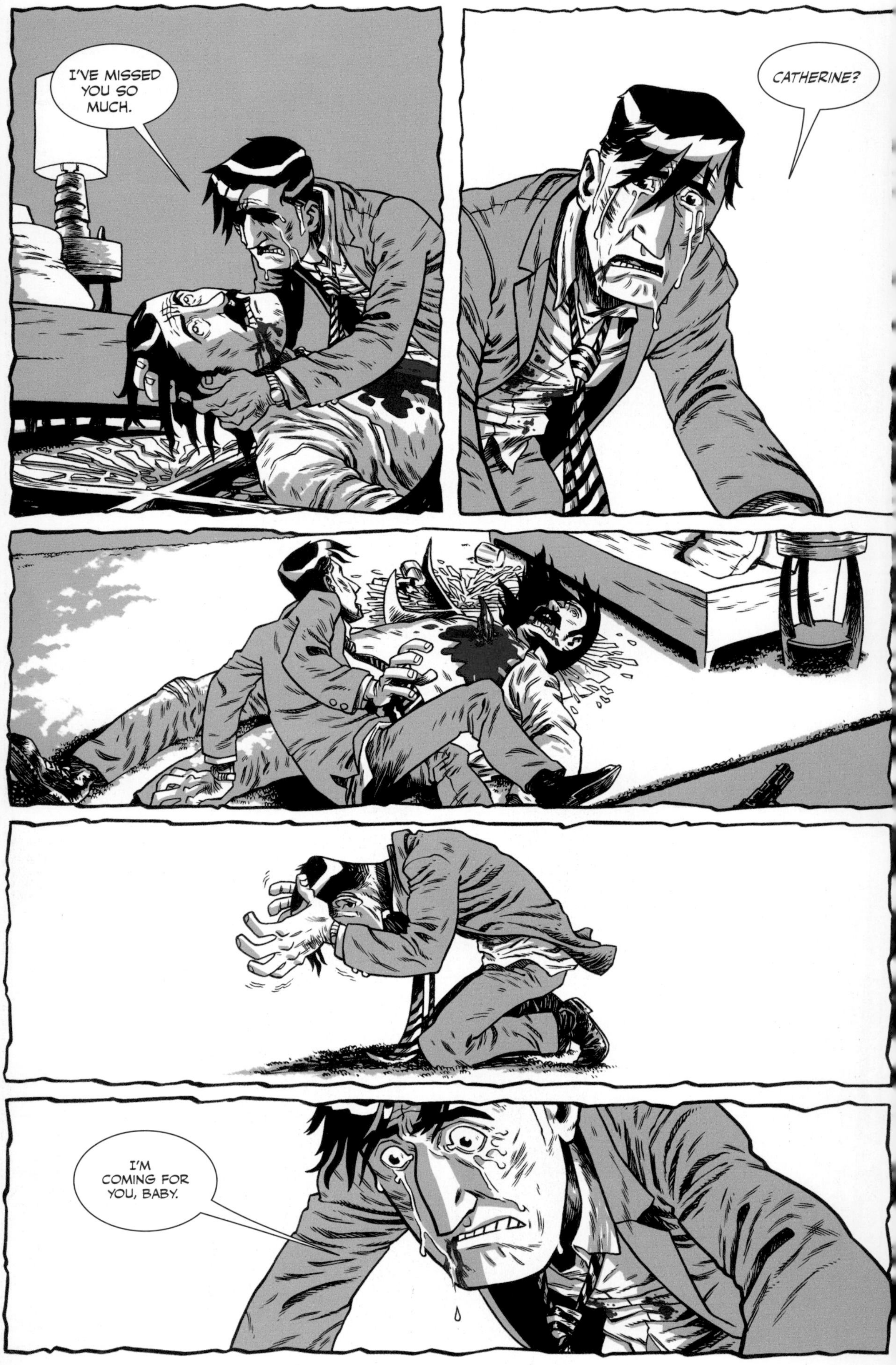
I'VE MISSED YOU SO MUCH.
CATHERINE?
I'M COMING FOR YOU, BABY.

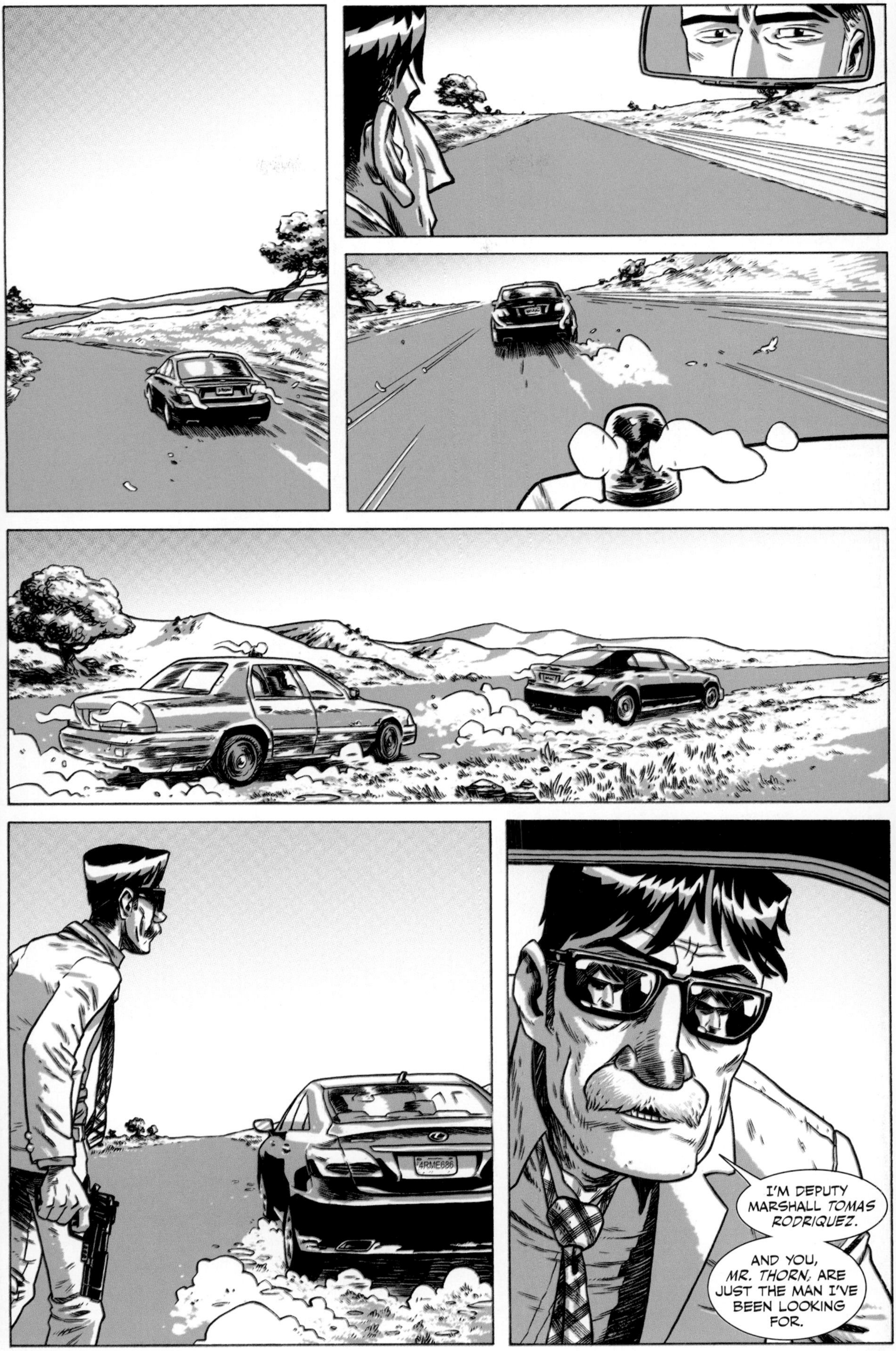

4RME686
I'M DEPUTY MARSHALL TOMAS RODRIQUEZ.
AND YOU, MR. THORN, ARE JUST THE MAN I'VE BEEN LOOKING FOR.

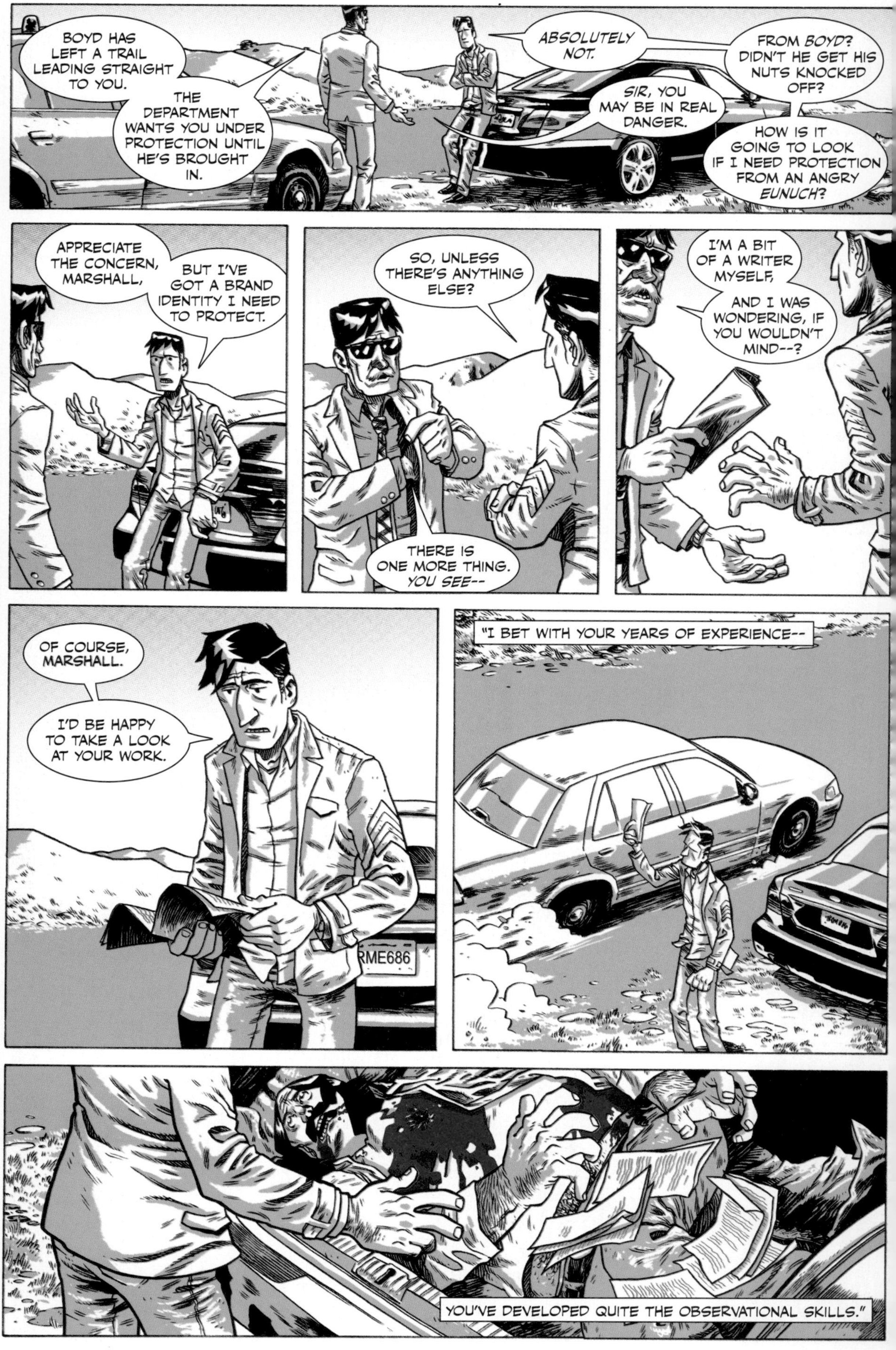
BOYD HAS LEFT A TRAIL LEADING STRAIGHT TO YOU.
THE DEPARTMENT WANTS YOU UNDER PROTECTION UNTIL HE'S BROUGHT IN.
ABSOLUTELY NOT.
SIR, YOU MAY BE IN REAL DANGER.
FROM BOYD? DIDN'T HE GET HIS NUTS KNOCKED OFF?
HOW IS IT GOING TO LOOK IF I NEED PROTECTION FROM AN ANGRY EUNUCH?
APPRECIATE THE CONCERN, MARSHALL,
BUT I'VE GOT A BRAND IDENTITY I NEED TO PROTECT.
SO, UNLESS THERE'S ANYTHING ELSE?
THERE IS ONE MORE THING. YOU SEE--
I'M A BIT OF A WRITER MYSELF,
AND I WAS WONDERING, IF YOU WOULDN'T MIND--?
OF COURSE, MARSHALL.
I'D BE HAPPY TO TAKE A LOOK AT YOUR WORK.
RME686
"I BET WITH YOUR YEARS OF EXPERIENCE--
YOU'VE DEVELOPED QUITE THE OBSERVATIONAL SKILLS."

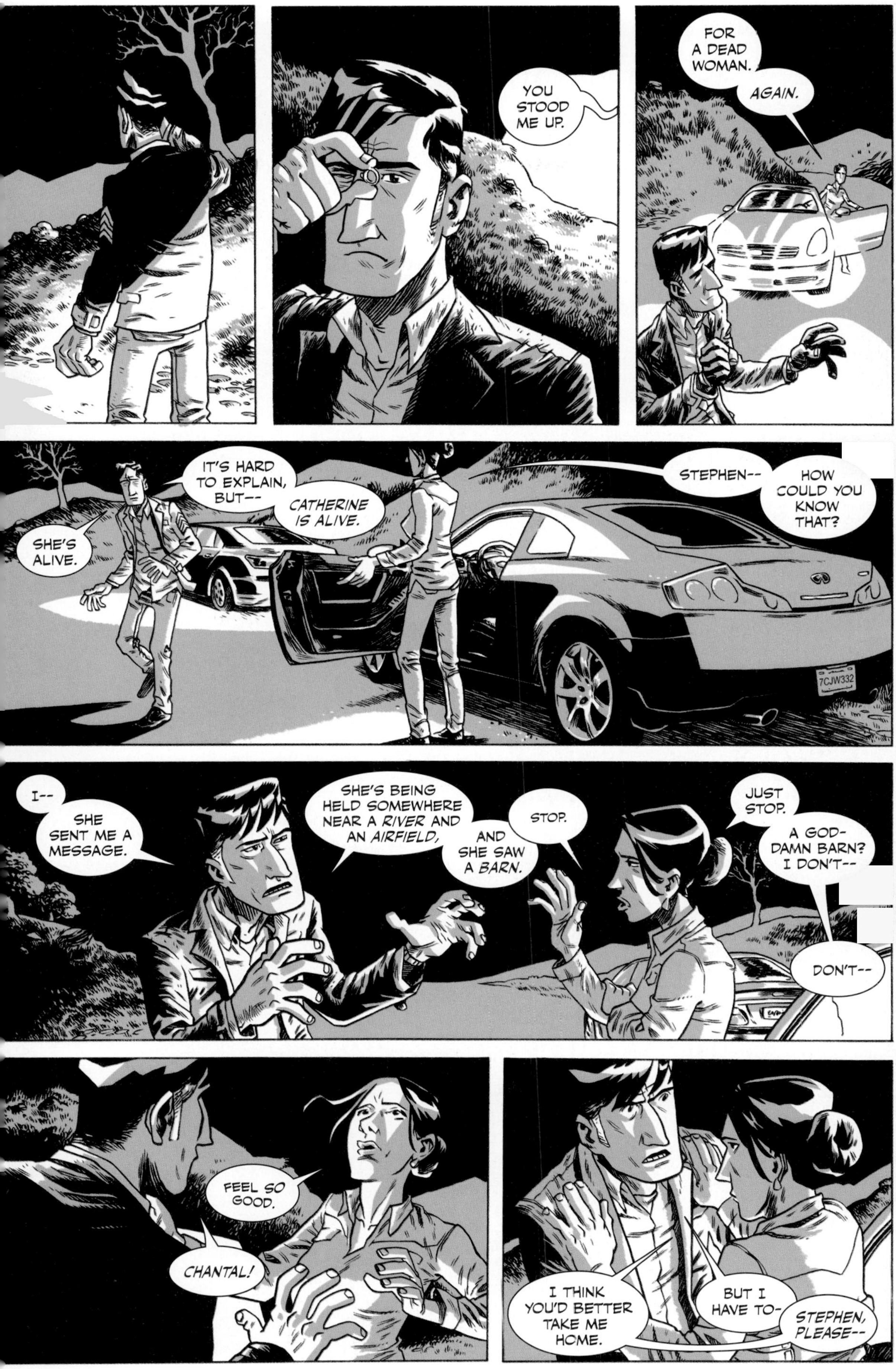
YOU STOOD ME UP.
FOR A DEAD WOMAN.
AGAIN.
IT'S HARD TO EXPLAIN, BUT--
SHE'S ALIVE.
CATHERINE IS ALIVE.
STEPHEN--
HOW COULD YOU KNOW THAT?
7CJW332
I--
SHE SENT ME A MESSAGE.
SHE'S BEING HELD SOMEWHERE NEAR A RIVER AND AN AIRFIELD,
AND SHE SAW A BARN.
STOP.
JUST STOP.
A GOD-DAMN BARN? I DON'T--
DON'T--
FEEL SO GOOD.
CHANTAL!
I THINK YOU'D BETTER TAKE ME HOME.
BUT I HAVE TO-
STEPHEN, PLEASE--

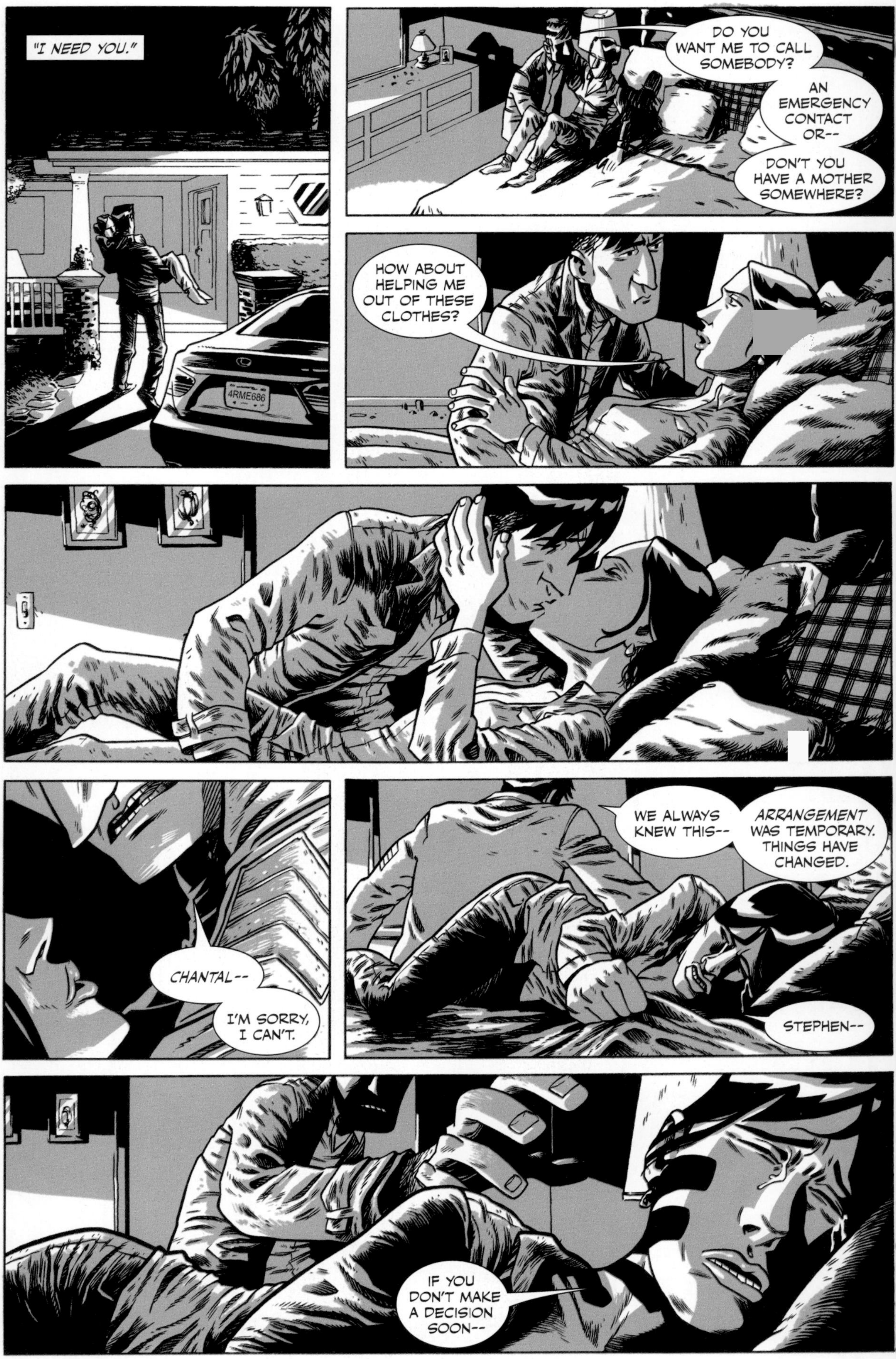
"I NEED YOU."
4RME686
DO YOU WANT ME TO CALL SOMEBODY?
AN EMERGENCY CONTACT OR--
DON'T YOU HAVE A MOTHER SOMEWHERE?
HOW ABOUT HELPING ME OUT OF THESE CLOTHES?
CHANTAL--
I'M SORRY, I CAN'T.
WE ALWAYS KNEW THIS--
ARRANGEMENT WAS TEMPORARY. THINGS HAVE CHANGED.
STEPHEN--
IF YOU DON'T MAKE A DECISION SOON--

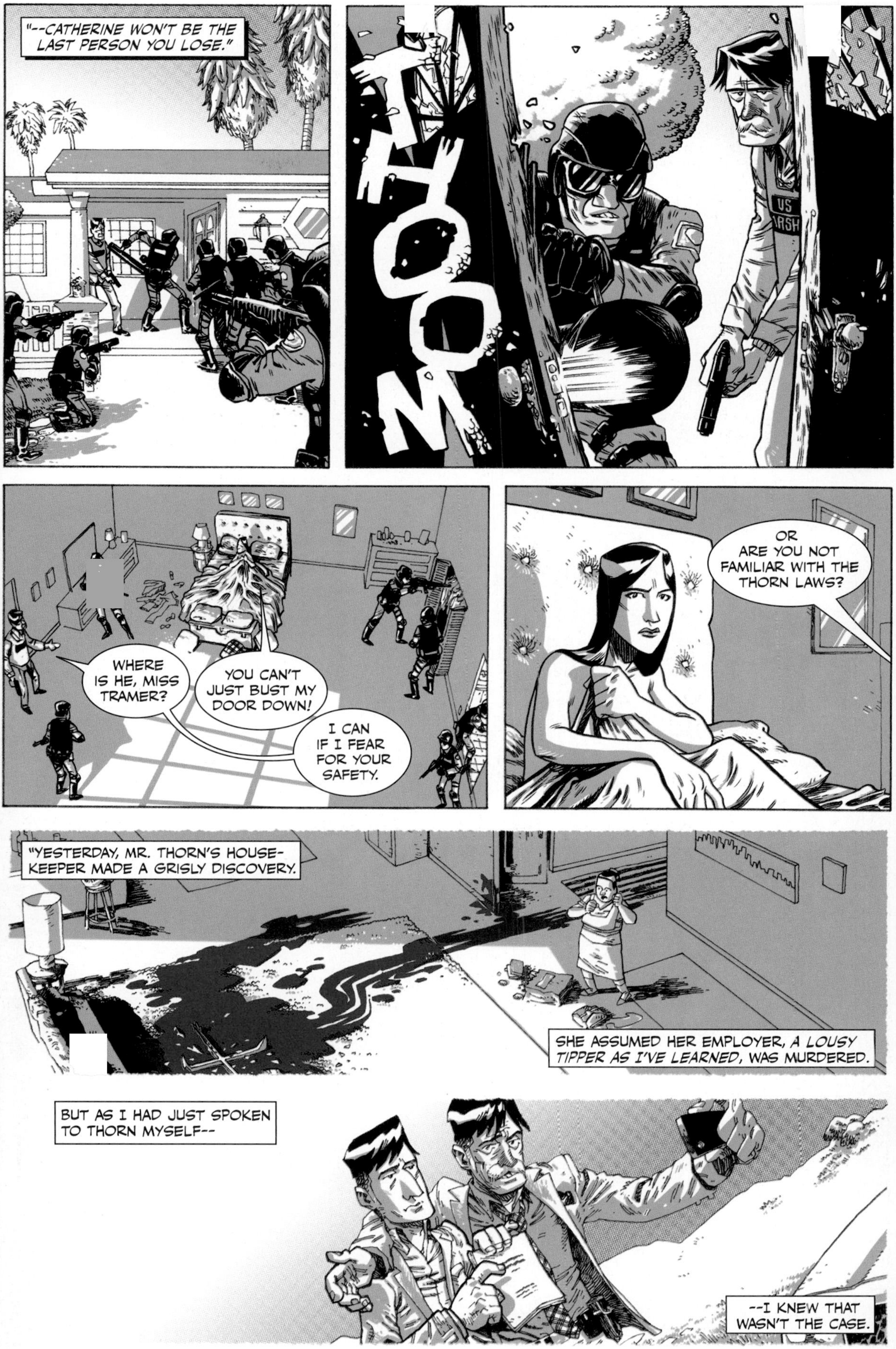

"--CATHERINE WON'T BE THE LAST PERSON YOU LOSE."
THOOM
US MARSH
WHERE IS HE, MISS TRAMER?
YOU CAN'T JUST BUST MY DOOR DOWN!
I CAN IF I FEAR FOR YOUR SAFETY.
OR ARE YOU NOT FAMILIAR WITH THE THORN LAWS?
"YESTERDAY, MR. THORN'S HOUSE-KEEPER MADE A GRISLY DISCOVERY.
SHE ASSUMED HER EMPLOYER, A LOUSY TIPPER AS I'VE LEARNED, WAS MURDERED.
BUT AS I HAD JUST SPOKEN TO THORN MYSELF--
--I KNEW THAT WASN'T THE CASE.

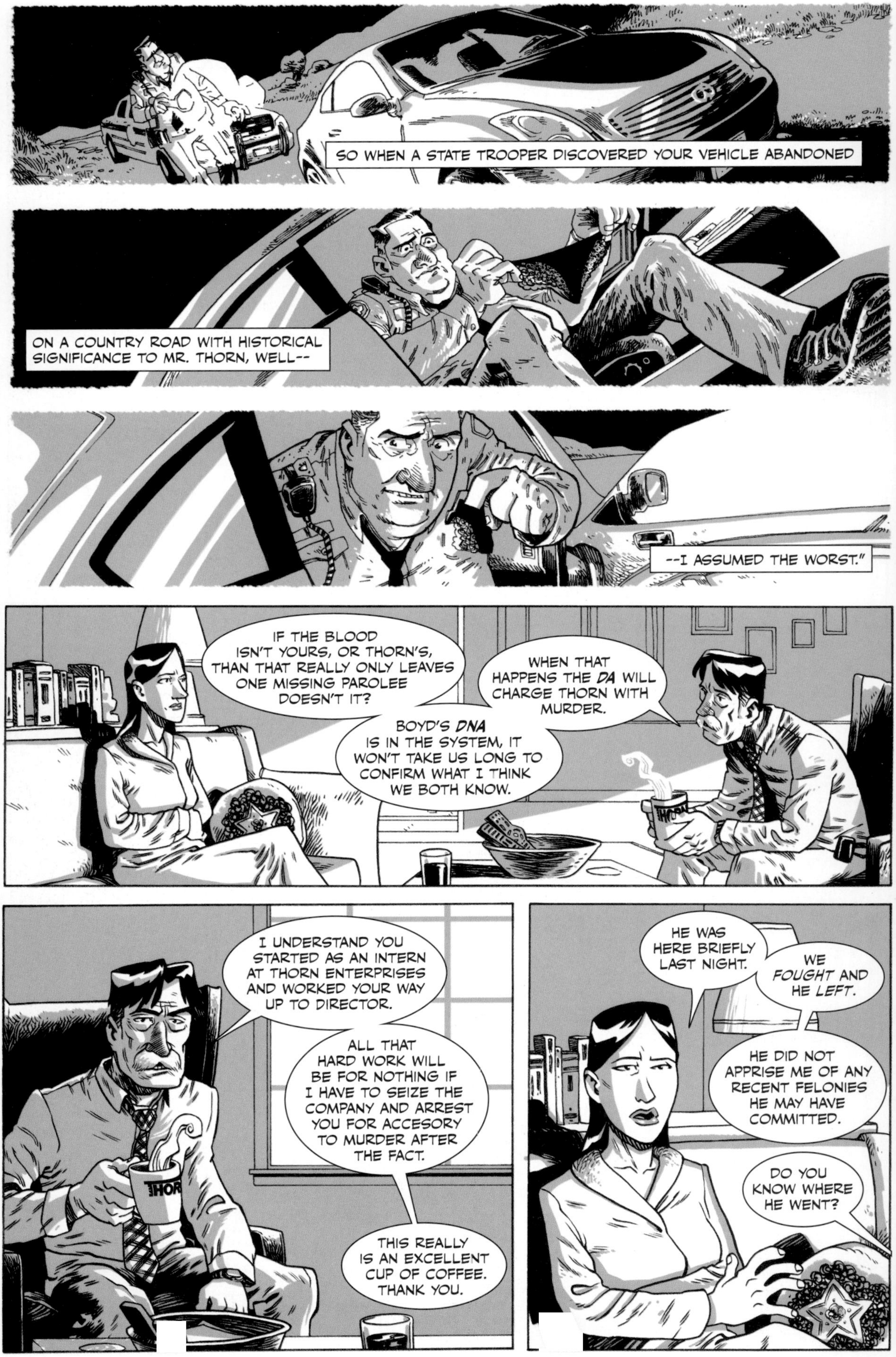
SO WHEN A STATE TROOPER DISCOVERED YOUR VEHICLE ABANDONED
ON A COUNTRY ROAD WITH HISTORICAL SIGNIFICANCE TO MR. THORN, WELL--
--I ASSUMED THE WORST."
IF THE BLOOD ISN'T YOURS, OR THORN'S, THAN THAT REALLY ONLY LEAVES ONE MISSING PAROLEE DOESN'T IT?
BOYD'S *DNA* IS IN THE SYSTEM, IT WON'T TAKE US LONG TO CONFIRM WHAT I THINK WE BOTH KNOW.
WHEN THAT HAPPENS THE *DA* WILL CHARGE THORN WITH MURDER.
I UNDERSTAND YOU STARTED AS AN INTERN AT THORN ENTERPRISES AND WORKED YOUR WAY UP TO DIRECTOR.
ALL THAT HARD WORK WILL BE FOR NOTHING IF I HAVE TO SEIZE THE COMPANY AND ARREST YOU FOR ACCESORY TO MURDER AFTER THE FACT.
THIS REALLY IS AN EXCELLENT CUP OF COFFEE. THANK YOU.
HE WAS HERE BRIEFLY LAST NIGHT.
WE *FOUGHT* AND HE *LEFT*.
HE DID NOT APPRISE ME OF ANY RECENT FELONIES HE MAY HAVE COMMITTED.
DO YOU KNOW WHERE HE WENT?

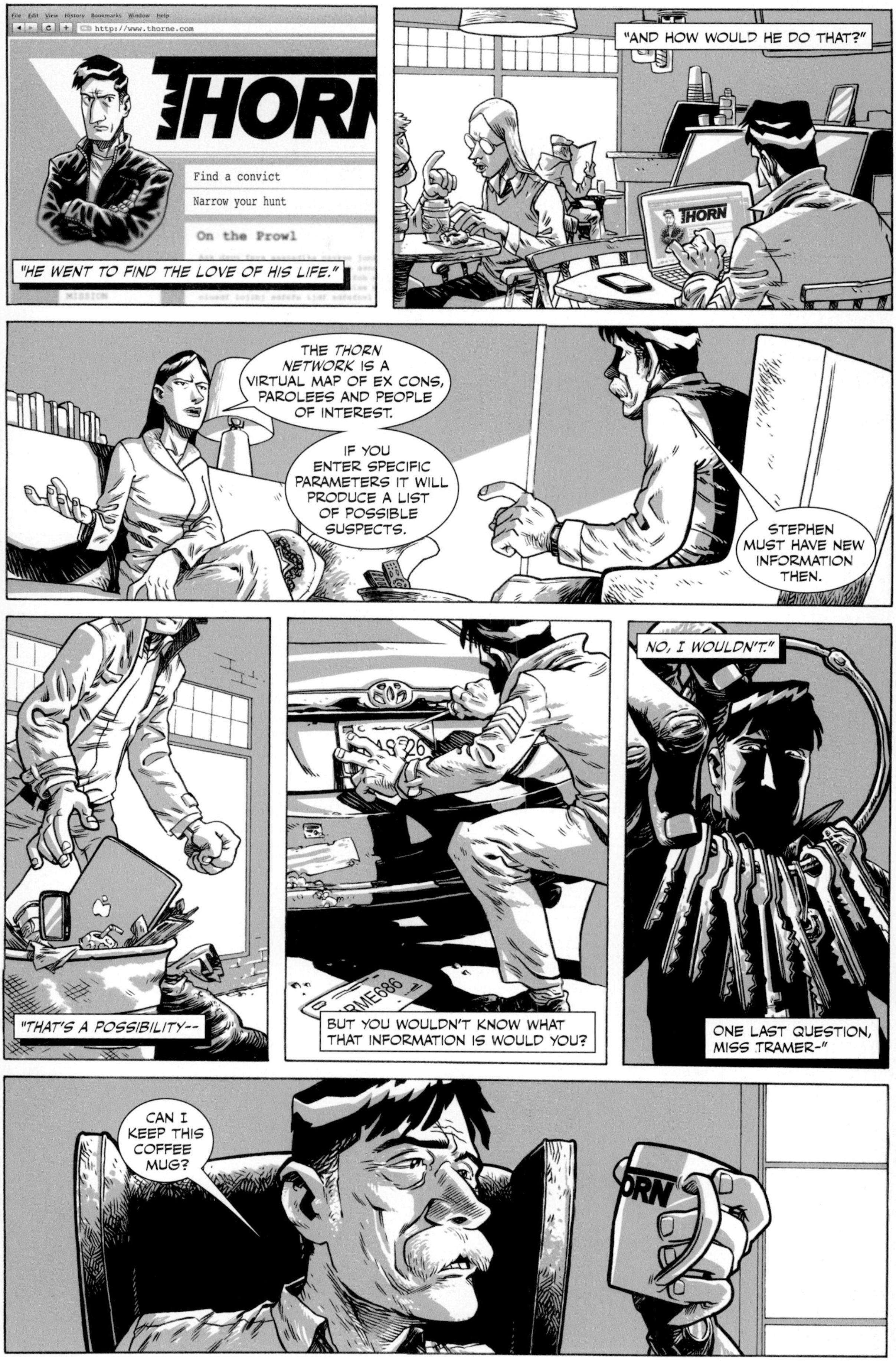
File Edit View History Bookmarks Window Help
http://www.thorne.com
THORN
Find a convict
Narrow your hunt
On the Prowl
MISSION
"HE WENT TO FIND THE LOVE OF HIS LIFE."
"AND HOW WOULD HE DO THAT?"
THORN
THE THORN NETWORK IS A VIRTUAL MAP OF EX CONS, PAROLEES AND PEOPLE OF INTEREST.
IF YOU ENTER SPECIFIC PARAMETERS IT WILL PRODUCE A LIST OF POSSIBLE SUSPECTS.
STEPHEN MUST HAVE NEW INFORMATION THEN.
"THAT'S A POSSIBILITY--
BUT YOU WOULDN'T KNOW WHAT THAT INFORMATION IS WOULD YOU?
NO, I WOULDN'T."
ONE LAST QUESTION, MISS TRAMER-"
CAN I KEEP THIS COFFEE MUG?
ORN

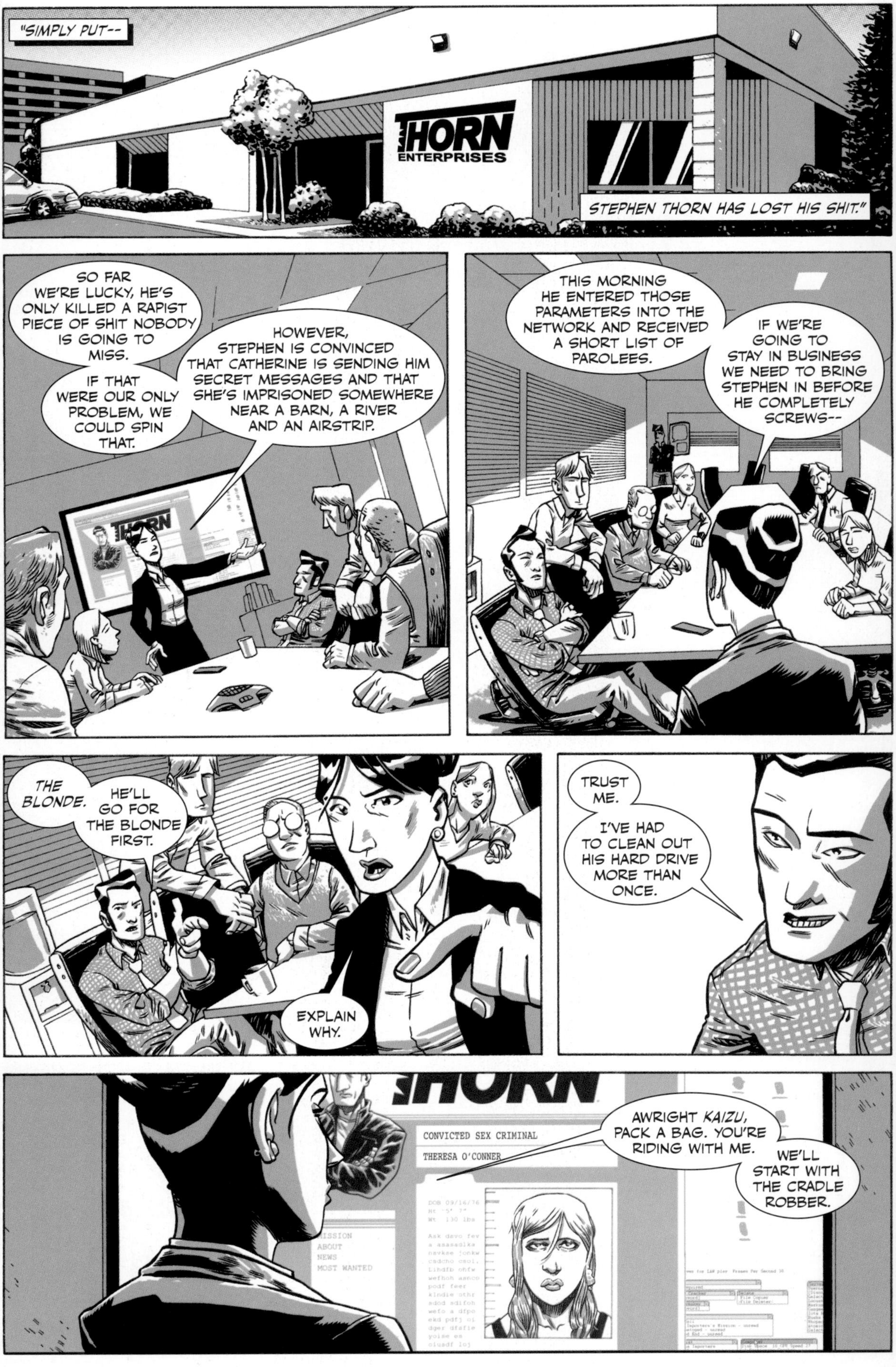
"SIMPLY PUT--
THORN ENTERPRISES
STEPHEN THORN HAS LOST HIS SHIT."
SO FAR WE'RE LUCKY, HE'S ONLY KILLED A RAPIST PIECE OF SHIT NOBODY IS GOING TO MISS.
IF THAT WERE OUR ONLY PROBLEM, WE COULD SPIN THAT.
HOWEVER, STEPHEN IS CONVINCED THAT CATHERINE IS SENDING HIM SECRET MESSAGES AND THAT SHE'S IMPRISONED SOMEWHERE NEAR A BARN, A RIVER AND AN AIRSTRIP.
THORN
THIS MORNING HE ENTERED THOSE PARAMETERS INTO THE NETWORK AND RECEIVED A SHORT LIST OF PAROLEES.
IF WE'RE GOING TO STAY IN BUSINESS WE NEED TO BRING STEPHEN IN BEFORE HE COMPLETELY SCREWS--
THE BLONDE.
HE'LL GO FOR THE BLONDE FIRST.
EXPLAIN WHY.
TRUST ME.
I'VE HAD TO CLEAN OUT HIS HARD DRIVE MORE THAN ONCE.
THORN
CONVICTED SEX CRIMINAL
THERESA O'CONNER
MISSION
ABOUT
NEWS
MOST WANTED
AWRIGHT KAIZU, PACK A BAG. YOU'RE RIDING WITH ME.
WE'LL START WITH THE CRADLE ROBBER.

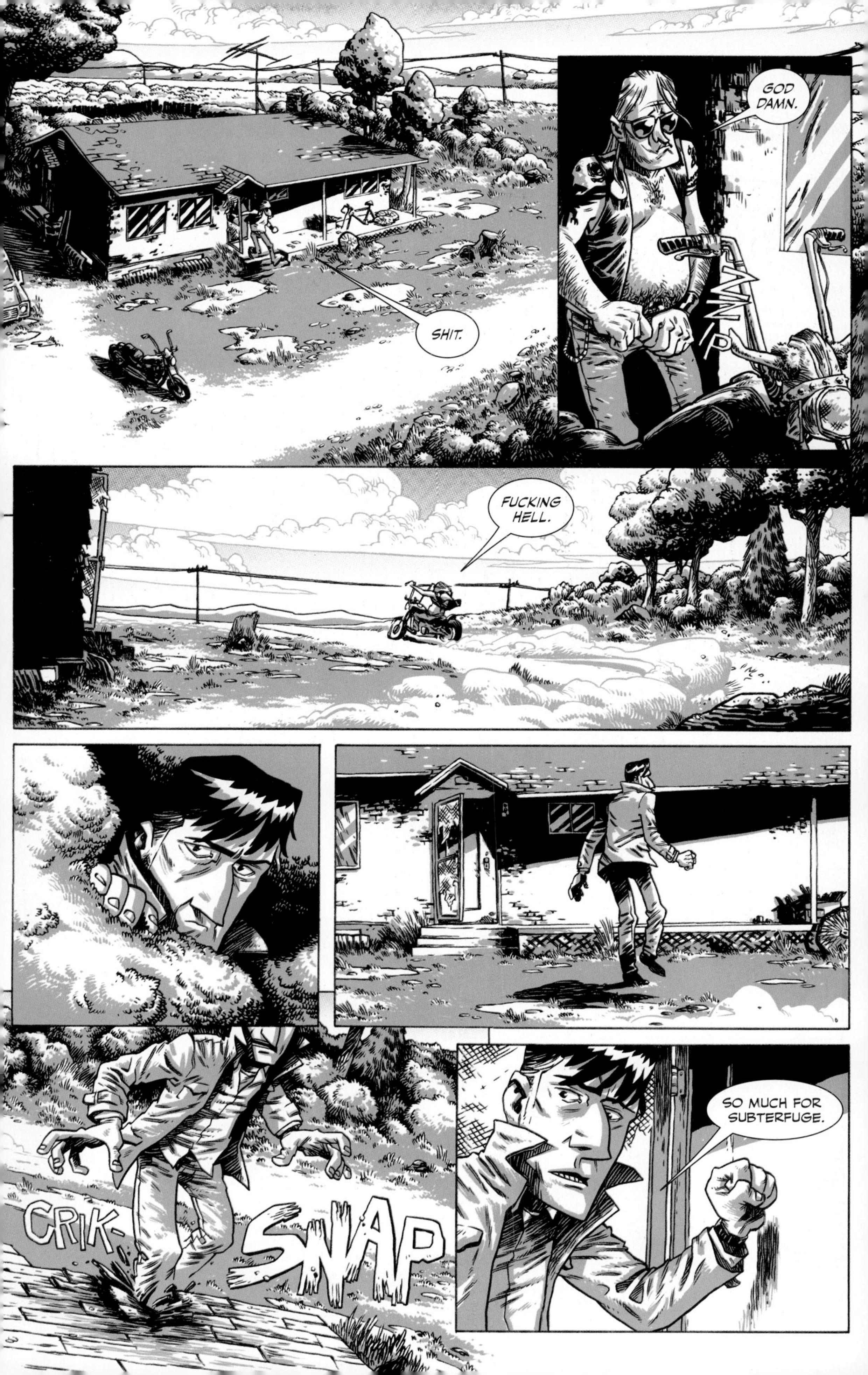
SHIT.
GOD DAMN.
ZZZIP
FUCKING HELL.
CRIK-
SNAP
SO MUCH FOR SUBTERFUGE.

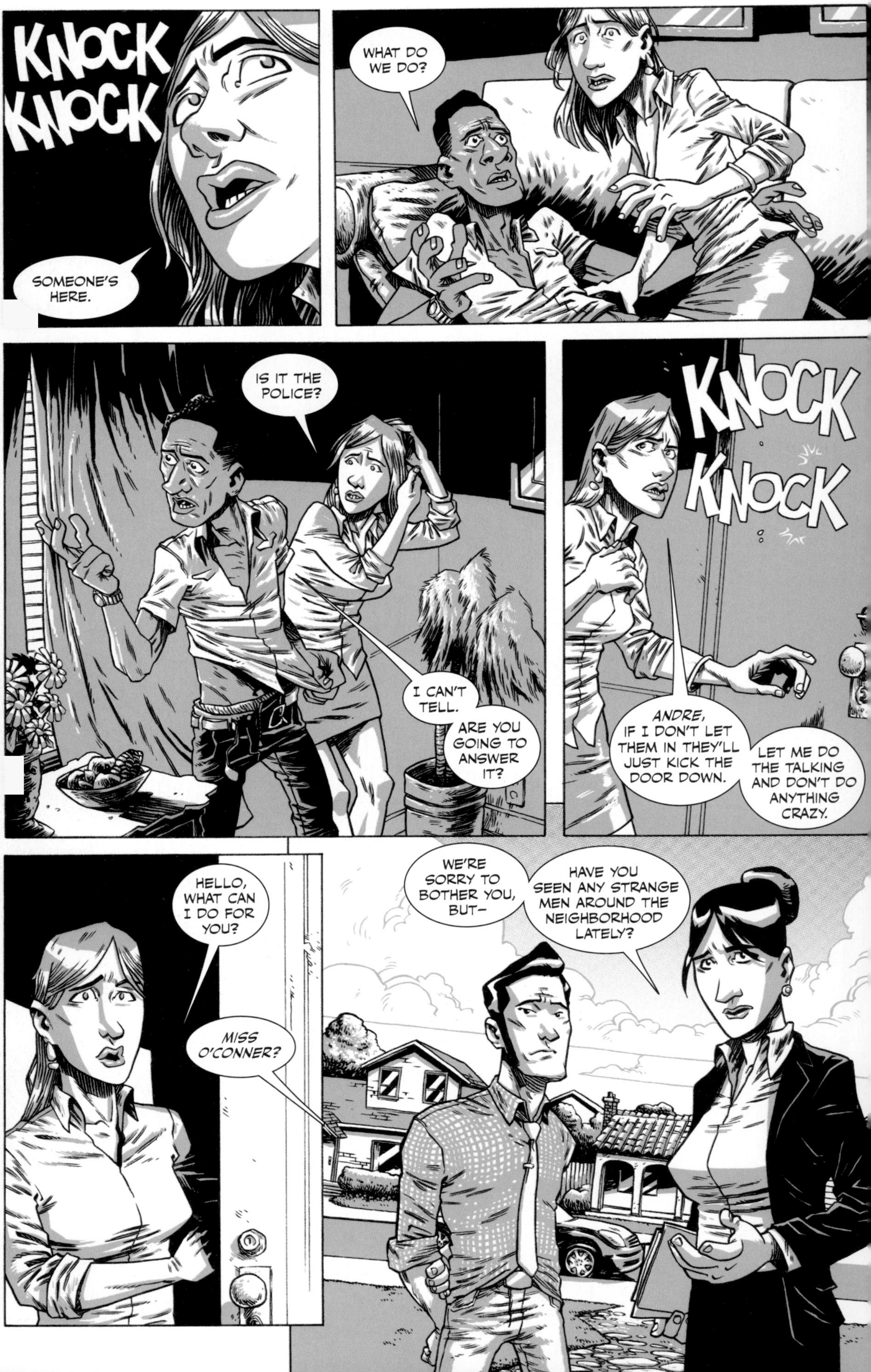
KNOCK KNOCK
SOMEONE'S HERE.
WHAT DO WE DO?
IS IT THE POLICE?
I CAN'T TELL.
ARE YOU GOING TO ANSWER IT?
KNOCK KNOCK
ANDRE, IF I DON'T LET THEM IN THEY'LL JUST KICK THE DOOR DOWN.
LET ME DO THE TALKING AND DON'T DO ANYTHING CRAZY.
HELLO, WHAT CAN I DO FOR YOU?
MISS O'CONNER?
WE'RE SORRY TO BOTHER YOU, BUT—
HAVE YOU SEEN ANY STRANGE MEN AROUND THE NEIGHBORHOOD LATELY?

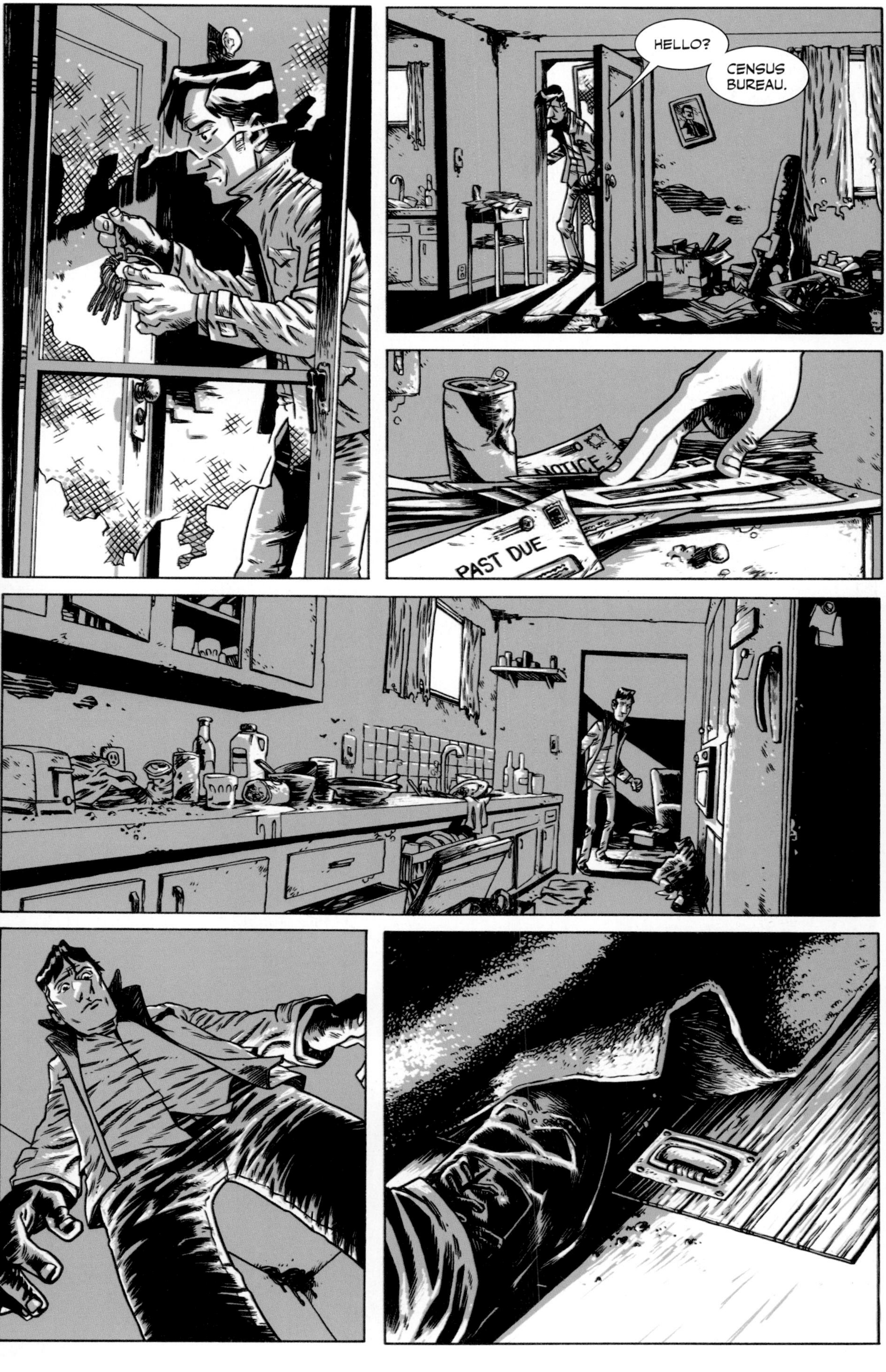
HELLO?
CENSUS BUREAU.
NOTICE
PAST DUE

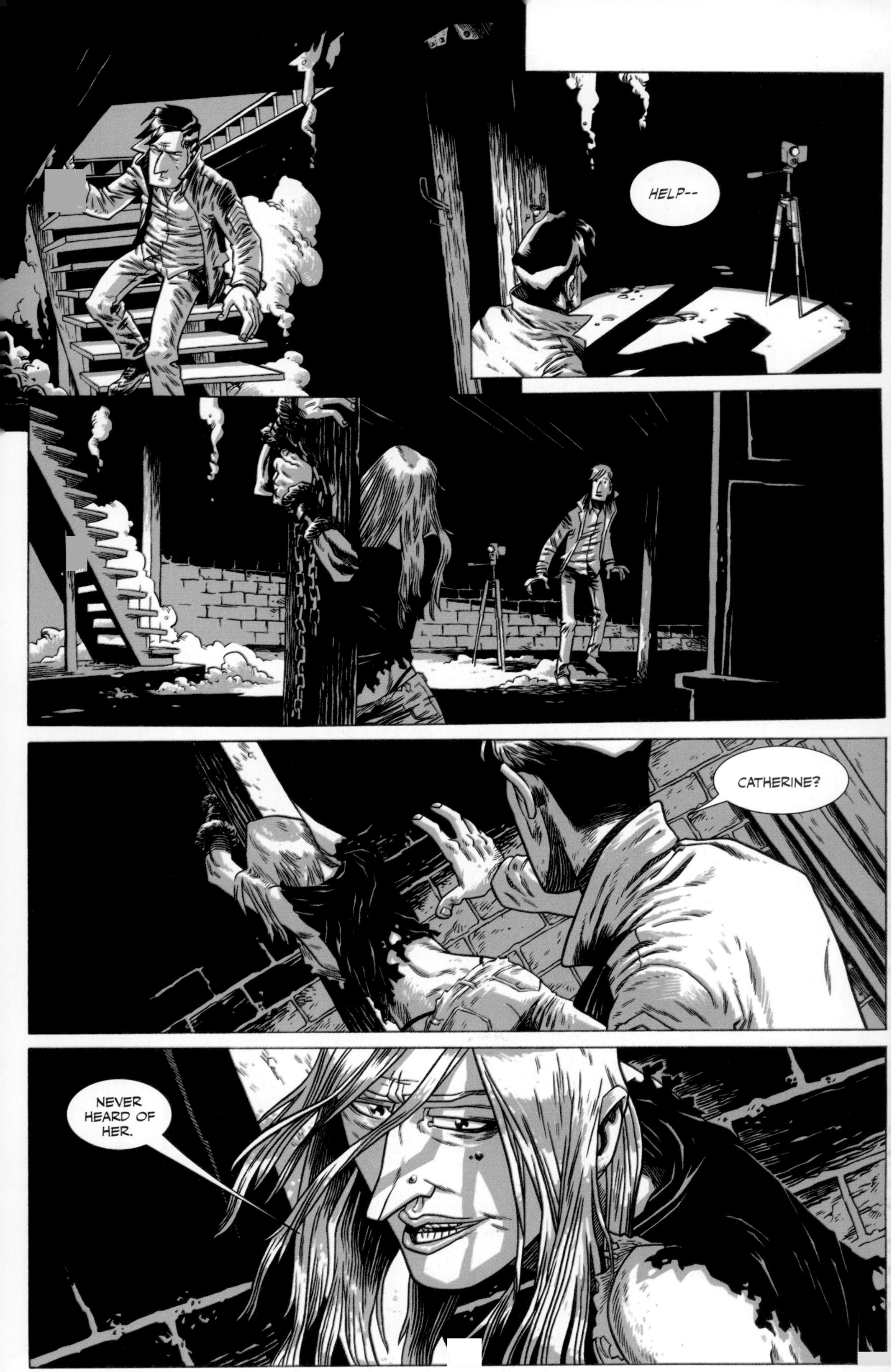
HELP--
CATHERINE?
NEVER HEARD OF HER.

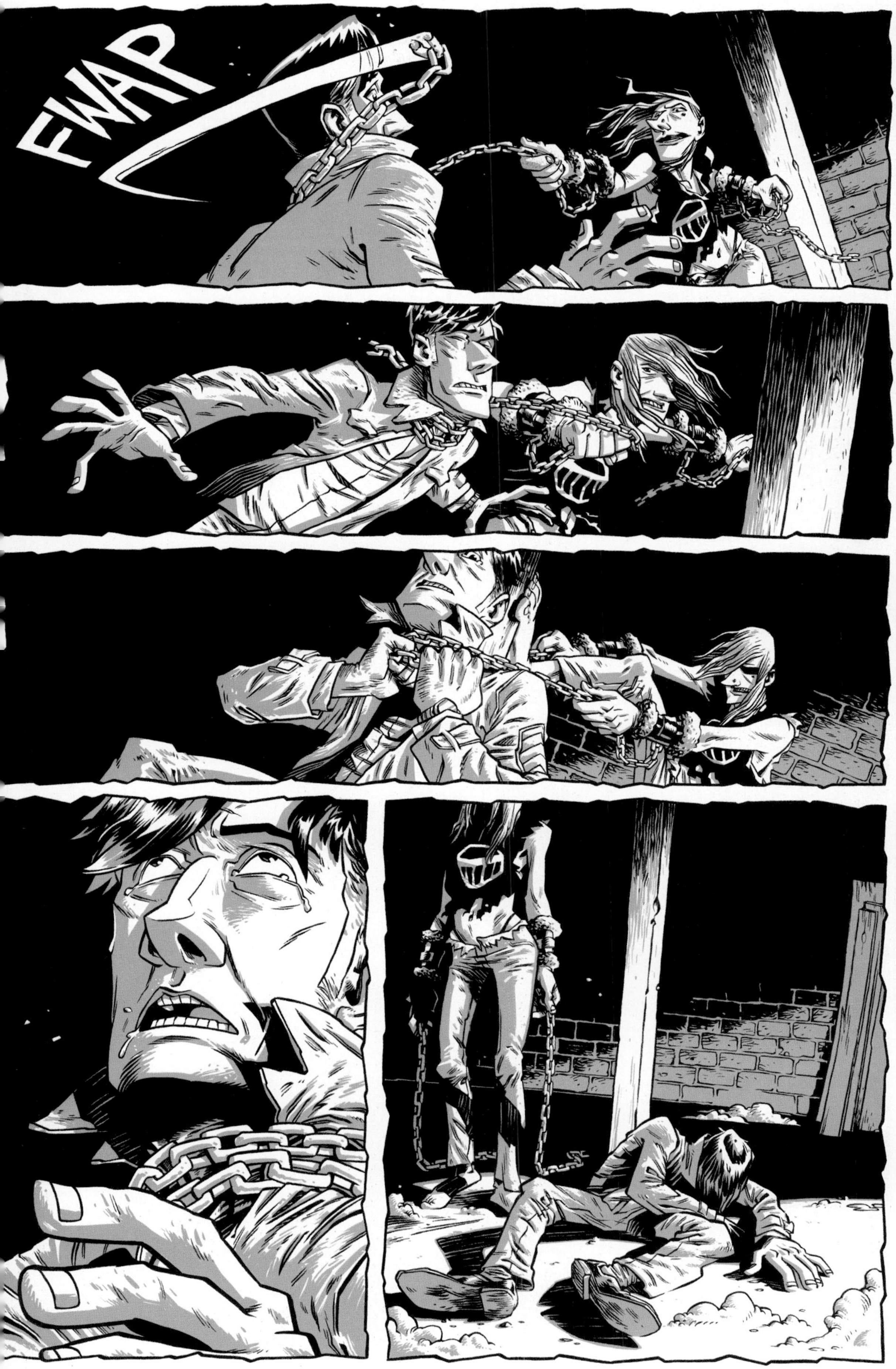
FWAP

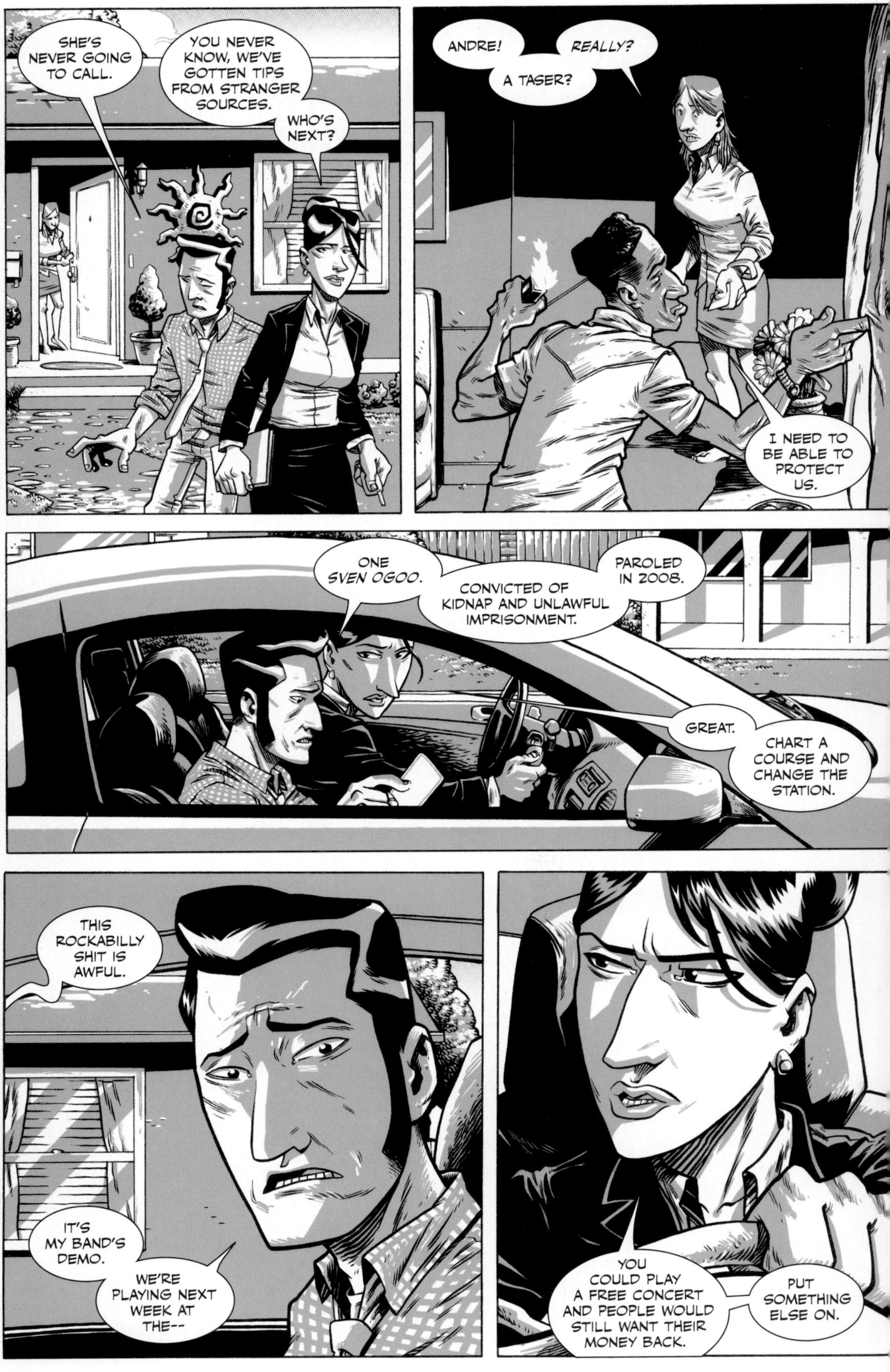
SHE'S NEVER GOING TO CALL.
YOU NEVER KNOW, WE'VE GOTTEN TIPS FROM STRANGER SOURCES.
WHO'S NEXT?
ANDRE!
A TASER?
REALLY?
I NEED TO BE ABLE TO PROTECT US.
ONE SVEN OGOO.
CONVICTED OF KIDNAP AND UNLAWFUL IMPRISONMENT.
PAROLED IN 2008.
GREAT.
CHART A COURSE AND CHANGE THE STATION.
THIS ROCKABILLY SHIT IS AWFUL.
IT'S MY BAND'S DEMO.
WE'RE PLAYING NEXT WEEK AT THE--
YOU COULD PLAY A FREE CONCERT AND PEOPLE WOULD STILL WANT THEIR MONEY BACK.
PUT SOMETHING ELSE ON.

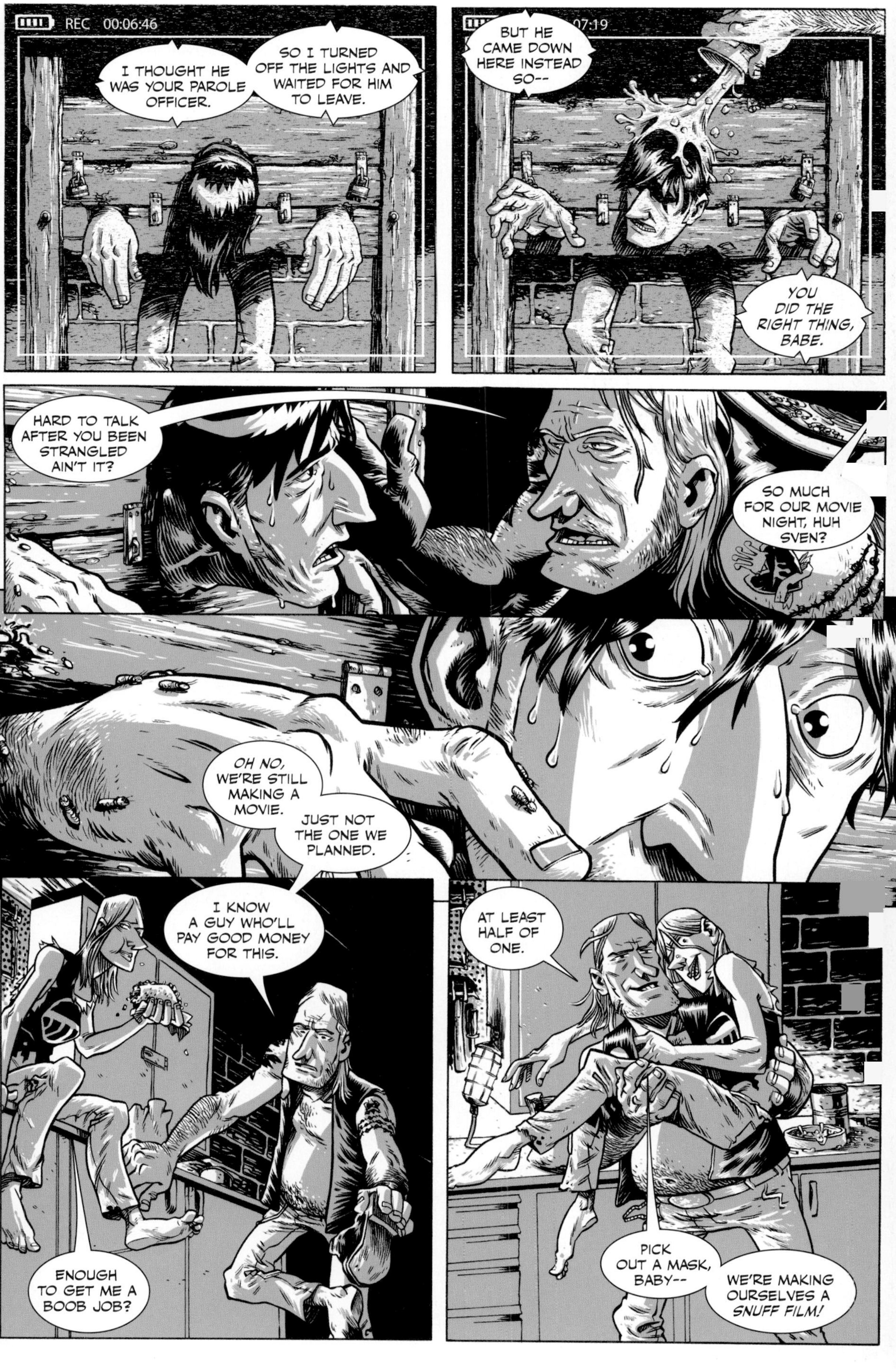
REC 00:06:46
I THOUGHT HE WAS YOUR PAROLE OFFICER.
SO I TURNED OFF THE LIGHTS AND WAITED FOR HIM TO LEAVE.
07:19
BUT HE CAME DOWN HERE INSTEAD SO--
YOU DID THE RIGHT THING, BABE.
HARD TO TALK AFTER YOU BEEN STRANGLED AIN'T IT?
SO MUCH FOR OUR MOVIE NIGHT, HUH SVEN?
OH NO, WE'RE STILL MAKING A MOVIE.
JUST NOT THE ONE WE PLANNED.
I KNOW A GUY WHO'LL PAY GOOD MONEY FOR THIS.
ENOUGH TO GET ME A BOOB JOB?
AT LEAST HALF OF ONE.
PICK OUT A MASK, BABY--
WE'RE MAKING OURSELVES A SNUFF FILM!

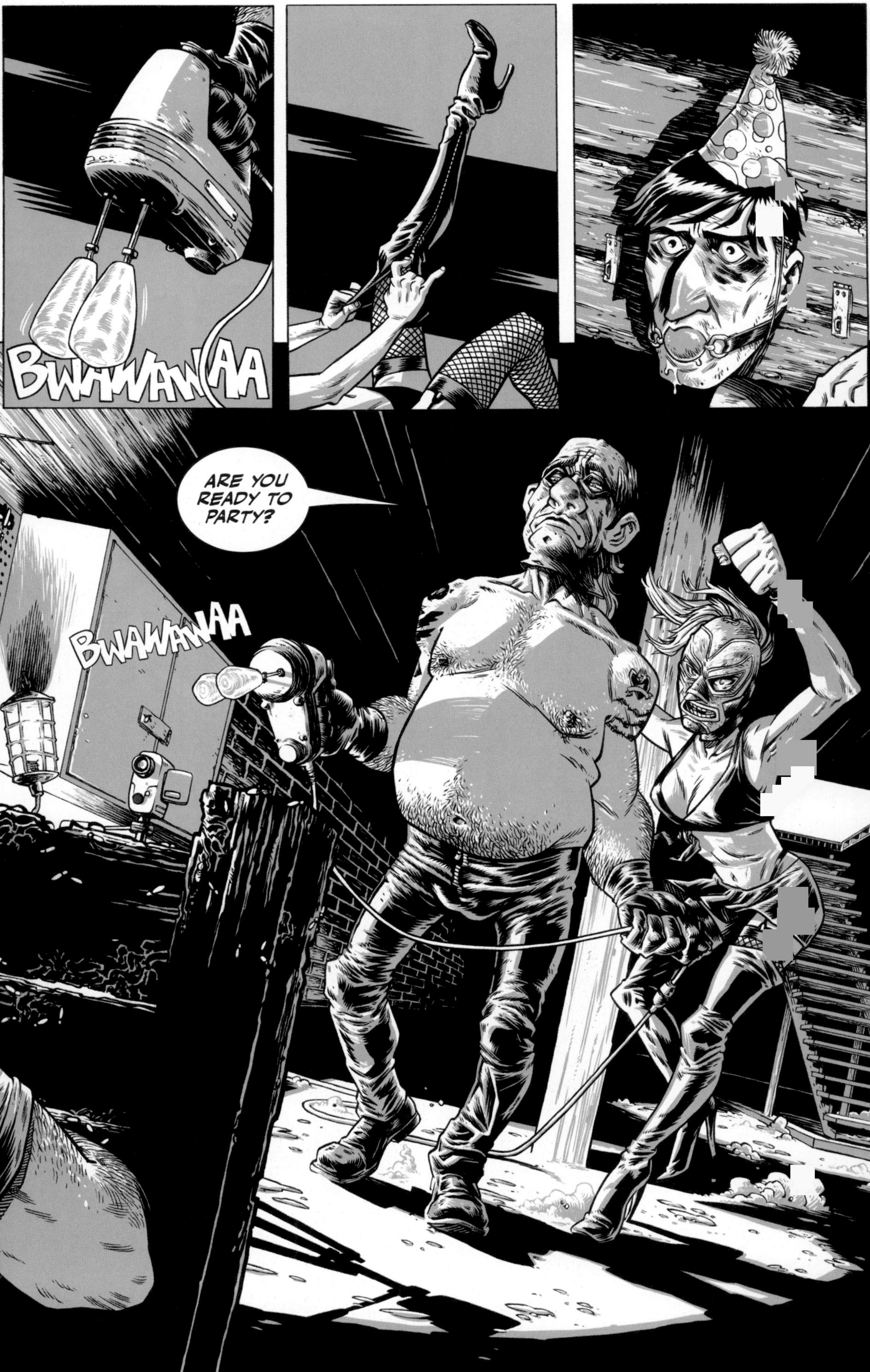
BWAWAWAA
ARE YOU READY TO PARTY?
BWAWAWAA

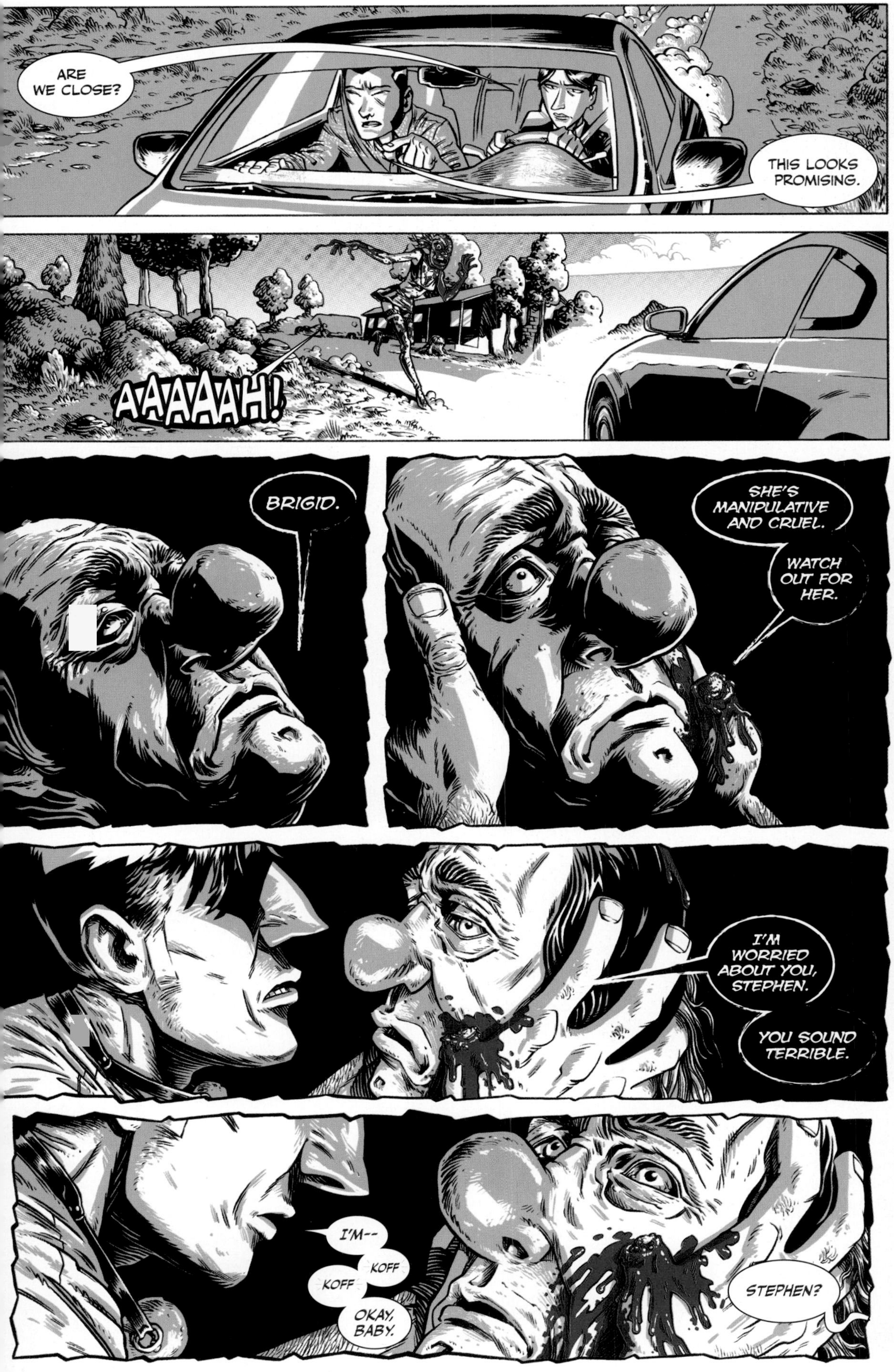
ARE WE CLOSE?
THIS LOOKS PROMISING.
AAAAAH!
BRIGID.
SHE'S MANIPULATIVE AND CRUEL.
WATCH OUT FOR HER.
I'M WORRIED ABOUT YOU, STEPHEN.
YOU SOUND TERRIBLE.
I'M--
KOFF
KOFF
OKAY, BABY.
STEPHEN?

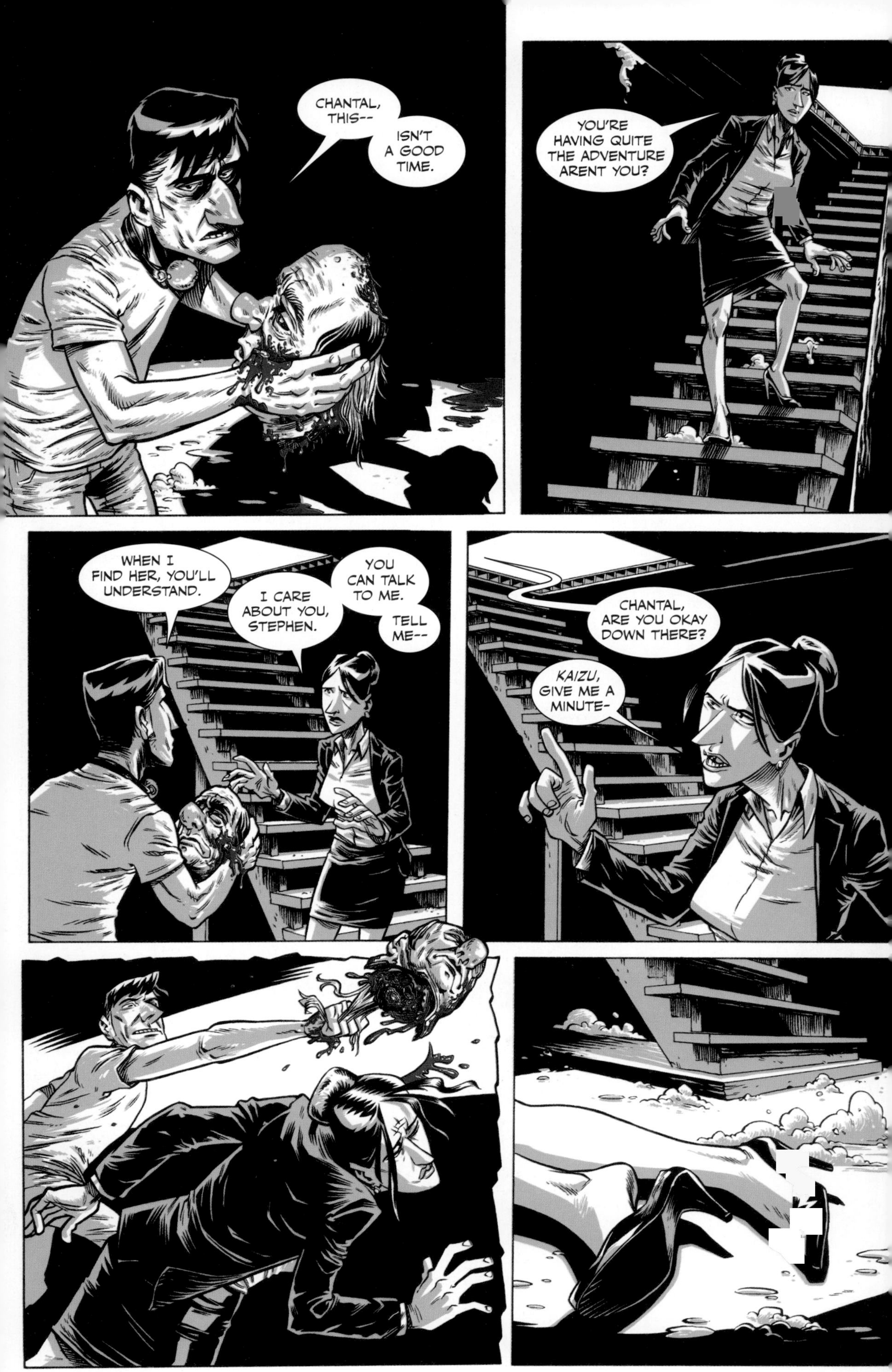
CHANTAL, THIS--
ISN'T A GOOD TIME.
YOU'RE HAVING QUITE THE ADVENTURE ARENT YOU?
WHEN I FIND HER, YOU'LL UNDERSTAND.
I CARE ABOUT YOU, STEPHEN.
YOU CAN TALK TO ME.
TELL ME--
CHANTAL, ARE YOU OKAY DOWN THERE?
KAIZU, GIVE ME A MINUTE-

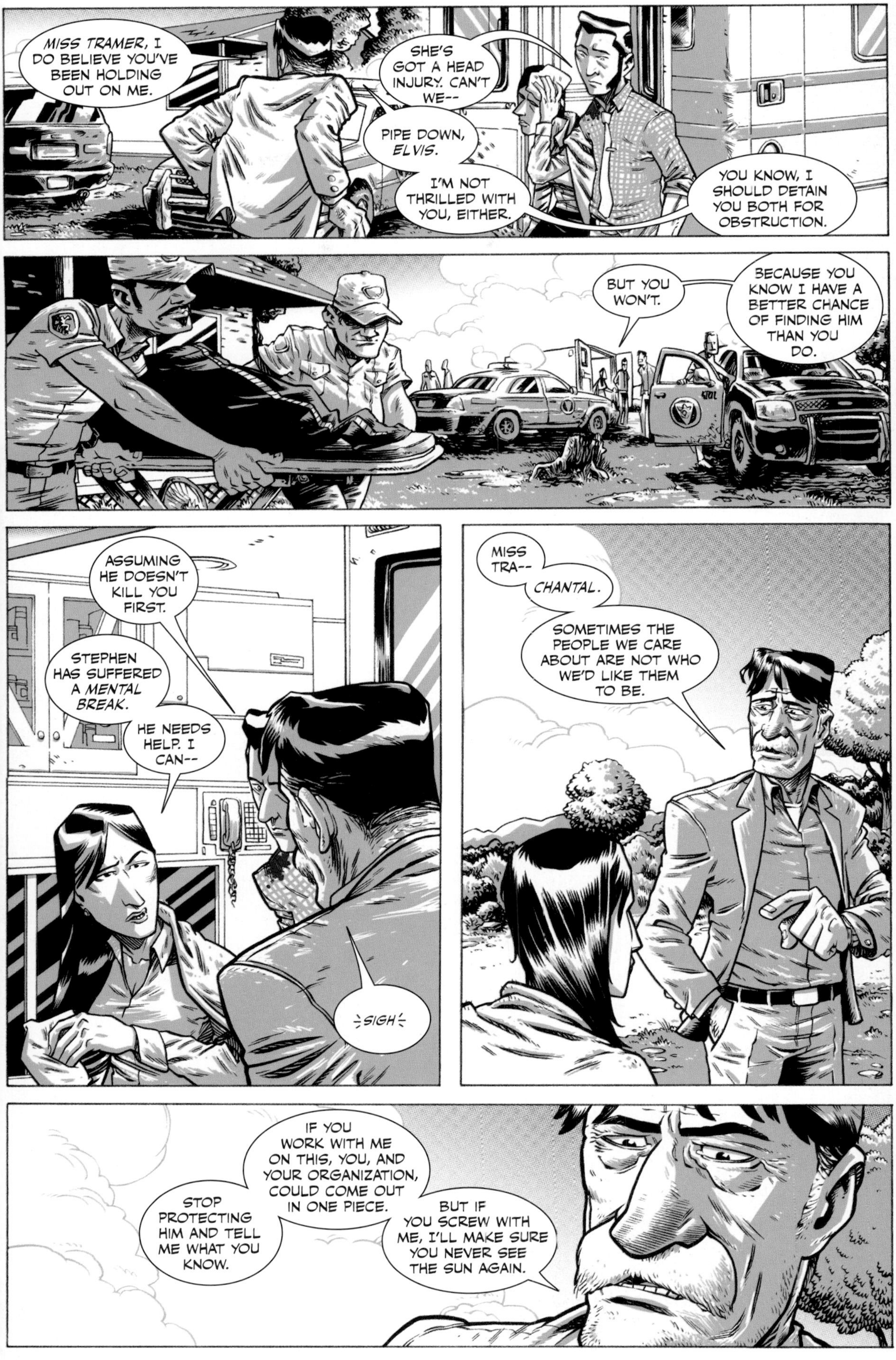
MISS TRAMER, I DO BELIEVE YOU'VE BEEN HOLDING OUT ON ME.
SHE'S GOT A HEAD INJURY. CAN'T WE--
PIPE DOWN, ELVIS.
I'M NOT THRILLED WITH YOU, EITHER.
YOU KNOW, I SHOULD DETAIN YOU BOTH FOR OBSTRUCTION.
BUT YOU WON'T.
BECAUSE YOU KNOW I HAVE A BETTER CHANCE OF FINDING HIM THAN YOU DO.
ASSUMING HE DOESN'T KILL YOU FIRST.
STEPHEN HAS SUFFERED A MENTAL BREAK.
HE NEEDS HELP. I CAN--
SIGH
MISS TRA--
CHANTAL.
SOMETIMES THE PEOPLE WE CARE ABOUT ARE NOT WHO WE'D LIKE THEM TO BE.
STOP PROTECTING HIM AND TELL ME WHAT YOU KNOW.
IF YOU WORK WITH ME ON THIS, YOU, AND YOUR ORGANIZATION, COULD COME OUT IN ONE PIECE.
BUT IF YOU SCREW WITH ME, I'LL MAKE SURE YOU NEVER SEE THE SUN AGAIN.

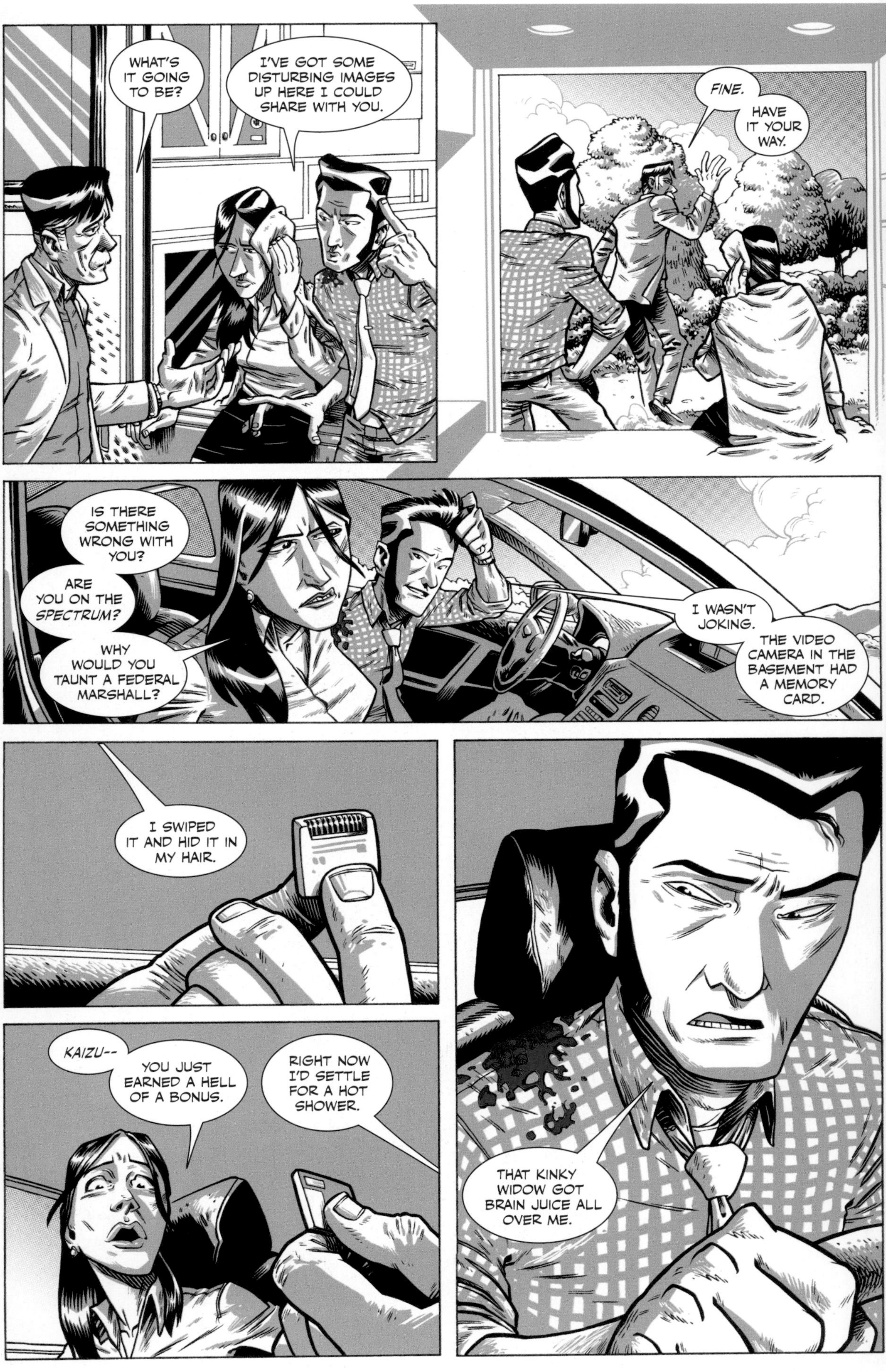
WHAT'S IT GOING TO BE?
I'VE GOT SOME DISTURBING IMAGES UP HERE I COULD SHARE WITH YOU.
FINE.
HAVE IT YOUR WAY.
IS THERE SOMETHING WRONG WITH YOU?
ARE YOU ON THE SPECTRUM?
WHY WOULD YOU TAUNT A FEDERAL MARSHALL?
I WASN'T JOKING.
THE VIDEO CAMERA IN THE BASEMENT HAD A MEMORY CARD.
I SWIPED IT AND HID IT IN MY HAIR.
KAIZU--
YOU JUST EARNED A HELL OF A BONUS.
RIGHT NOW I'D SETTLE FOR A HOT SHOWER.
THAT KINKY WIDOW GOT BRAIN JUICE ALL OVER ME.

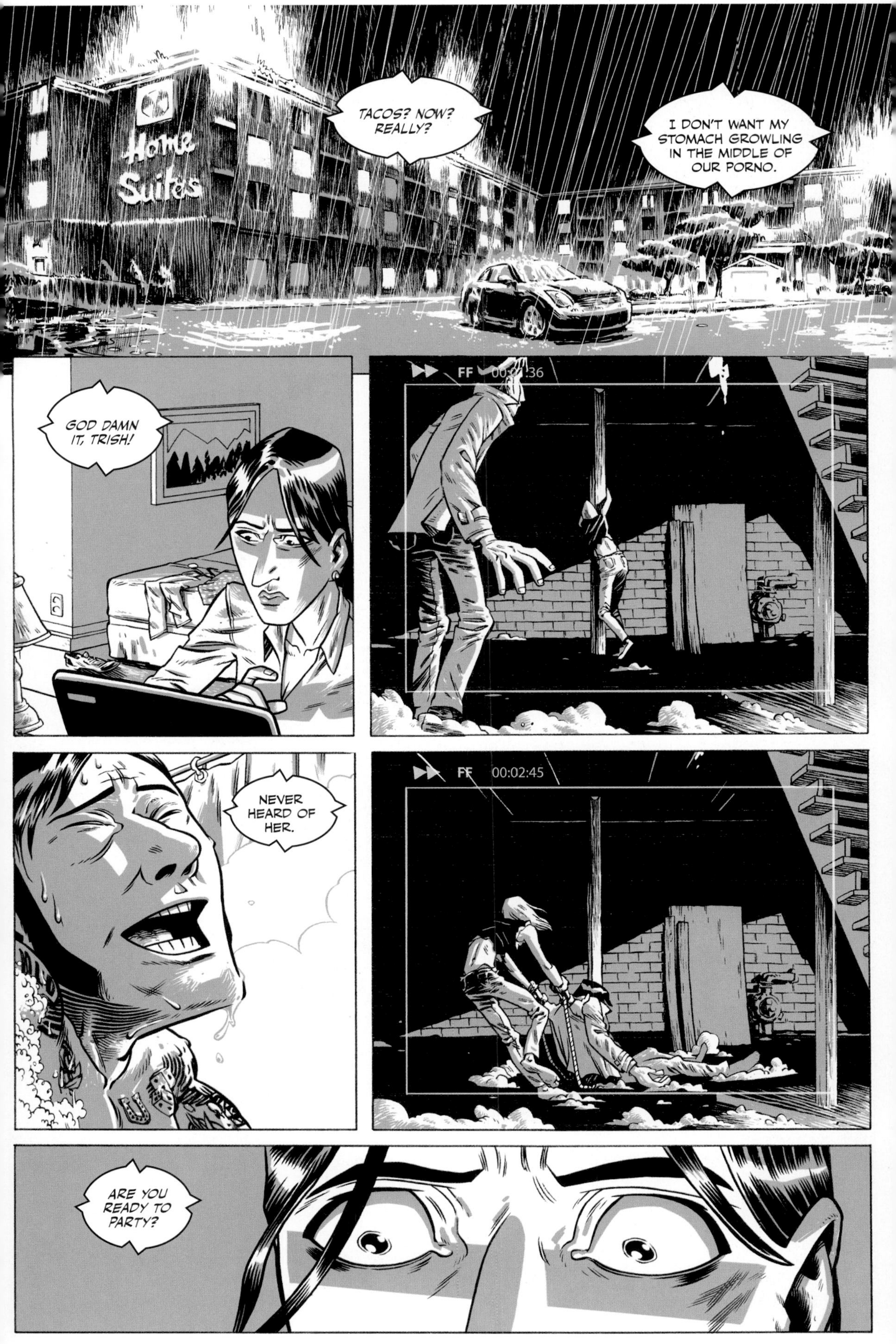
Home Suites
TACOS? NOW? REALLY?
I DON'T WANT MY STOMACH GROWLING IN THE MIDDLE OF OUR PORNO.
GOD DAMN IT, TRISH!
FF
NEVER HEARD OF HER.
FF 00:02:45
ARE YOU READY TO PARTY?

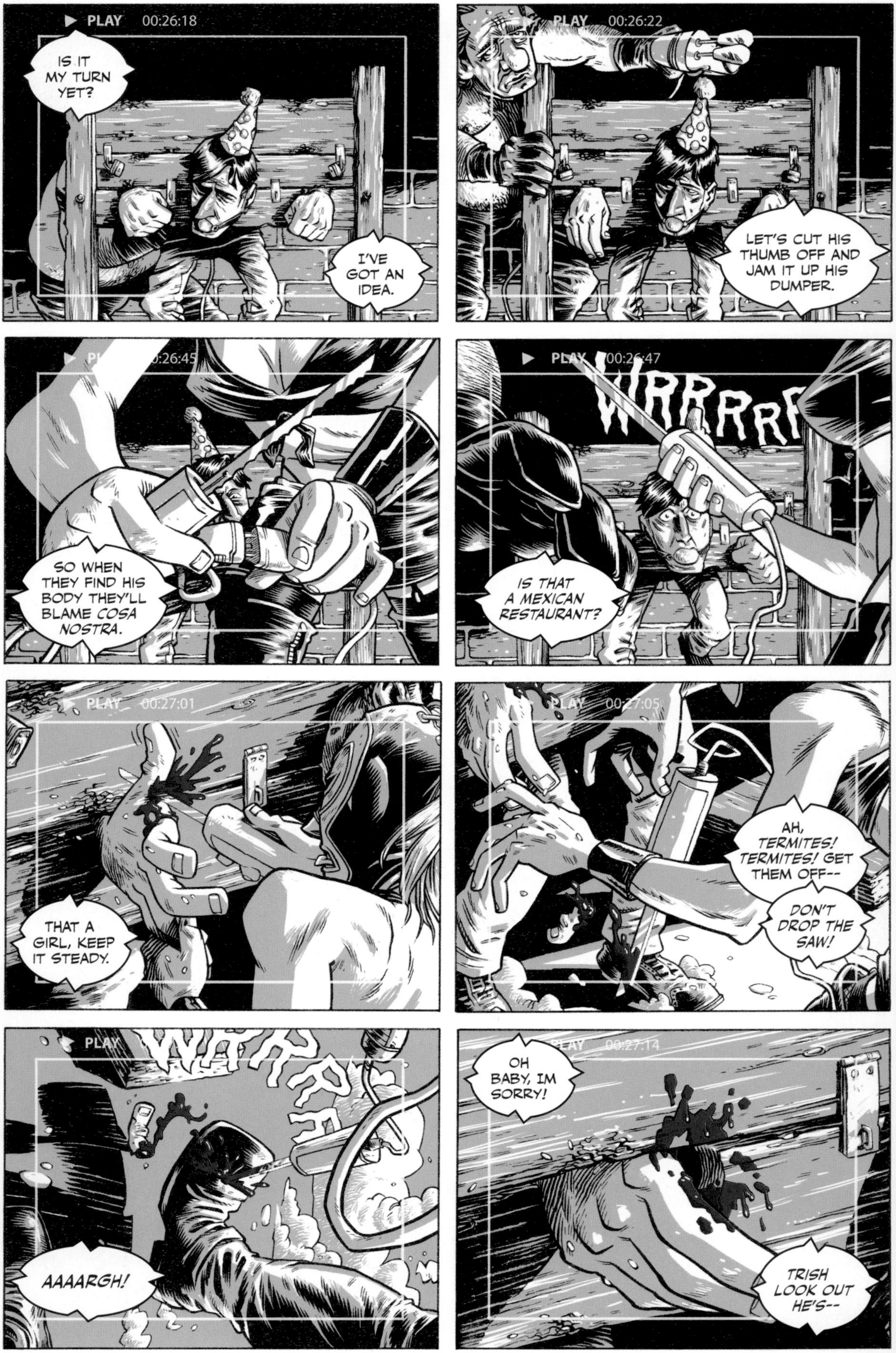
PLAY 00:26:18
IS IT MY TURN YET?
I'VE GOT AN IDEA.
PLAY 00:26:22
LET'S CUT HIS THUMB OFF AND JAM IT UP HIS DUMPER.
SO WHEN THEY FIND HIS BODY THEY'LL BLAME COSA NOSTRA.
PLAY
WRRRRR
IS THAT A MEXICAN RESTAURANT?
PLAY 00:27:01
THAT A GIRL, KEEP IT STEADY.
PLAY
AH, TERMITES! TERMITES! GET THEM OFF--
DON'T DROP THE SAW!
PLAY
AAAARGH!
OH BABY, IM SORRY!
TRISH LOOK OUT HE'S--

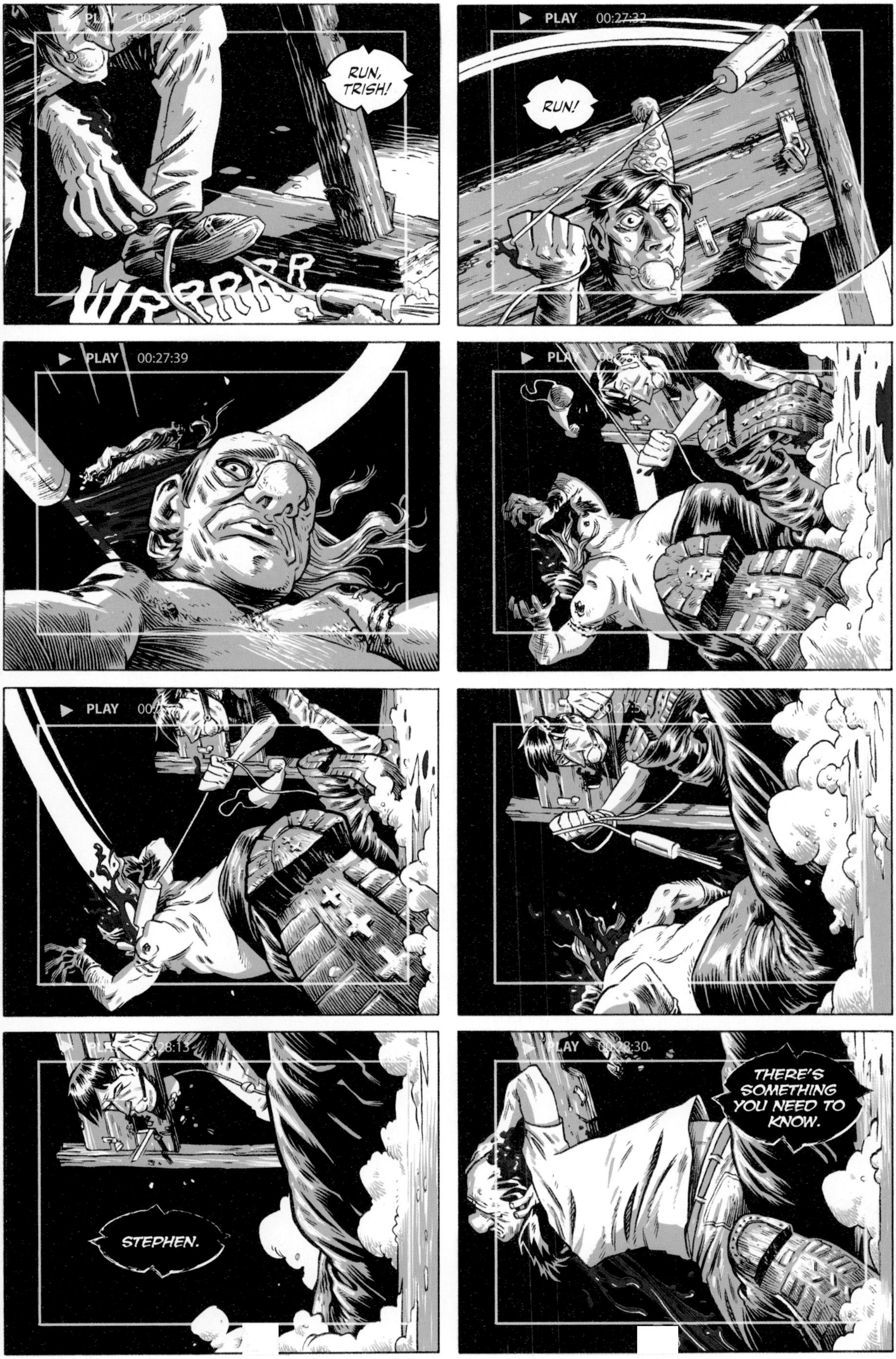
RUN, TRISH!
WRRRRR
PLAY 00:27:32
RUN!
PLAY 00:27:39
STEPHEN.
PLAY 00:28:30
THERE'S SOMETHING YOU NEED TO KNOW.

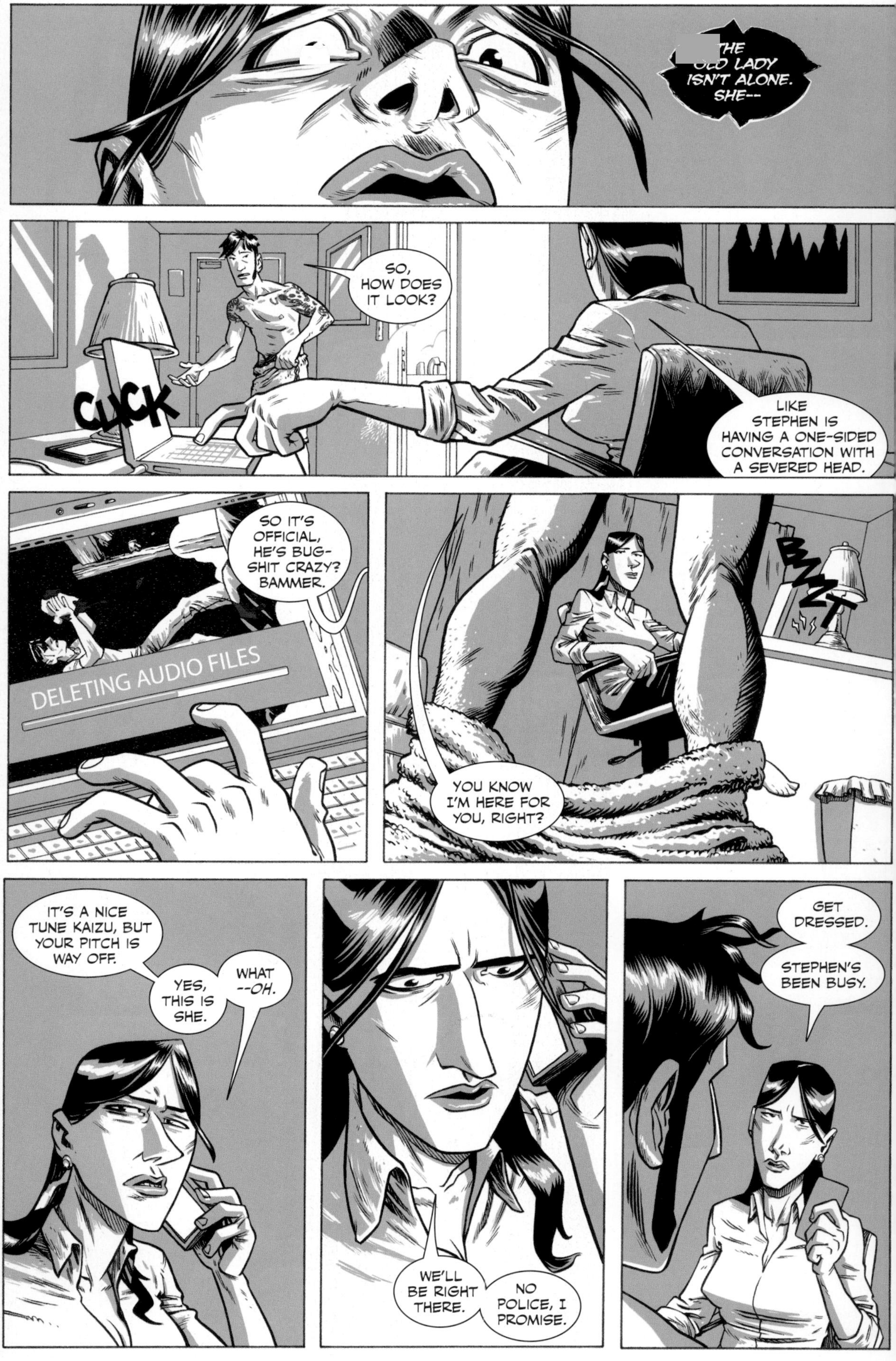
THE OLD LADY ISN'T ALONE. SHE--
SO, HOW DOES IT LOOK?
CLICK
LIKE STEPHEN IS HAVING A ONE-SIDED CONVERSATION WITH A SEVERED HEAD.
SO IT'S OFFICIAL, HE'S BUG-SHIT CRAZY? BAMMER.
DELETING AUDIO FILES
BZZZT
YOU KNOW I'M HERE FOR YOU, RIGHT?
IT'S A NICE TUNE KAIZU, BUT YOUR PITCH IS WAY OFF.
YES, THIS IS SHE.
WHAT --OH.
WE'LL BE RIGHT THERE.
NO POLICE, I PROMISE.
GET DRESSED.
STEPHEN'S BEEN BUSY.

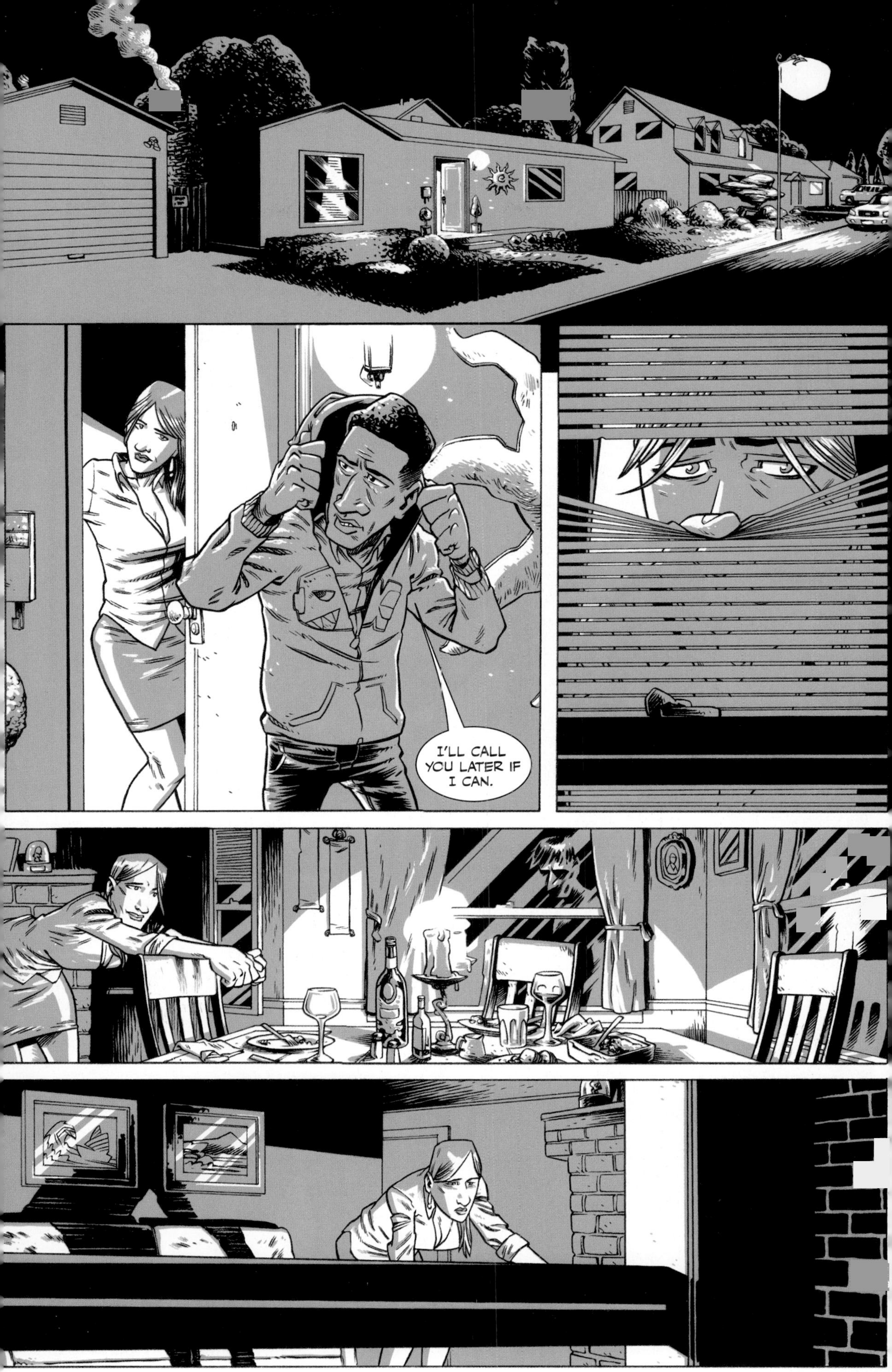
I'LL CALL YOU LATER IF I CAN.

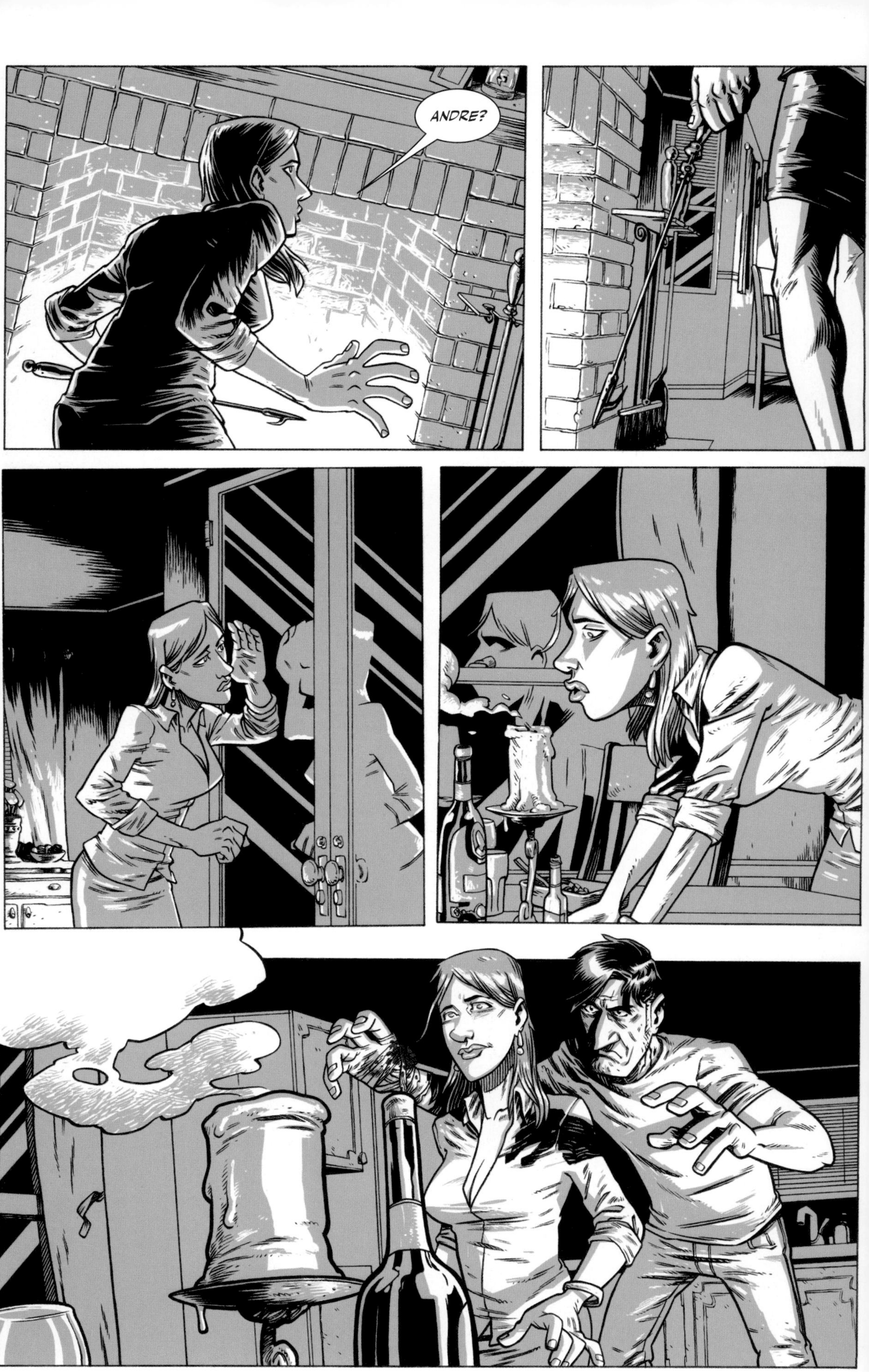
ANDRE?

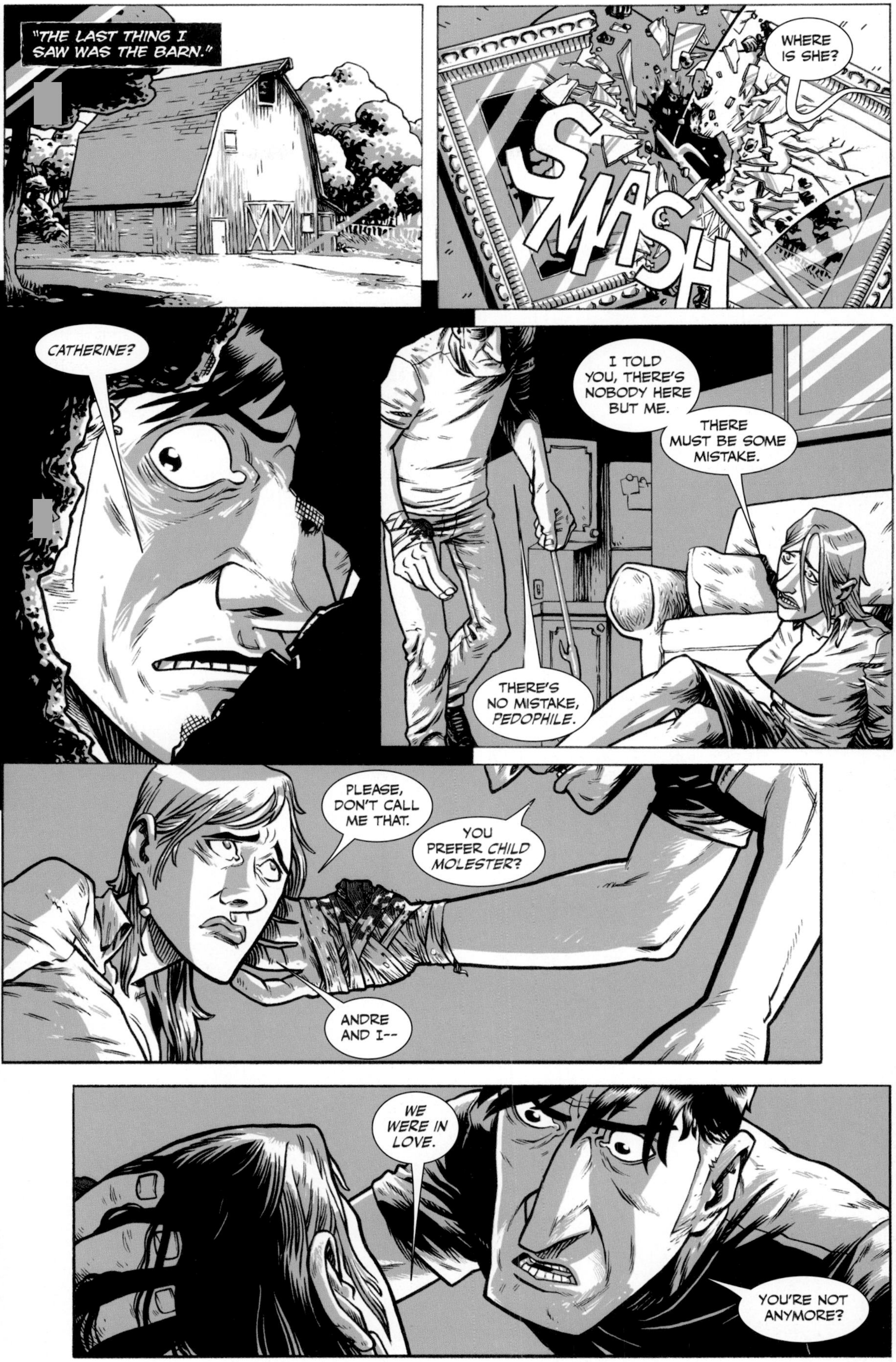
"THE LAST THING I SAW WAS THE BARN."
WHERE IS SHE?
SMASH
CATHERINE?
I TOLD YOU, THERE'S NOBODY HERE BUT ME.
THERE MUST BE SOME MISTAKE.
THERE'S NO MISTAKE, *PEDOPHILE*.
PLEASE, DON'T CALL ME THAT.
YOU PREFER *CHILD MOLESTER*?
ANDRE AND I--
WE WERE IN LOVE.
YOU'RE NOT ANYMORE?

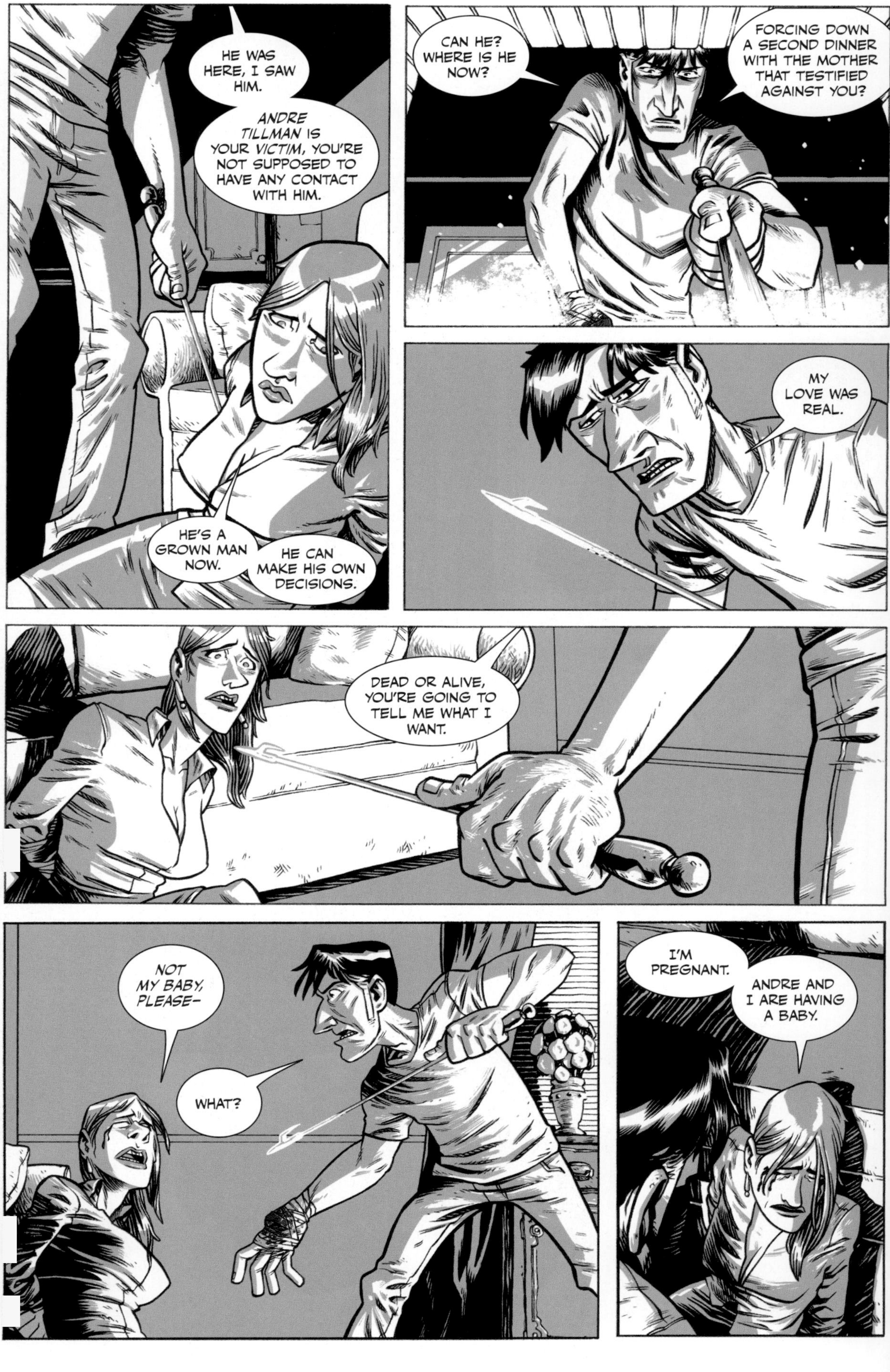
HE WAS HERE, I SAW HIM.
ANDRE TILLMAN IS YOUR *VICTIM*, YOU'RE NOT SUPPOSED TO HAVE ANY CONTACT WITH HIM.
HE'S A GROWN MAN NOW.
HE CAN MAKE HIS OWN DECISIONS.
CAN HE? WHERE IS HE NOW?
FORCING DOWN A SECOND DINNER WITH THE MOTHER THAT TESTIFIED AGAINST YOU?
MY LOVE WAS REAL.
DEAD OR ALIVE, YOU'RE GOING TO TELL ME WHAT I WANT.
NOT MY BABY, PLEASE-
WHAT?
I'M PREGNANT.
ANDRE AND I ARE HAVING A BABY.

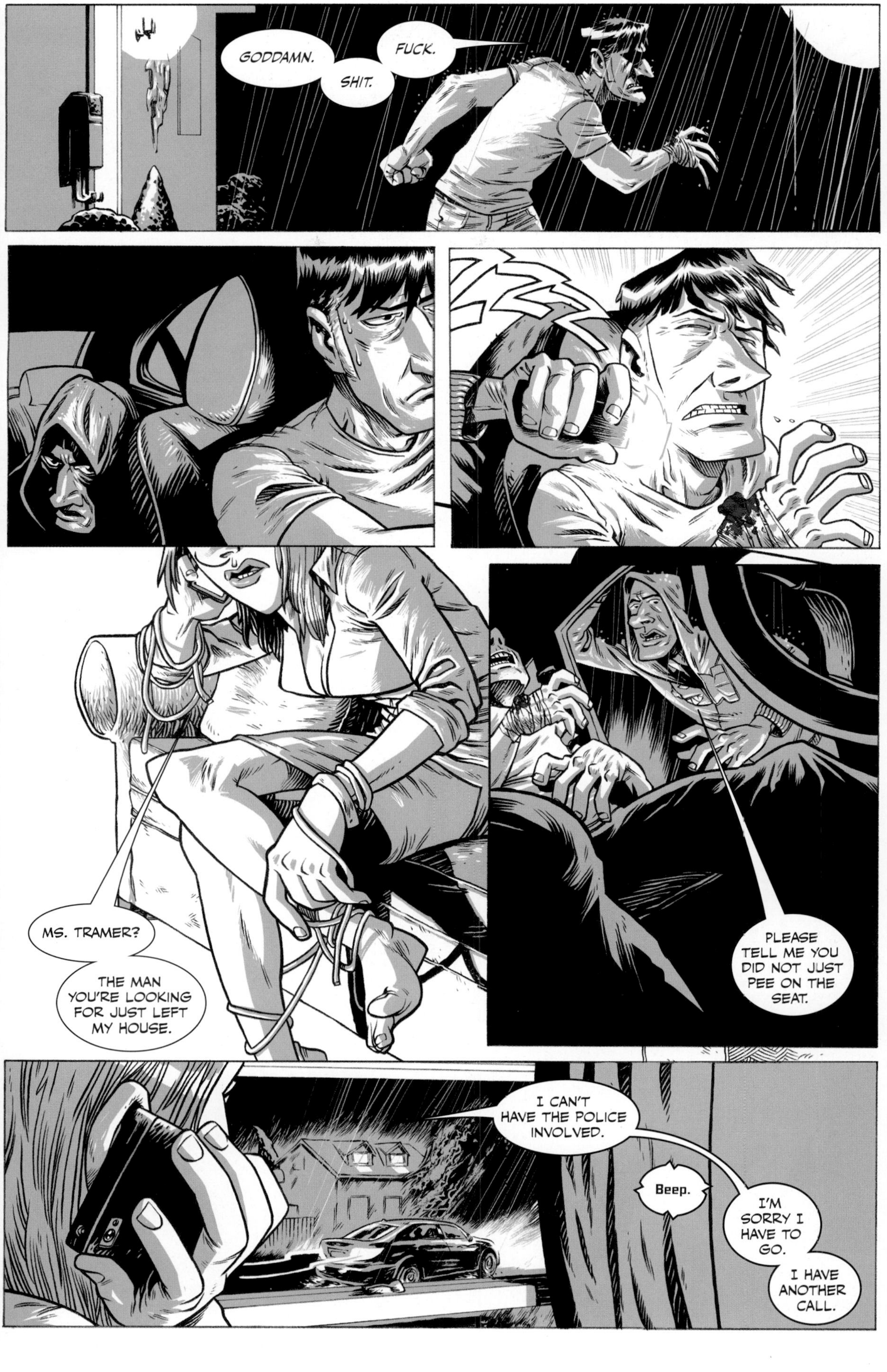
GODDAMN.
SHIT.
FUCK.
MS. TRAMER?
THE MAN YOU'RE LOOKING FOR JUST LEFT MY HOUSE.
PLEASE TELL ME YOU DID NOT JUST PEE ON THE SEAT.
I CAN'T HAVE THE POLICE INVOLVED.
Beep.
I'M SORRY I HAVE TO GO.
I HAVE ANOTHER CALL.

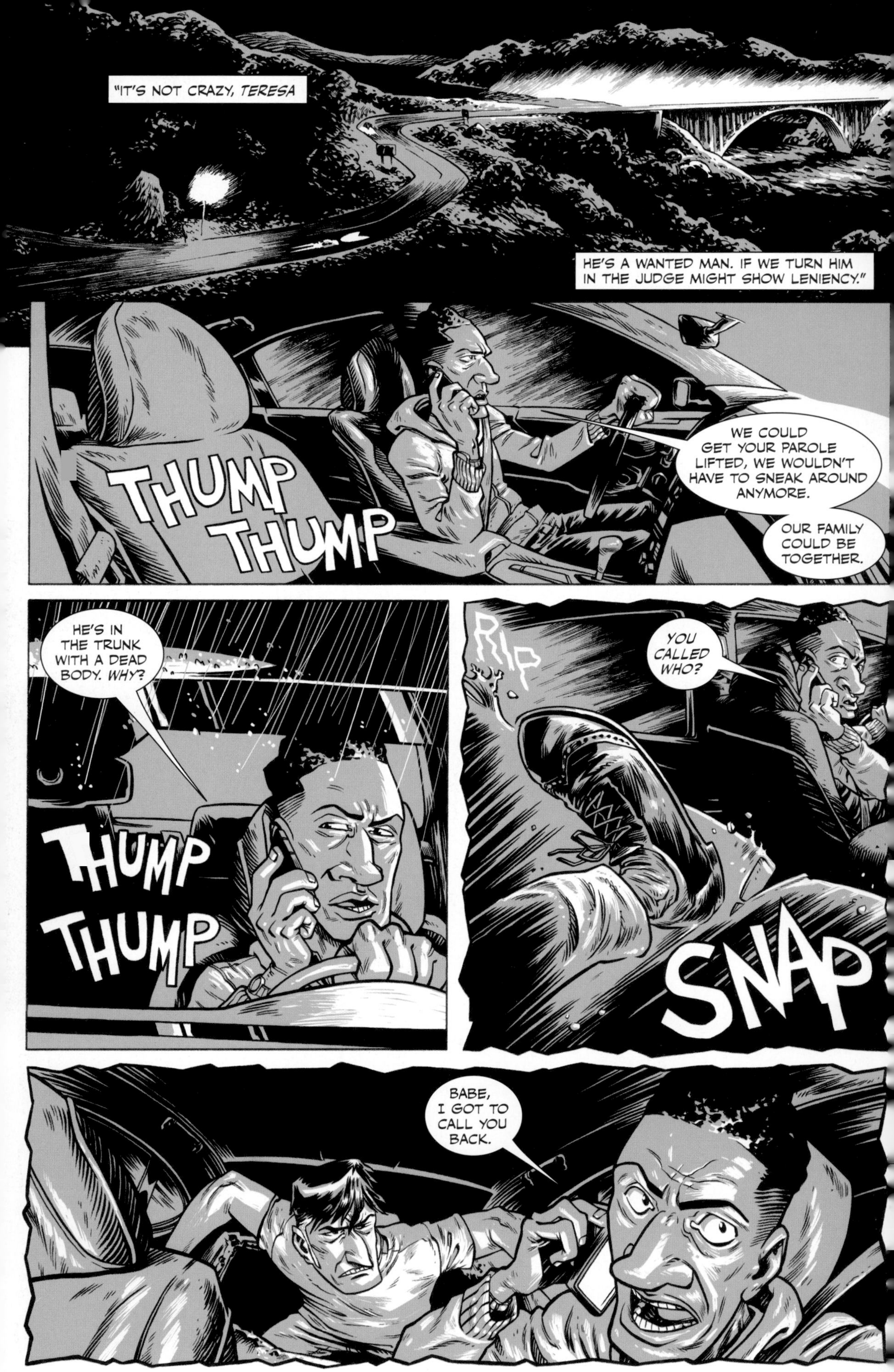
"IT'S NOT CRAZY, *TERESA*
HE'S A WANTED MAN. IF WE TURN HIM IN THE JUDGE MIGHT SHOW LENIENCY."
THUMP THUMP
WE COULD GET YOUR PAROLE LIFTED, WE WOULDN'T HAVE TO SNEAK AROUND ANYMORE.
OUR FAMILY COULD BE TOGETHER.
HE'S IN THE TRUNK WITH A DEAD BODY. *WHY?*
THUMP THUMP
RIP
YOU CALLED WHO?
SNAP
BABE, I GOT TO CALL YOU BACK.

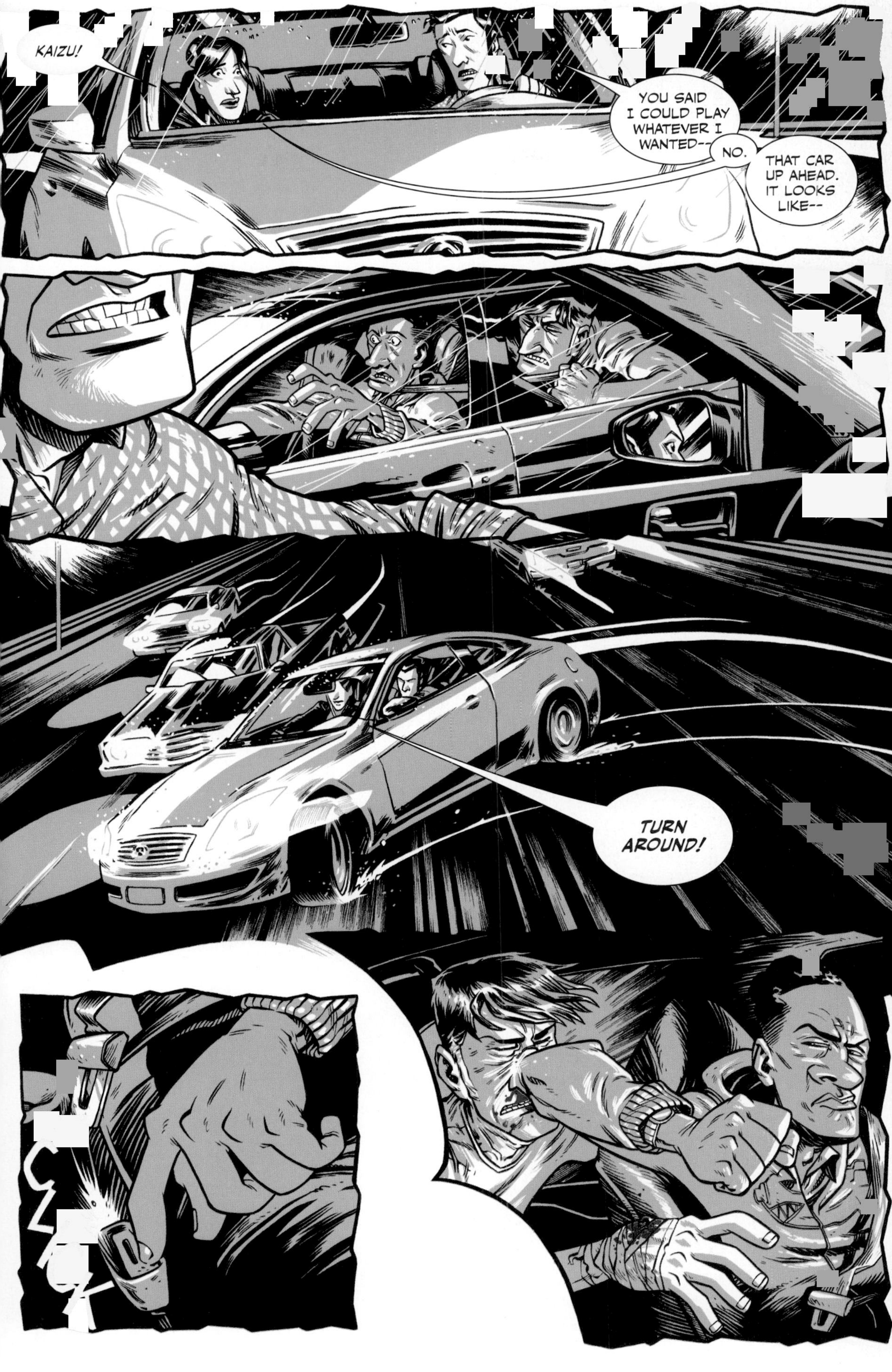
KAIZU!
YOU SAID I COULD PLAY WHATEVER I WANTED--
NO.
THAT CAR UP AHEAD. IT LOOKS LIKE--
TURN AROUND!

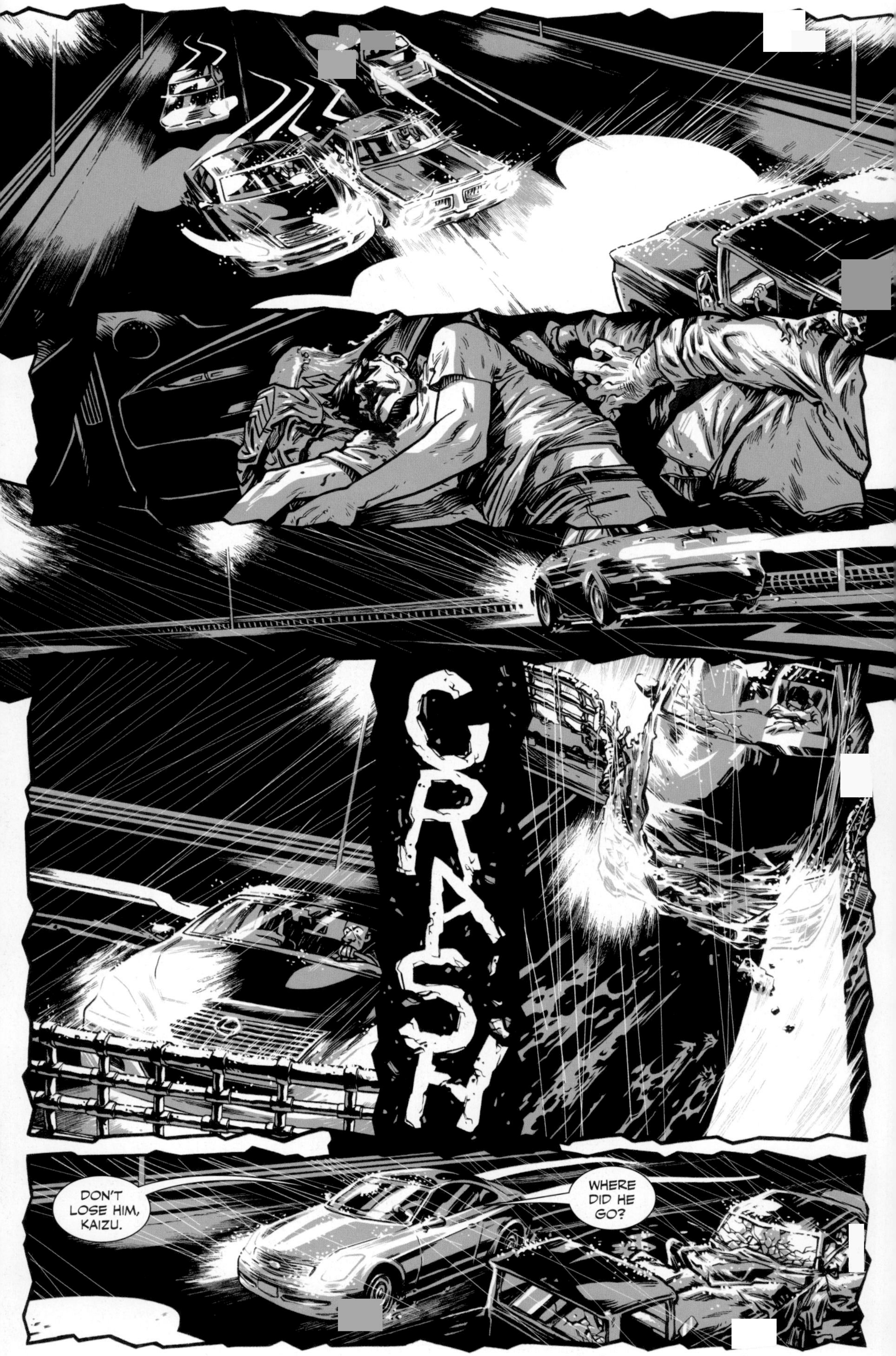
CRASH
DON'T LOSE HIM, KAIZU.
WHERE DID HE GO?

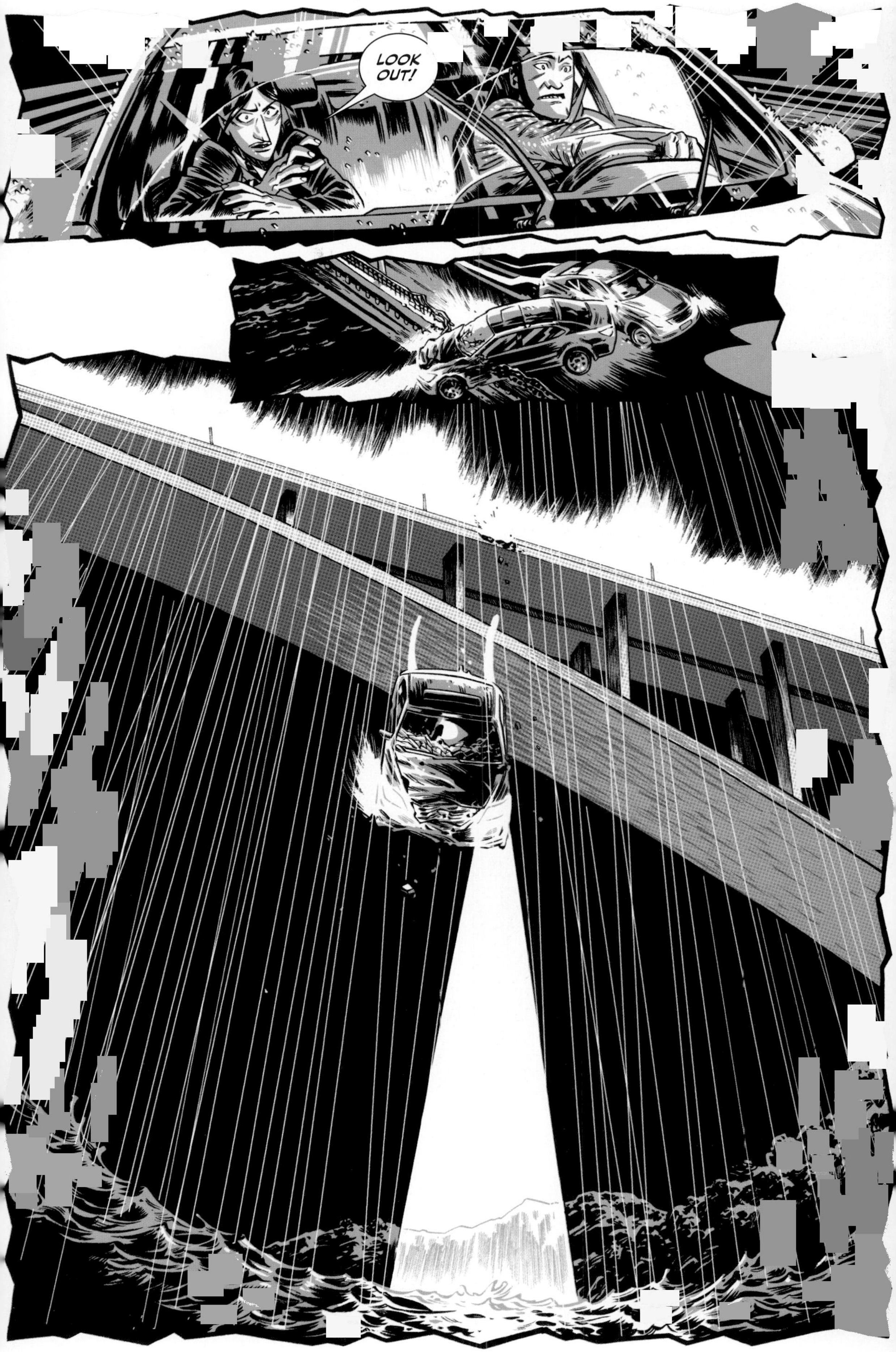
LOOK OUT!

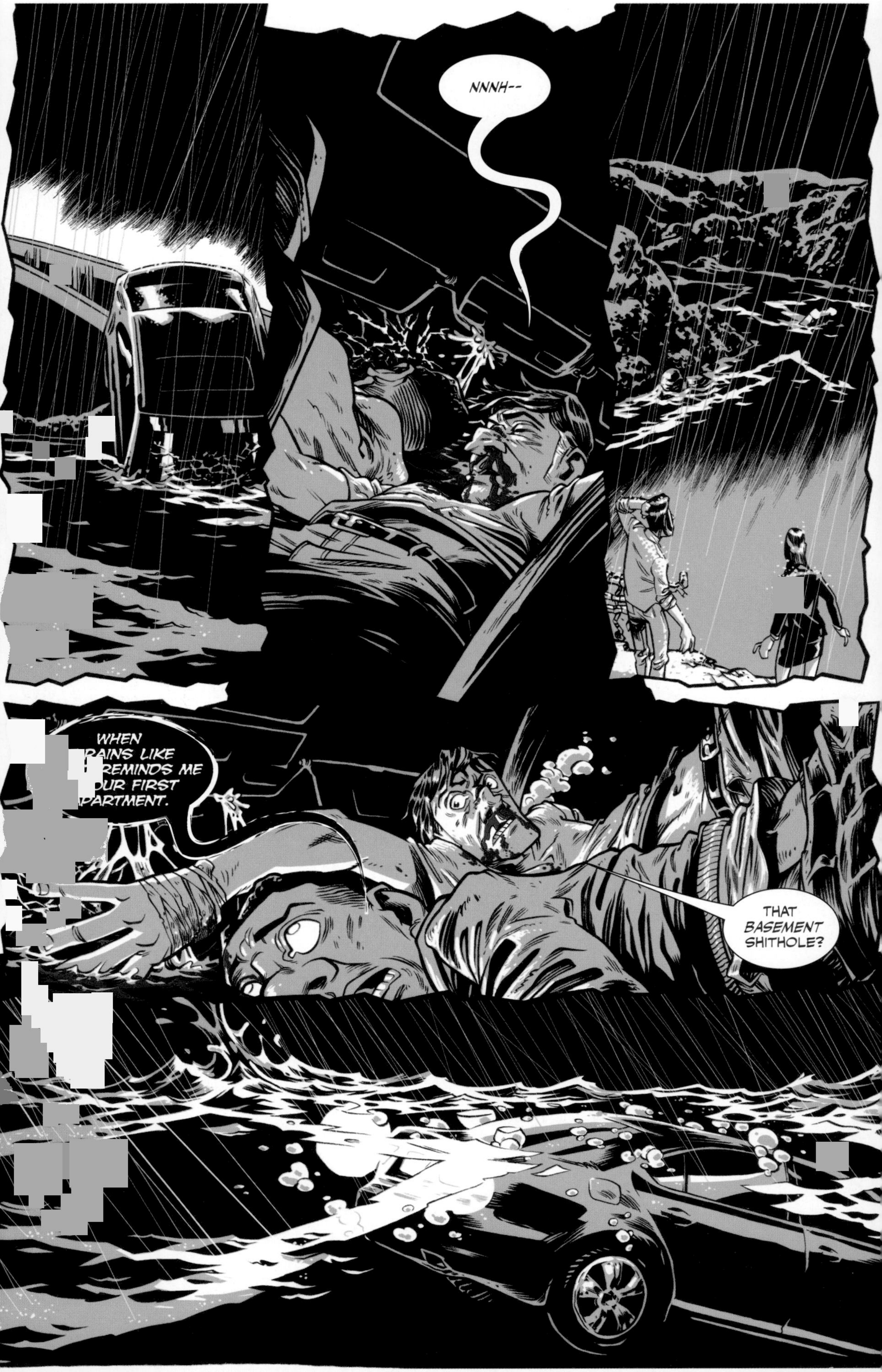
NNNH--
WHEN RAINS LIKE REMINDS ME OUR FIRST APARTMENT.
THAT BASEMENT SHITHOLE?

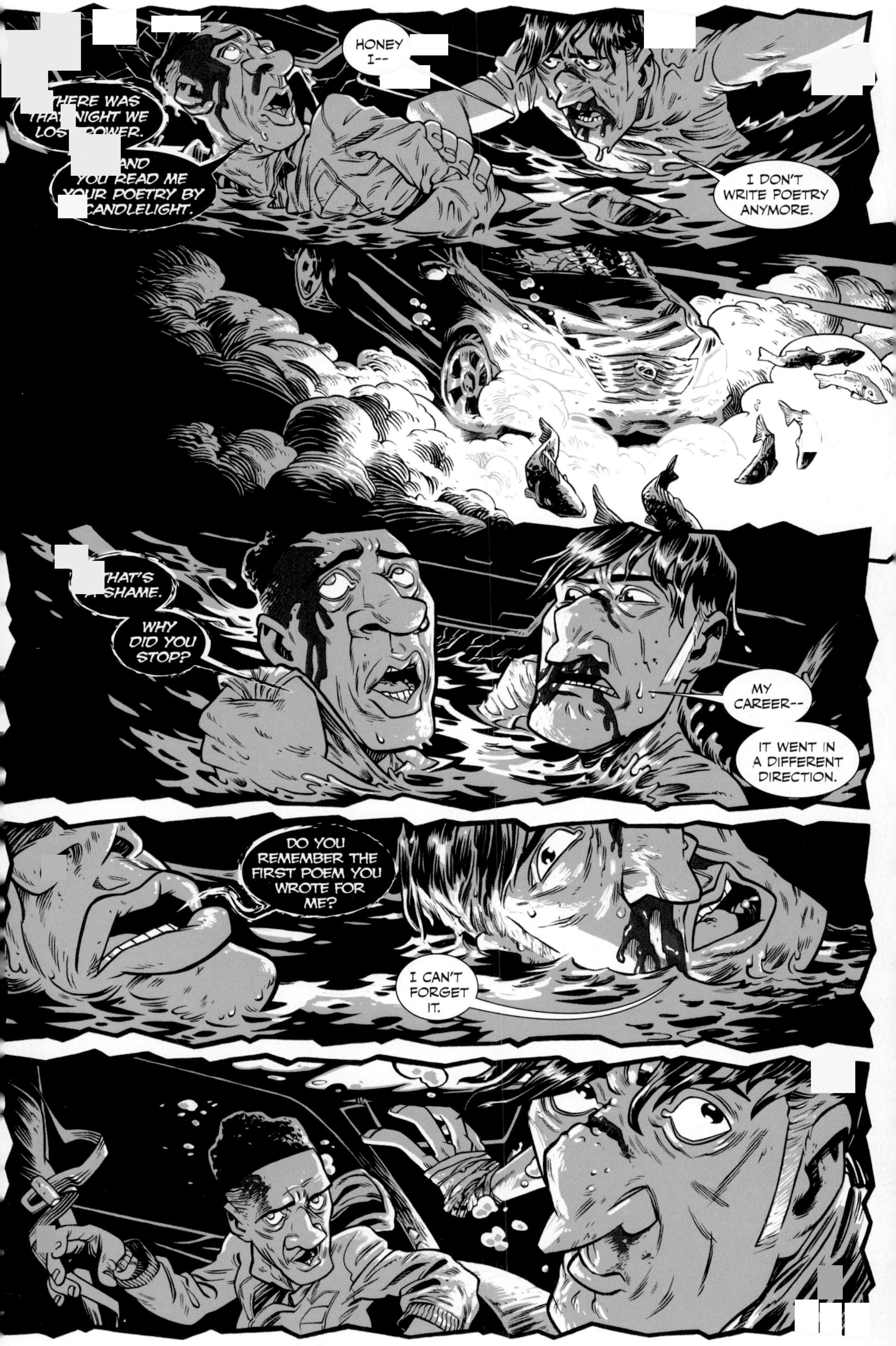
THERE WAS THAT NIGHT WE LOST POWER.
AND YOU READ ME YOUR POETRY BY CANDLELIGHT.
HONEY I--
I DON'T WRITE POETRY ANYMORE.
THAT'S A SHAME.
WHY DID YOU STOP?
MY CAREER--
IT WENT IN A DIFFERENT DIRECTION.
DO YOU REMEMBER THE FIRST POEM YOU WROTE FOR ME?
I CAN'T FORGET IT.

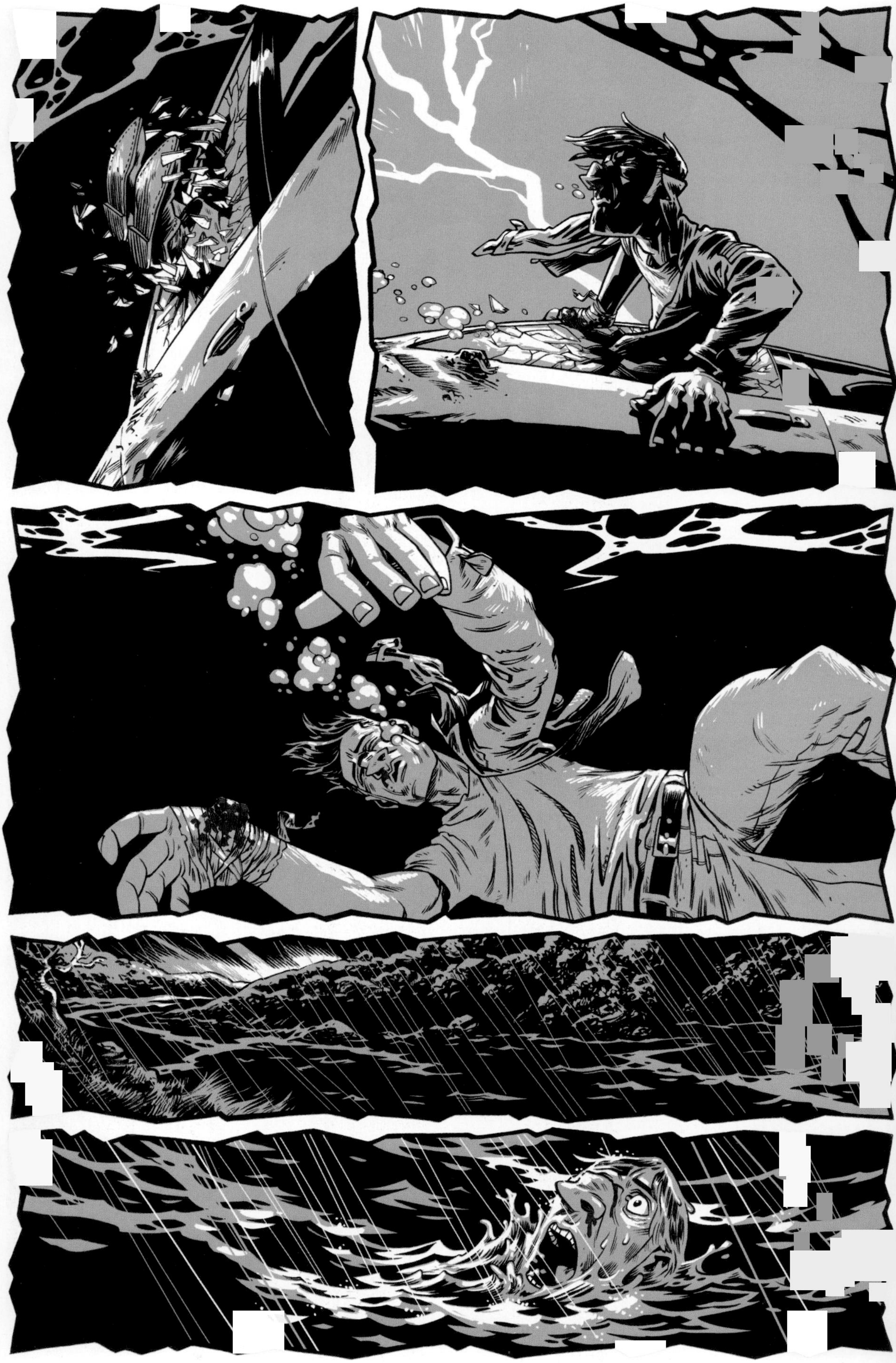

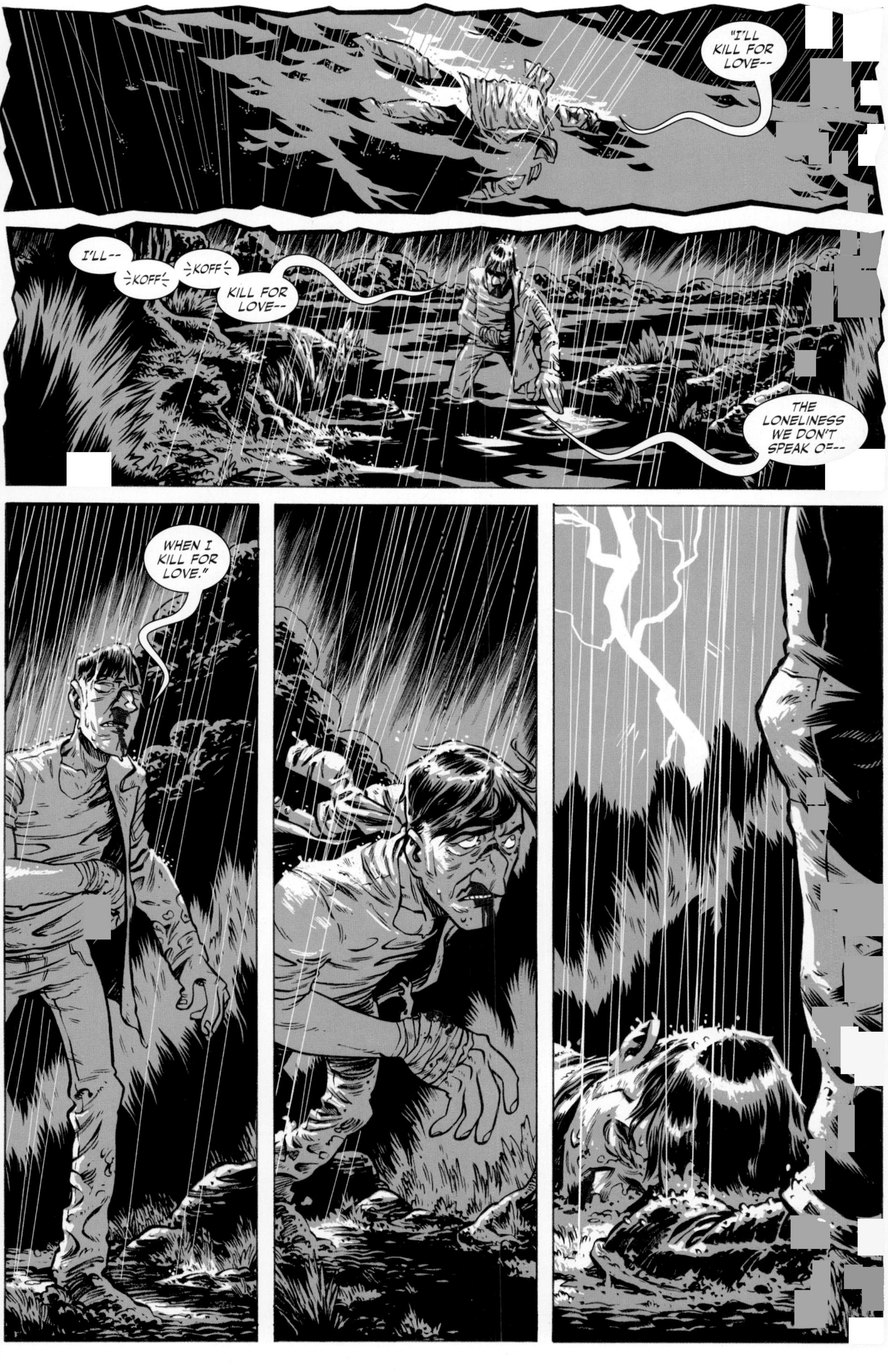
"I'LL KILL FOR LOVE--
I'LL--
KOFF
KOFF
KILL FOR LOVE--
THE LONELINESS WE DON'T SPEAK OF--
WHEN I KILL FOR LOVE."

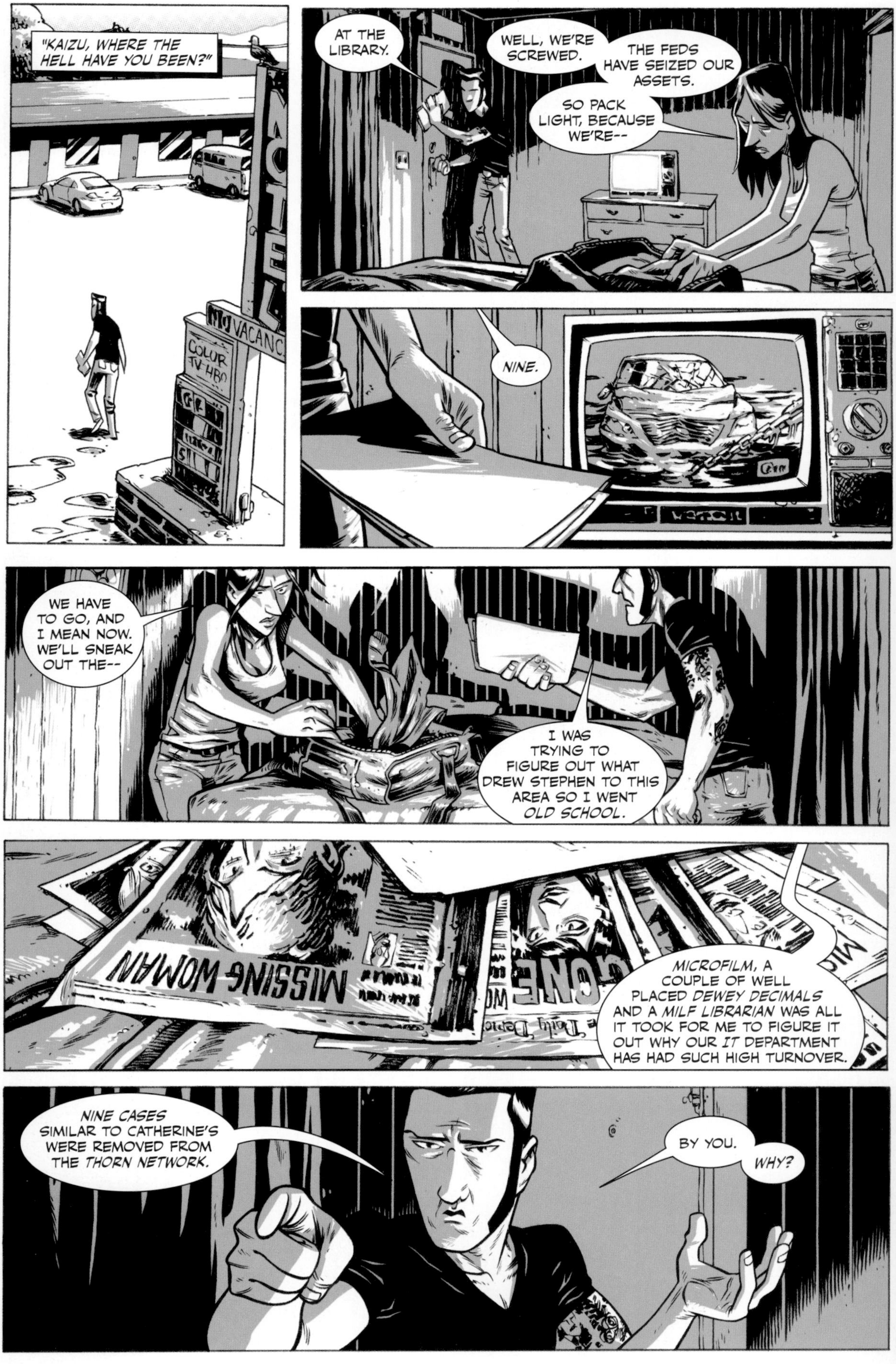
"KAIZU, WHERE THE HELL HAVE YOU BEEN?"
MOTEL
NO VACANC
COLOR TV HBO
AT THE LIBRARY.
WELL, WE'RE SCREWED.
THE FEDS HAVE SEIZED OUR ASSETS.
SO PACK LIGHT, BECAUSE WE'RE--
NINE.
WATCH
WE HAVE TO GO, AND I MEAN NOW. WE'LL SNEAK OUT THE--
I WAS TRYING TO FIGURE OUT WHAT DREW STEPHEN TO THIS AREA SO I WENT OLD SCHOOL.
MISSING WOMAN
GONE
MICROFILM, A COUPLE OF WELL PLACED DEWEY DECIMALS AND A MILF LIBRARIAN WAS ALL IT TOOK FOR ME TO FIGURE IT OUT WHY OUR IT DEPARTMENT HAS HAD SUCH HIGH TURNOVER.
NINE CASES SIMILAR TO CATHERINE'S WERE REMOVED FROM THE THORN NETWORK.
BY YOU.
WHY?

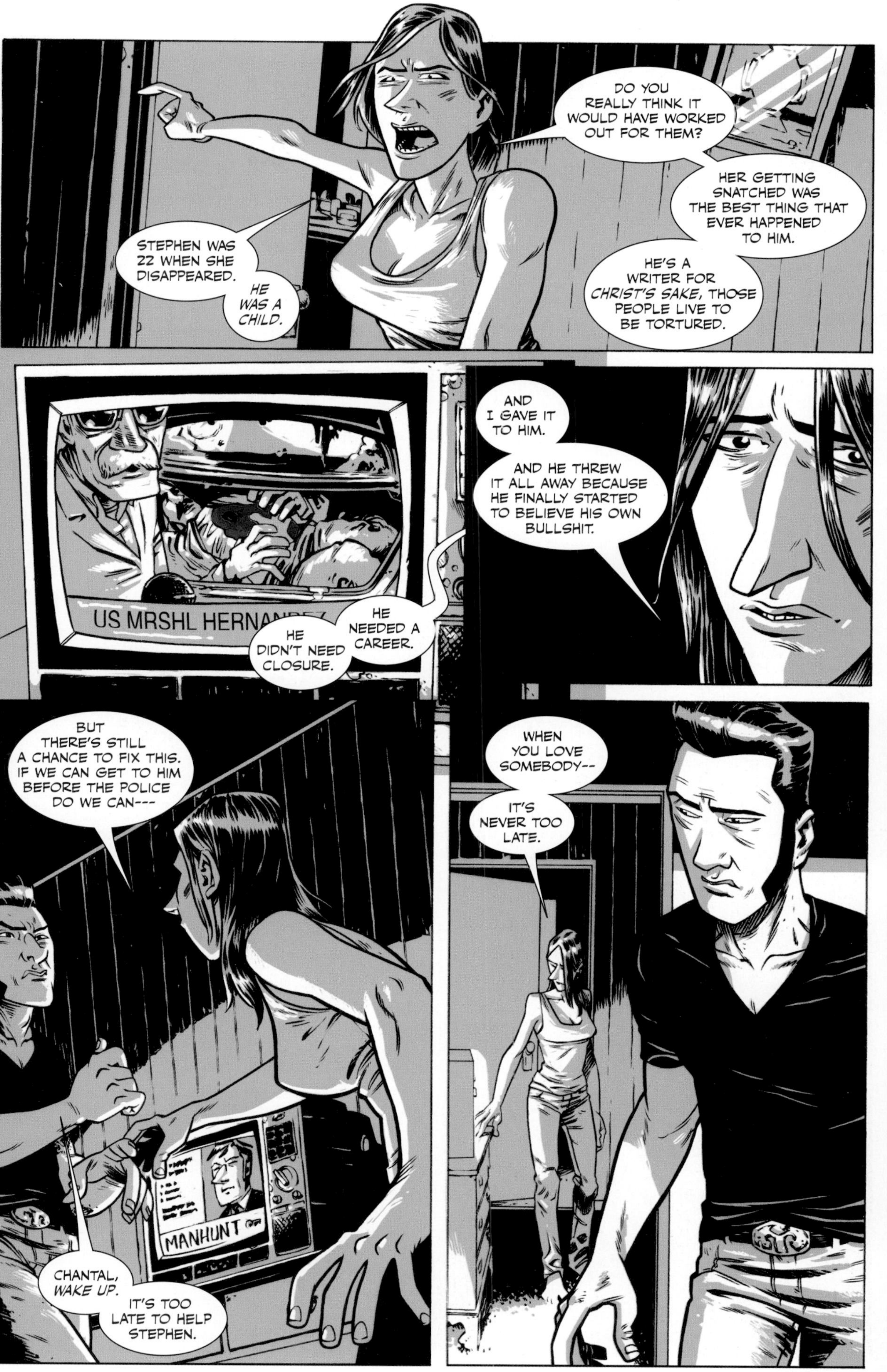

DO YOU REALLY THINK IT WOULD HAVE WORKED OUT FOR THEM?
HER GETTING SNATCHED WAS THE BEST THING THAT EVER HAPPENED TO HIM.
HE'S A WRITER FOR *CHRIST'S SAKE*, THOSE PEOPLE LIVE TO BE TORTURED.
STEPHEN WAS 22 WHEN SHE DISAPPEARED.
HE WAS A CHILD.
US MRSHL HERNANDEZ
HE NEEDED A CAREER.
HE DIDN'T NEED CLOSURE.
AND I GAVE IT TO HIM.
AND HE THREW IT ALL AWAY BECAUSE HE FINALLY STARTED TO BELIEVE HIS OWN BULLSHIT.
BUT THERE'S STILL A CHANCE TO FIX THIS. IF WE CAN GET TO HIM BEFORE THE POLICE DO WE CAN---
MANHUNT
CHANTAL, *WAKE UP*.
IT'S TOO LATE TO HELP STEPHEN.
WHEN YOU LOVE SOMEBODY--
IT'S NEVER TOO LATE.

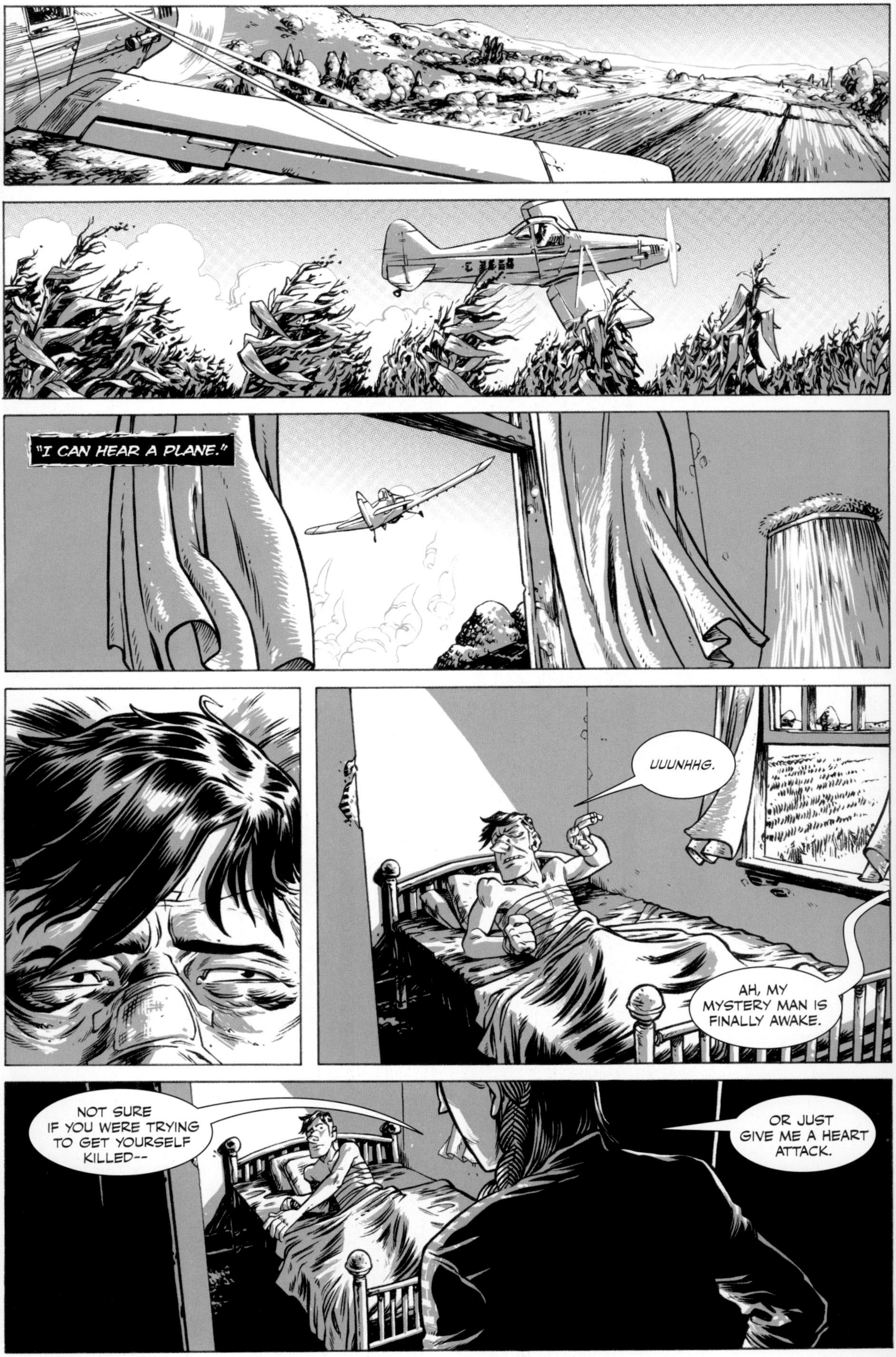
"I CAN HEAR A PLANE."
UUUNHHG.
AH, MY MYSTERY MAN IS FINALLY AWAKE.
NOT SURE IF YOU WERE TRYING TO GET YOURSELF KILLED--
OR JUST GIVE ME A HEART ATTACK.

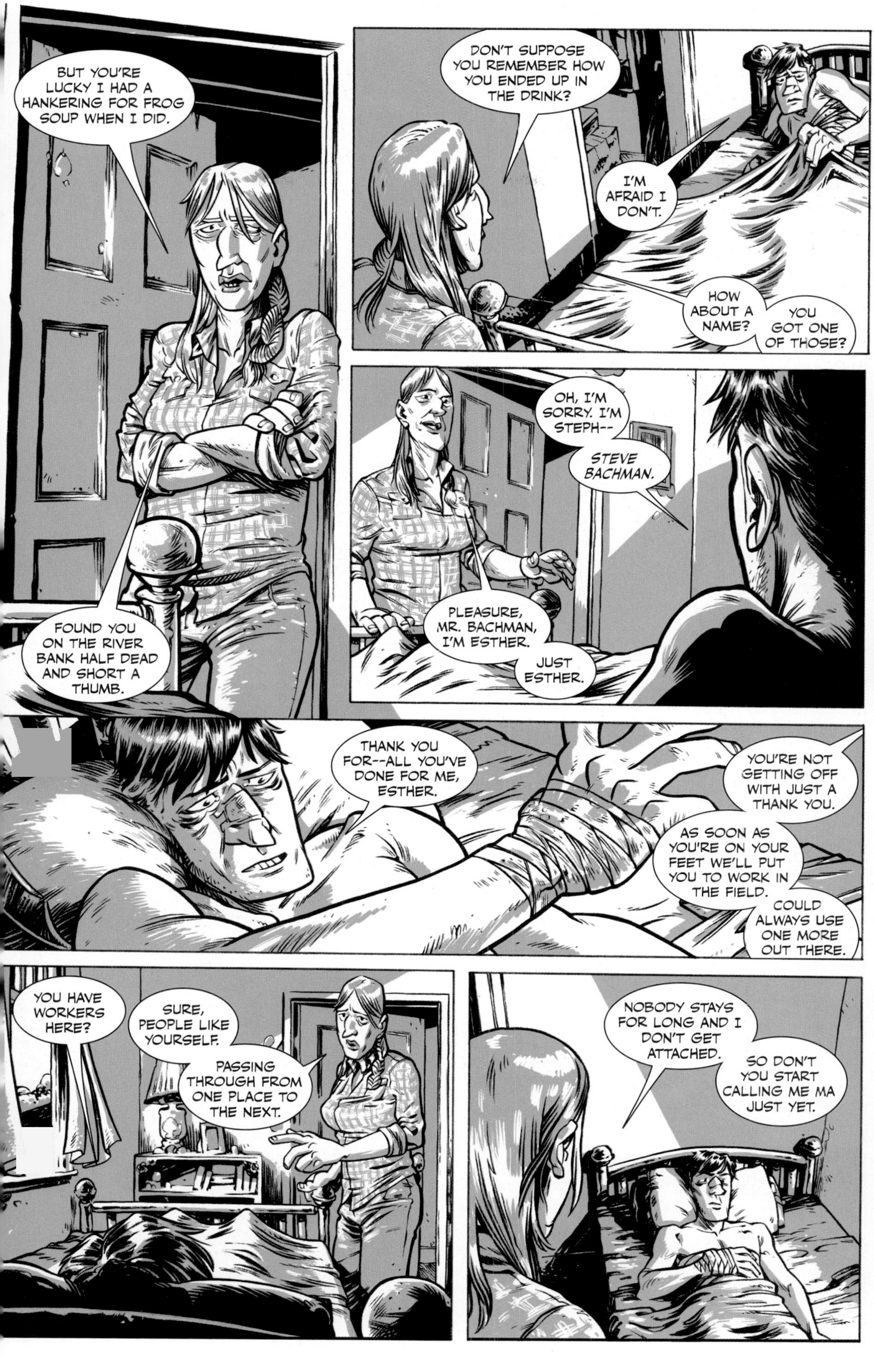
BUT YOU'RE LUCKY I HAD A HANKERING FOR FROG SOUP WHEN I DID.
FOUND YOU ON THE RIVER BANK HALF DEAD AND SHORT A THUMB.
DON'T SUPPOSE YOU REMEMBER HOW YOU ENDED UP IN THE DRINK?
I'M AFRAID I DON'T.
HOW ABOUT A NAME?
YOU GOT ONE OF THOSE?
OH, I'M SORRY. I'M STEPH--
STEVE BACHMAN.
PLEASURE, MR. BACHMAN, I'M ESTHER.
JUST ESTHER.
THANK YOU FOR--ALL YOU'VE DONE FOR ME, ESTHER.
YOU'RE NOT GETTING OFF WITH JUST A THANK YOU.
AS SOON AS YOU'RE ON YOUR FEET WE'LL PUT YOU TO WORK IN THE FIELD.
COULD ALWAYS USE ONE MORE OUT THERE.
YOU HAVE WORKERS HERE?
SURE, PEOPLE LIKE YOURSELF.
PASSING THROUGH FROM ONE PLACE TO THE NEXT.
NOBODY STAYS FOR LONG AND I DON'T GET ATTACHED.
SO DON'T YOU START CALLING ME MA JUST YET.

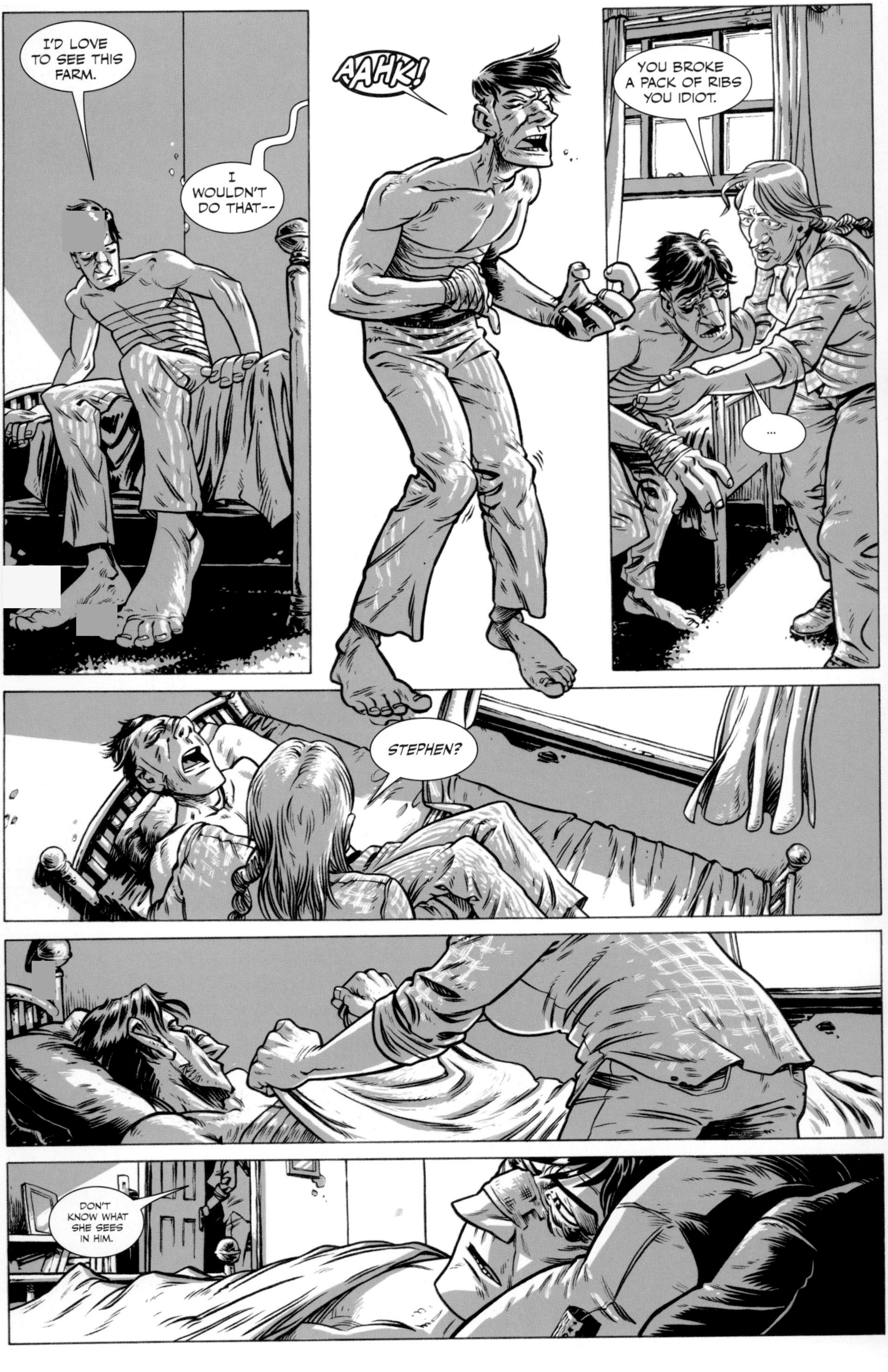
I'D LOVE TO SEE THIS FARM.
I WOULDN'T DO THAT--
AAHK!
YOU BROKE A PACK OF RIBS YOU IDIOT.
...
STEPHEN?
DON'T KNOW WHAT SHE SEES IN HIM.

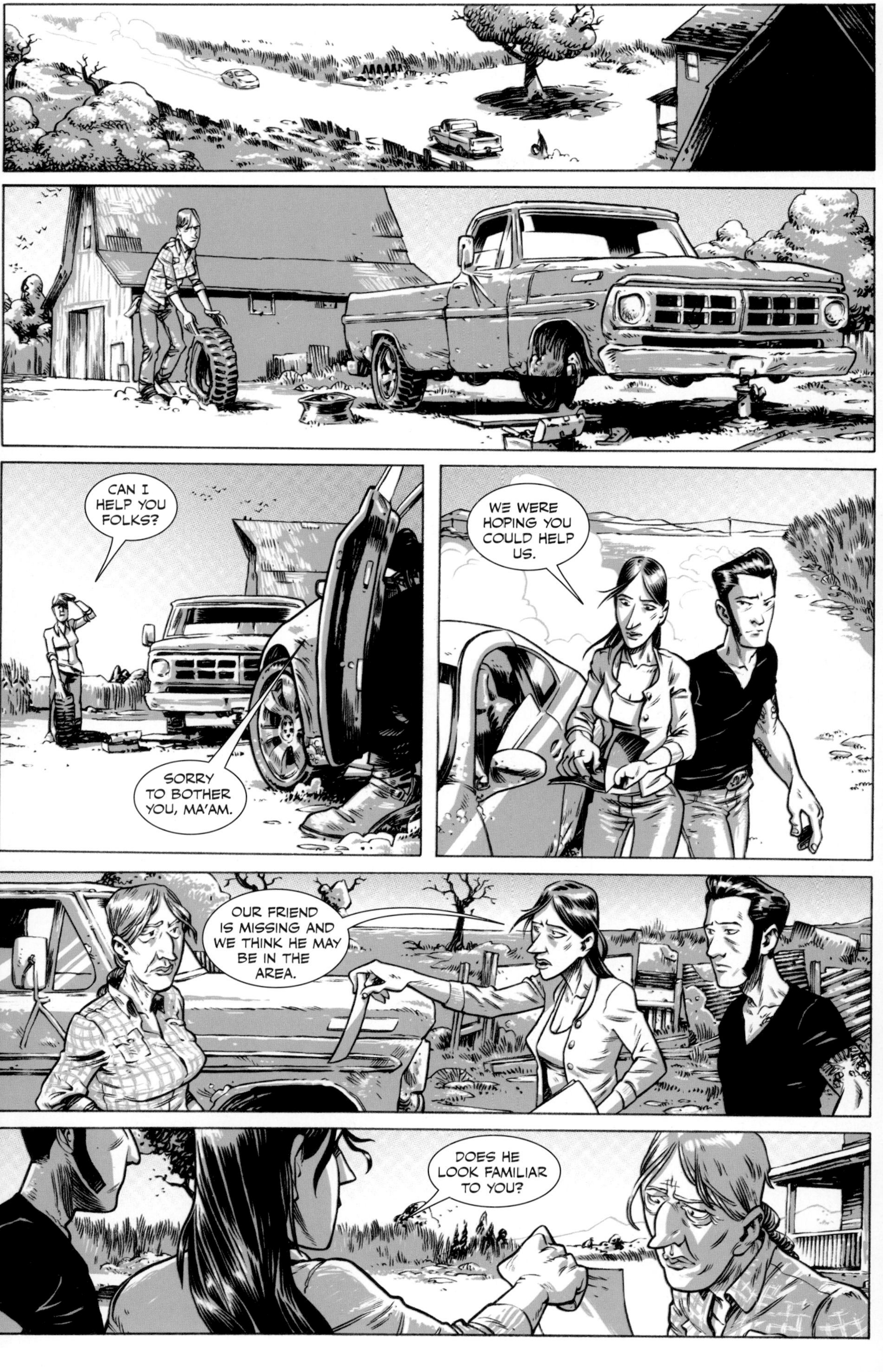
CAN I HELP YOU FOLKS?
SORRY TO BOTHER YOU, MA'AM.
WE WERE HOPING YOU COULD HELP US.
OUR FRIEND IS MISSING AND WE THINK HE MAY BE IN THE AREA.
DOES HE LOOK FAMILIAR TO YOU?

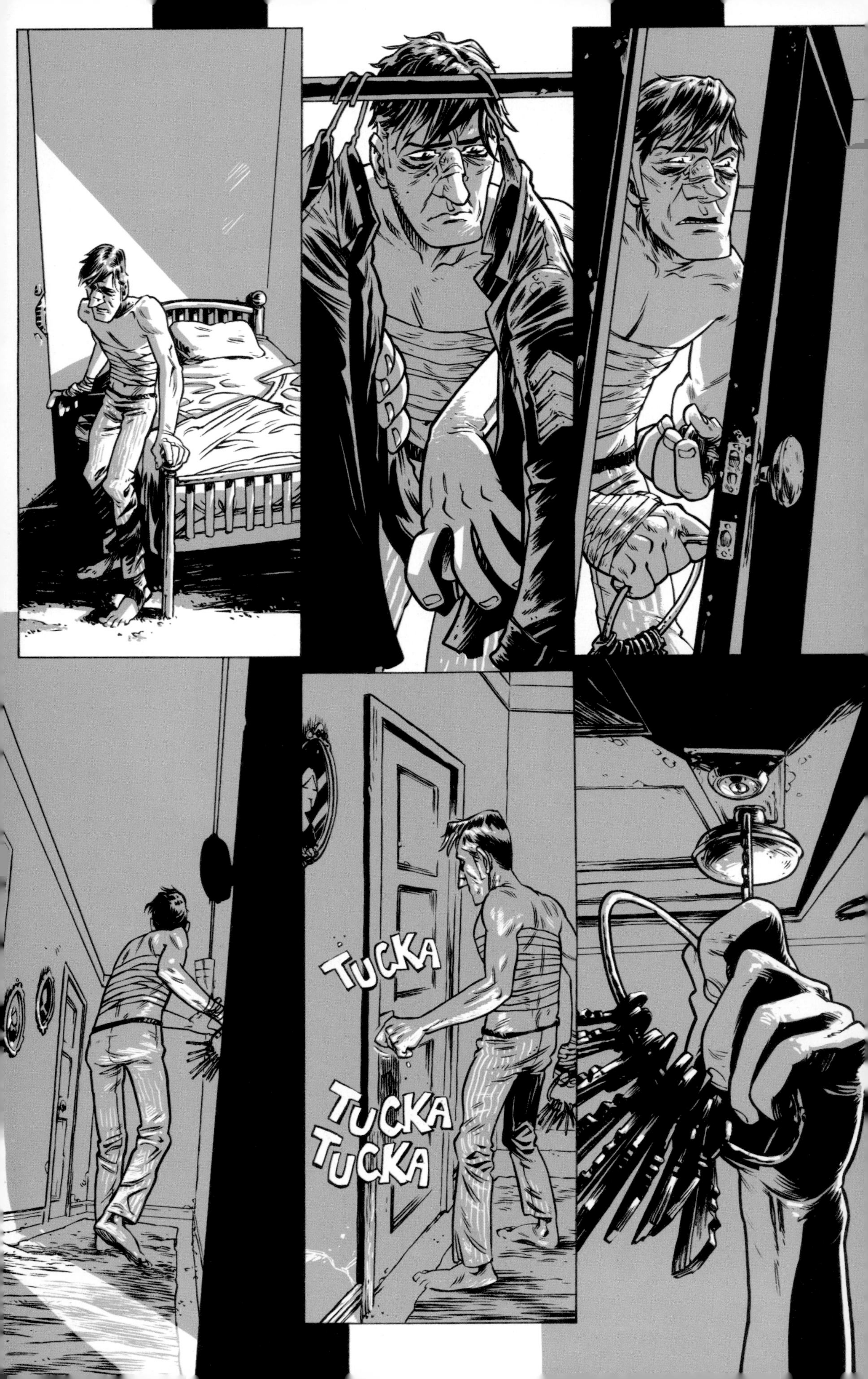
TUCKA
TUCKA
TUCKA

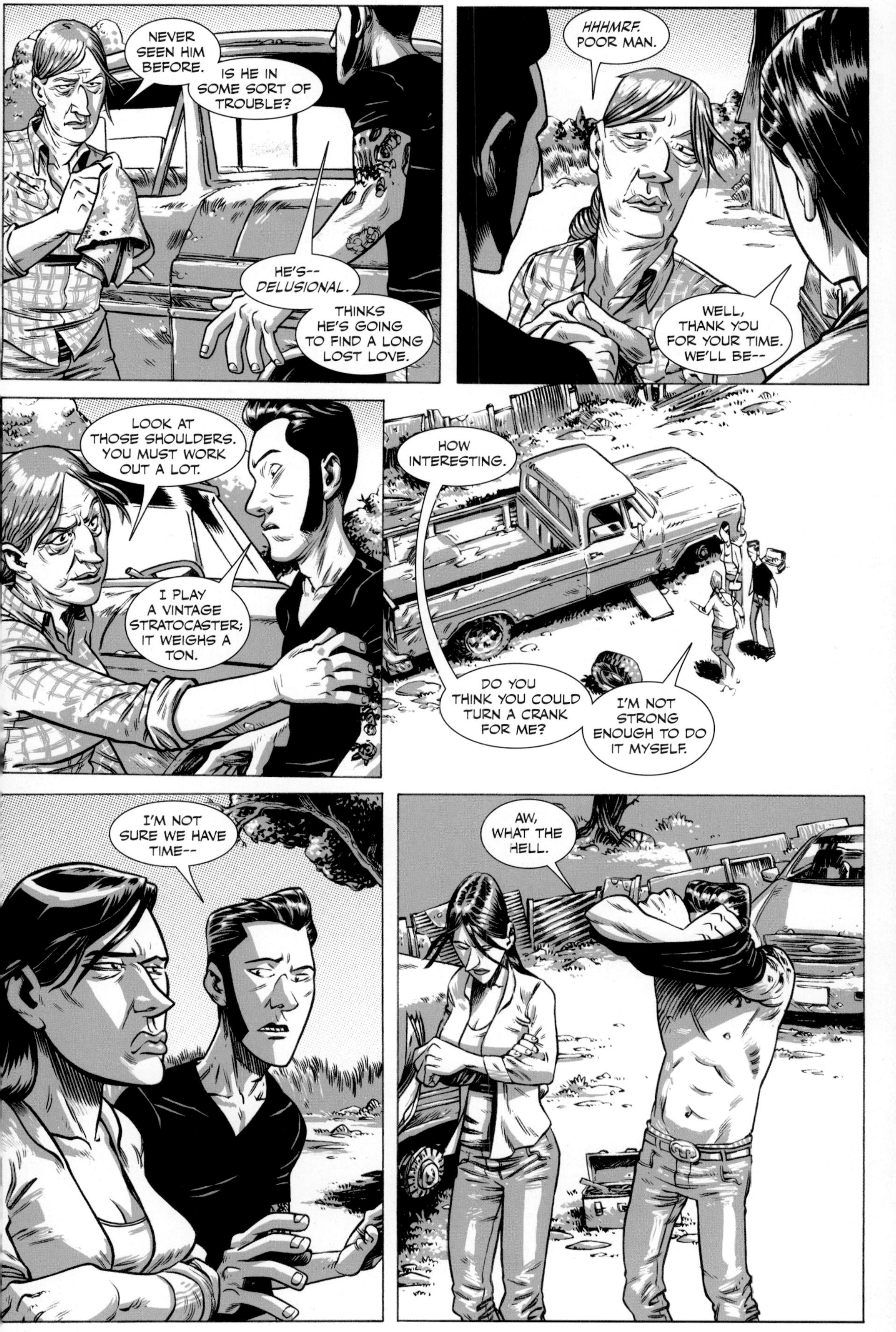
NEVER SEEN HIM BEFORE.
IS HE IN SOME SORT OF TROUBLE?
HE'S-- DELUSIONAL.
THINKS HE'S GOING TO FIND A LONG LOST LOVE.
HHHMRF. POOR MAN.
WELL, THANK YOU FOR YOUR TIME. WE'LL BE--
LOOK AT THOSE SHOULDERS. YOU MUST WORK OUT A LOT.
I PLAY A VINTAGE STRATOCASTER; IT WEIGHS A TON.
HOW INTERESTING.
DO YOU THINK YOU COULD TURN A CRANK FOR ME?
I'M NOT STRONG ENOUGH TO DO IT MYSELF.
I'M NOT SURE WE HAVE TIME--
AW, WHAT THE HELL.

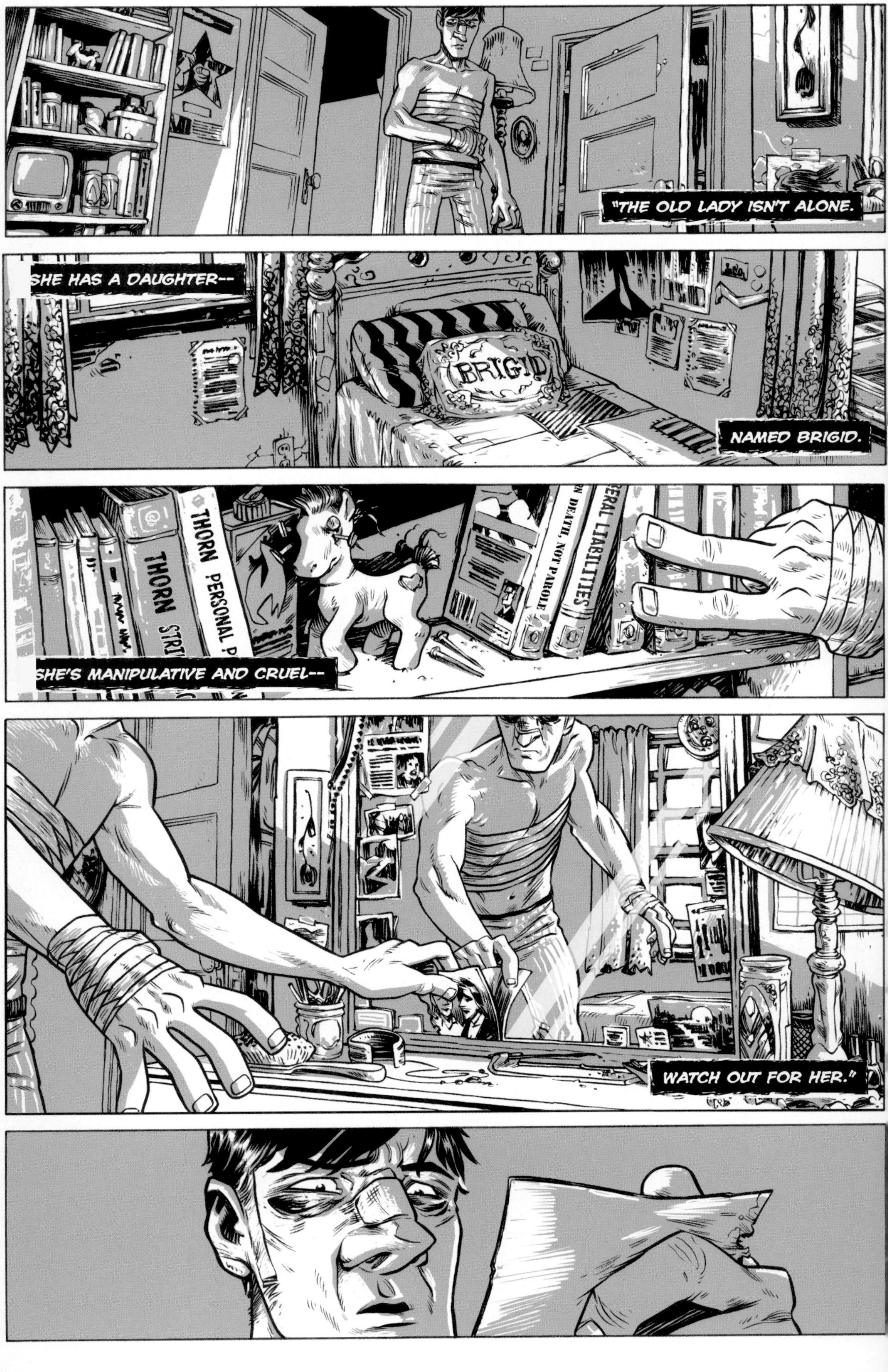
"THE OLD LADY ISN'T ALONE.
SHE HAS A DAUGHTER--
BRIGID
NAMED BRIGID.
THORN
DEATH, NOT PAROLE
SHE'S MANIPULATIVE AND CRUEL--
WATCH OUT FOR HER."

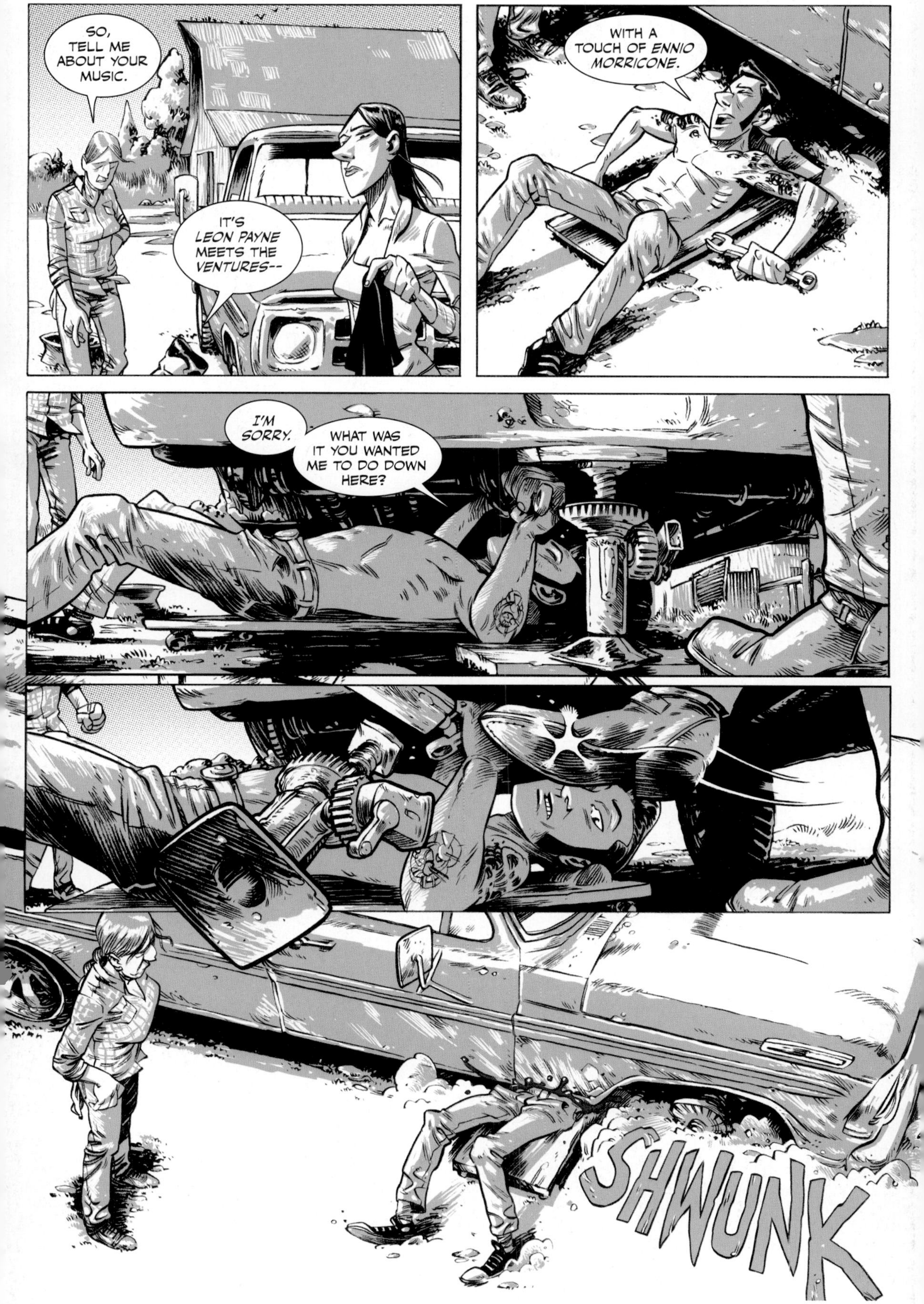
SO, TELL ME ABOUT YOUR MUSIC.
IT'S LEON PAYNE MEETS THE VENTURES--
WITH A TOUCH OF ENNIO MORRICONE.
I'M SORRY.
WHAT WAS IT YOU WANTED ME TO DO DOWN HERE?
SHWUNK

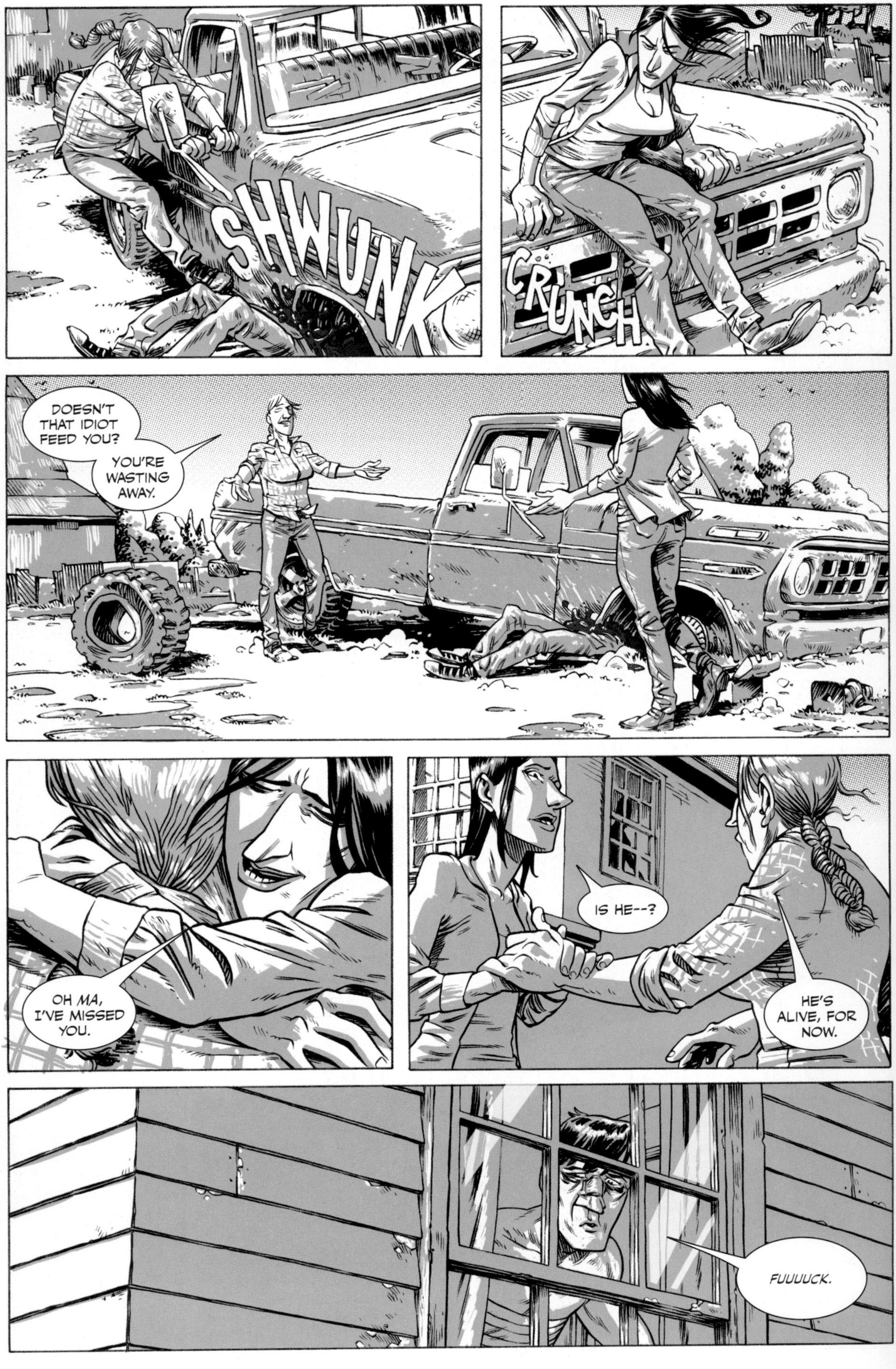
SHWUNK
CRUNCH
DOESN'T THAT IDIOT FEED YOU?
YOU'RE WASTING AWAY.
OH MA, I'VE MISSED YOU.
IS HE--?
HE'S ALIVE, FOR NOW.
FUUUUCK.

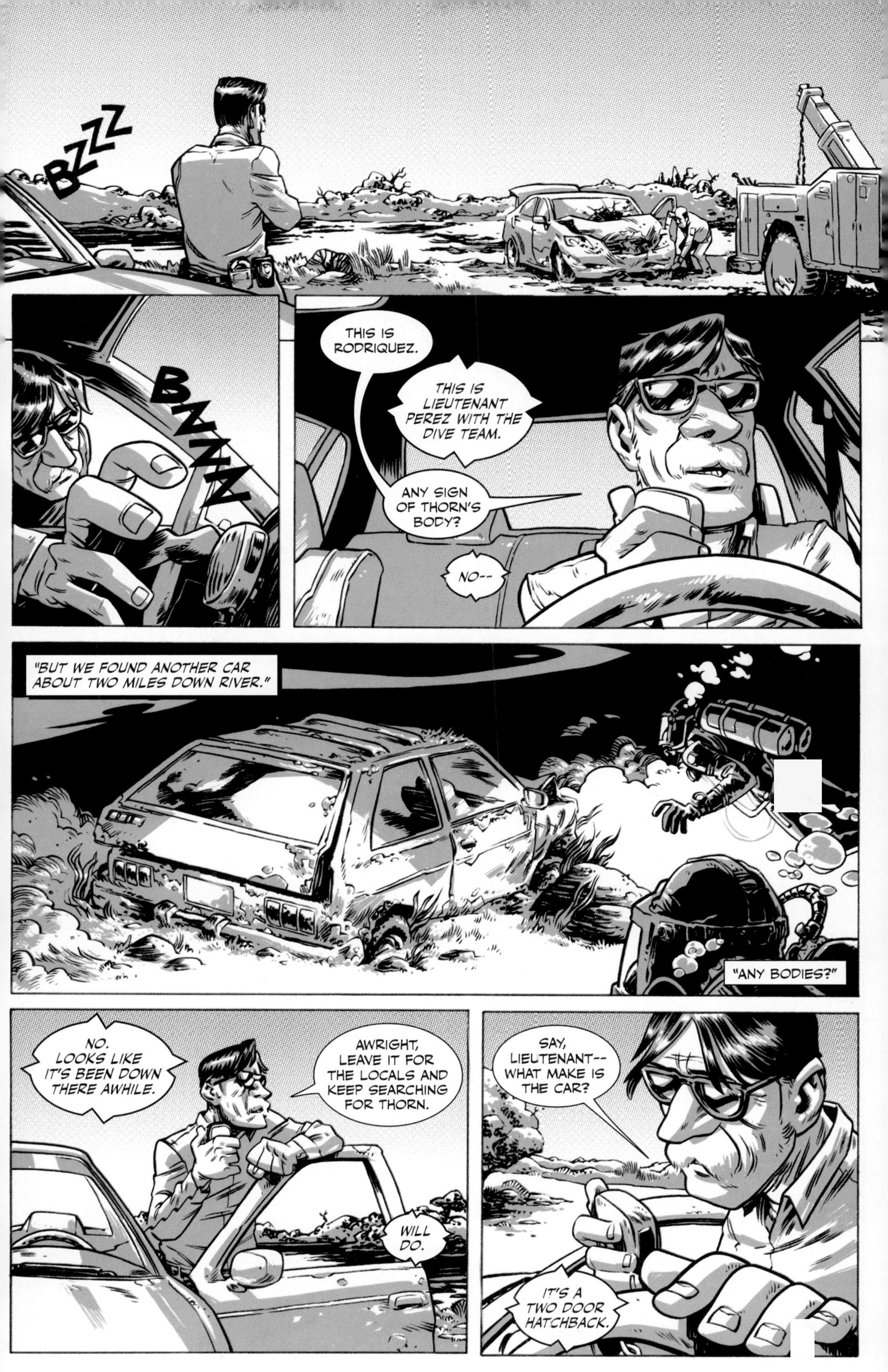
BZZZ
BZZZZ
THIS IS RODRIQUEZ.
THIS IS LIEUTENANT PEREZ WITH THE DIVE TEAM.
ANY SIGN OF THORN'S BODY?
NO--
"BUT WE FOUND ANOTHER CAR ABOUT TWO MILES DOWN RIVER."
"ANY BODIES?"
NO. LOOKS LIKE IT'S BEEN DOWN THERE AWHILE.
AWRIGHT, LEAVE IT FOR THE LOCALS AND KEEP SEARCHING FOR THORN.
WILL DO.
SAY, LIEUTENANT-- WHAT MAKE IS THE CAR?
IT'S A TWO DOOR HATCHBACK.

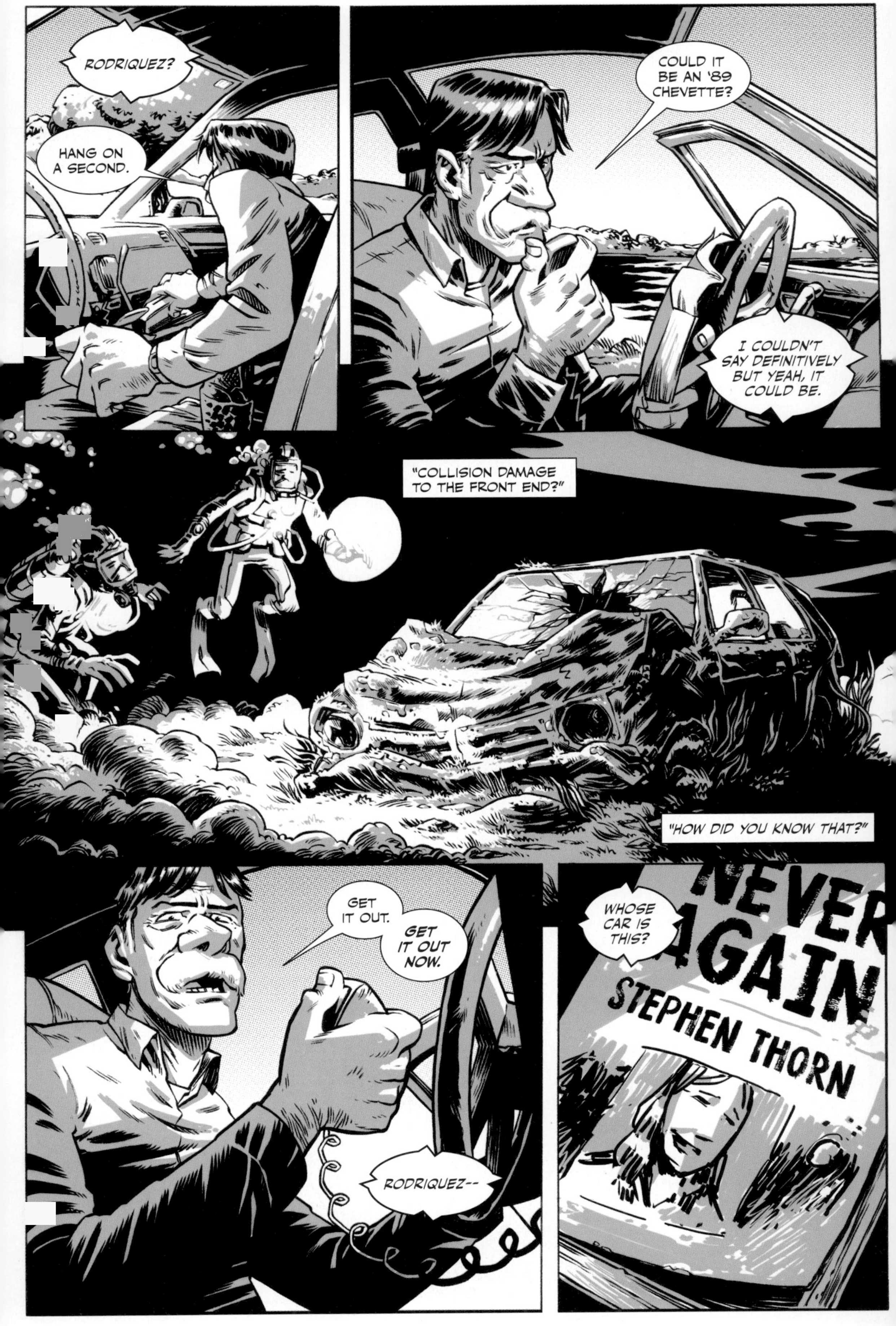
RODRIQUEZ?
HANG ON A SECOND.
COULD IT BE AN '89 CHEVETTE?
I COULDN'T SAY DEFINITIVELY BUT YEAH, IT COULD BE.
"COLLISION DAMAGE TO THE FRONT END?"
"HOW DID YOU KNOW THAT?"
GET IT OUT.
GET IT OUT NOW.
RODRIQUEZ--
WHOSE CAR IS THIS?
NEVER AGAIN
STEPHEN THORN

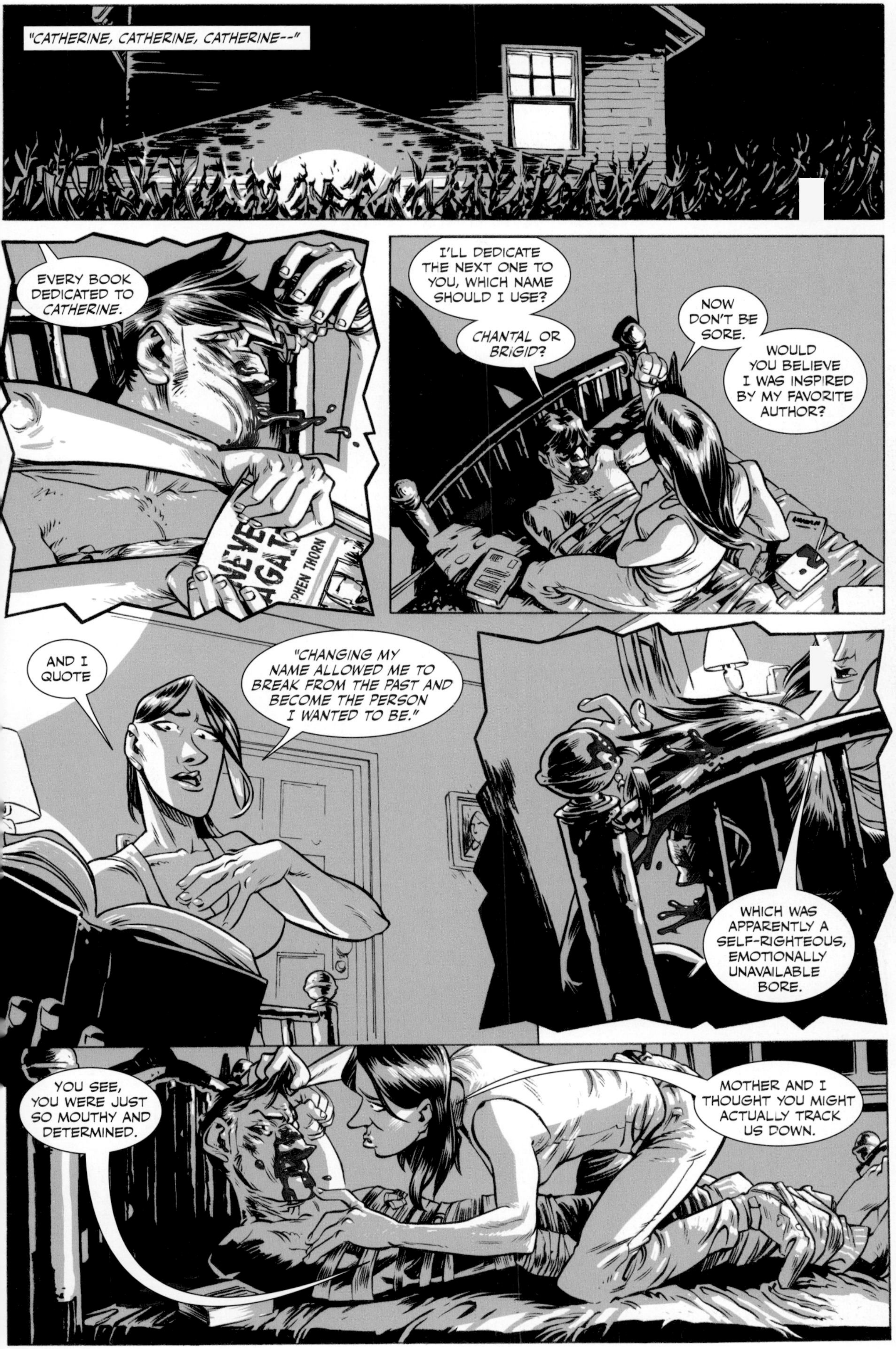
"CATHERINE, CATHERINE, CATHERINE--"
EVERY BOOK DEDICATED TO CATHERINE.
NEVER AGAIN
STEPHEN THORN
I'LL DEDICATE THE NEXT ONE TO YOU, WHICH NAME SHOULD I USE?
CHANTAL OR BRIGID?
NOW DON'T BE SORE.
WOULD YOU BELIEVE I WAS INSPIRED BY MY FAVORITE AUTHOR?
AND I QUOTE
"CHANGING MY NAME ALLOWED ME TO BREAK FROM THE PAST AND BECOME THE PERSON I WANTED TO BE."
WHICH WAS APPARENTLY A SELF-RIGHTEOUS, EMOTIONALLY UNAVAILABLE BORE.
YOU SEE, YOU WERE JUST SO MOUTHY AND DETERMINED.
MOTHER AND I THOUGHT YOU MIGHT ACTUALLY TRACK US DOWN.

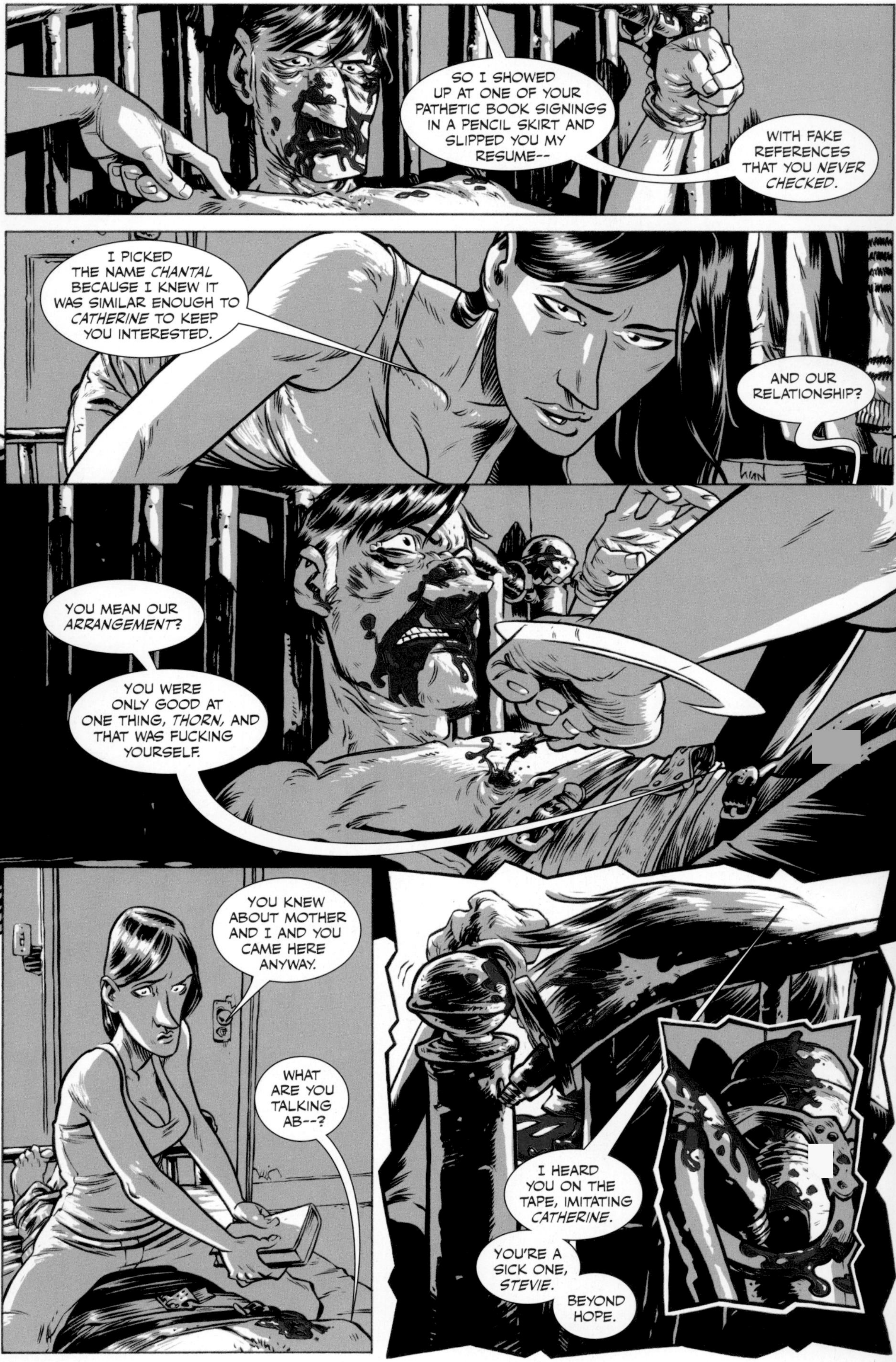
SO I SHOWED UP AT ONE OF YOUR PATHETIC BOOK SIGNINGS IN A PENCIL SKIRT AND SLIPPED YOU MY RESUME--
WITH FAKE REFERENCES THAT YOU NEVER CHECKED.
I PICKED THE NAME CHANTAL BECAUSE I KNEW IT WAS SIMILAR ENOUGH TO CATHERINE TO KEEP YOU INTERESTED.
AND OUR RELATIONSHIP?
YOU MEAN OUR ARRANGEMENT?
YOU WERE ONLY GOOD AT ONE THING, THORN, AND THAT WAS FUCKING YOURSELF.
YOU KNEW ABOUT MOTHER AND I AND YOU CAME HERE ANYWAY.
WHAT ARE YOU TALKING AB--?
I HEARD YOU ON THE TAPE, IMITATING CATHERINE.
YOU'RE A SICK ONE, STEVIE.
BEYOND HOPE.

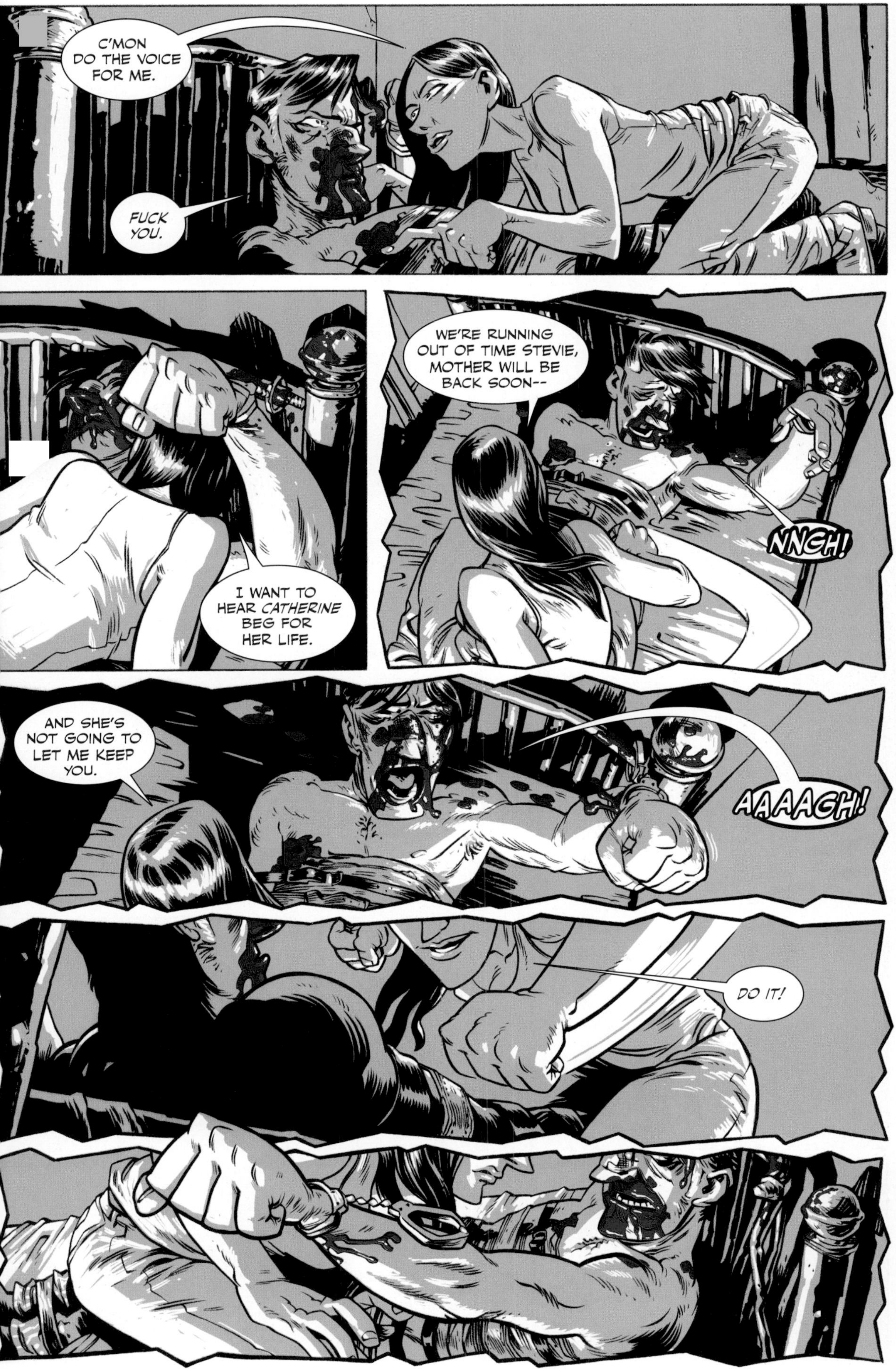
C'MON DO THE VOICE FOR ME.
FUCK YOU.
I WANT TO HEAR *CATHERINE* BEG FOR HER LIFE.
WE'RE RUNNING OUT OF TIME STEVIE, MOTHER WILL BE BACK SOON--
NNGH!
AND SHE'S NOT GOING TO LET ME KEEP YOU.
AAAAGH!
DO IT!

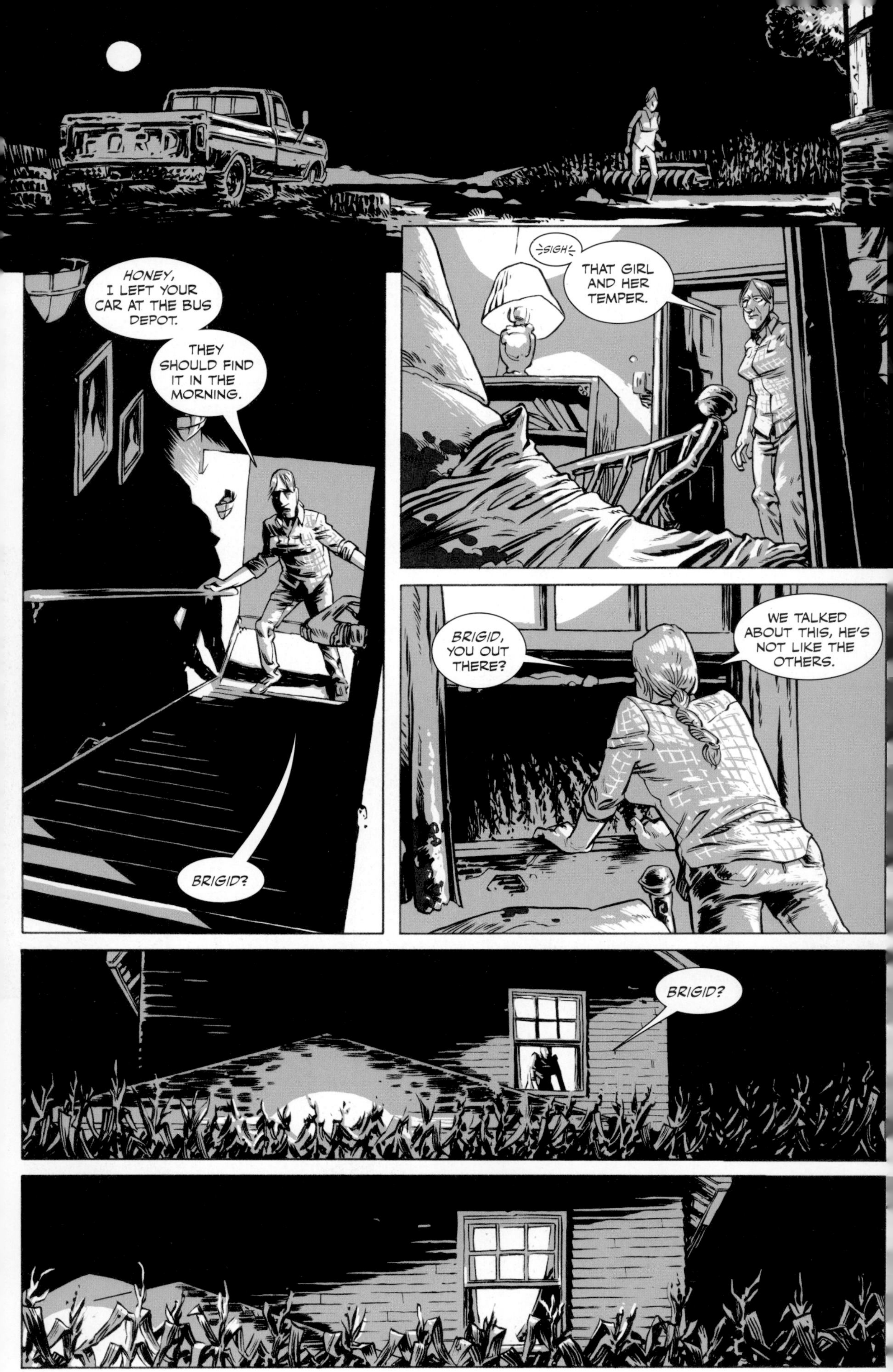
FORD
HONEY, I LEFT YOUR CAR AT THE BUS DEPOT.
THEY SHOULD FIND IT IN THE MORNING.
BRIGID?
SIGH
THAT GIRL AND HER TEMPER.
BRIGID, YOU OUT THERE?
WE TALKED ABOUT THIS, HE'S NOT LIKE THE OTHERS.
BRIGID?

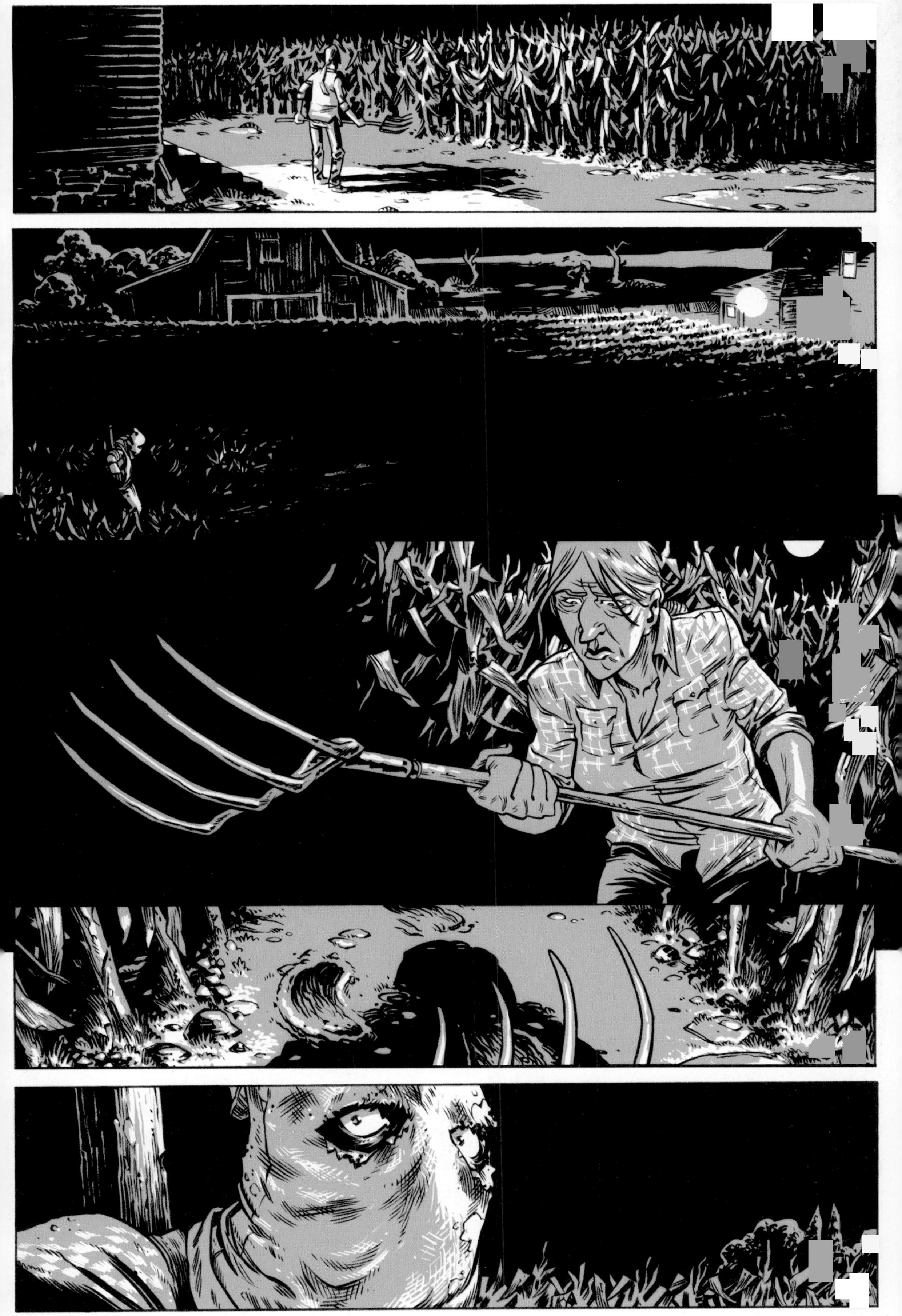

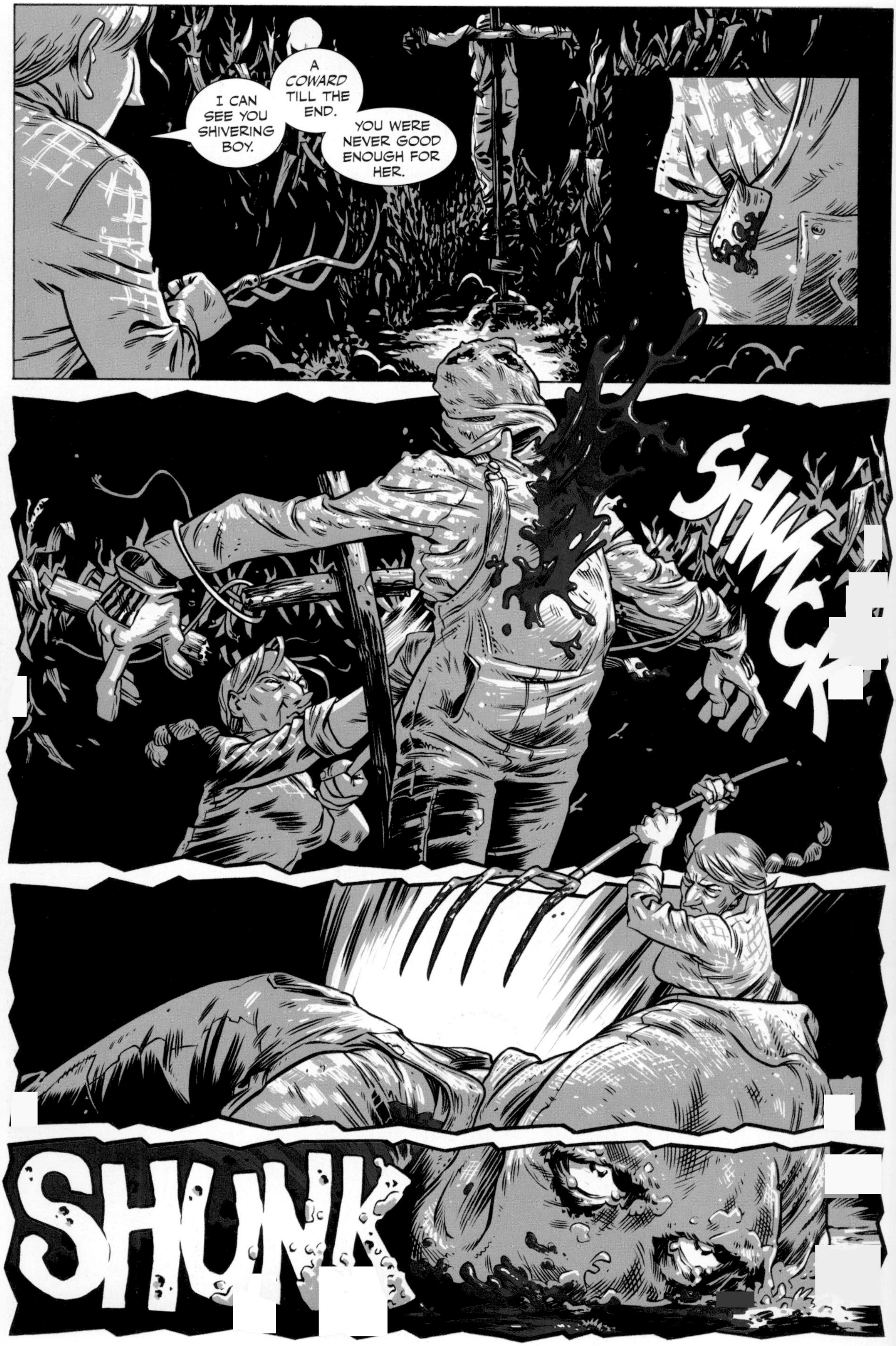
I CAN SEE YOU SHIVERING BOY.
A COWARD TILL THE END.
YOU WERE NEVER GOOD ENOUGH FOR HER.
SHUNCK
SHUNK

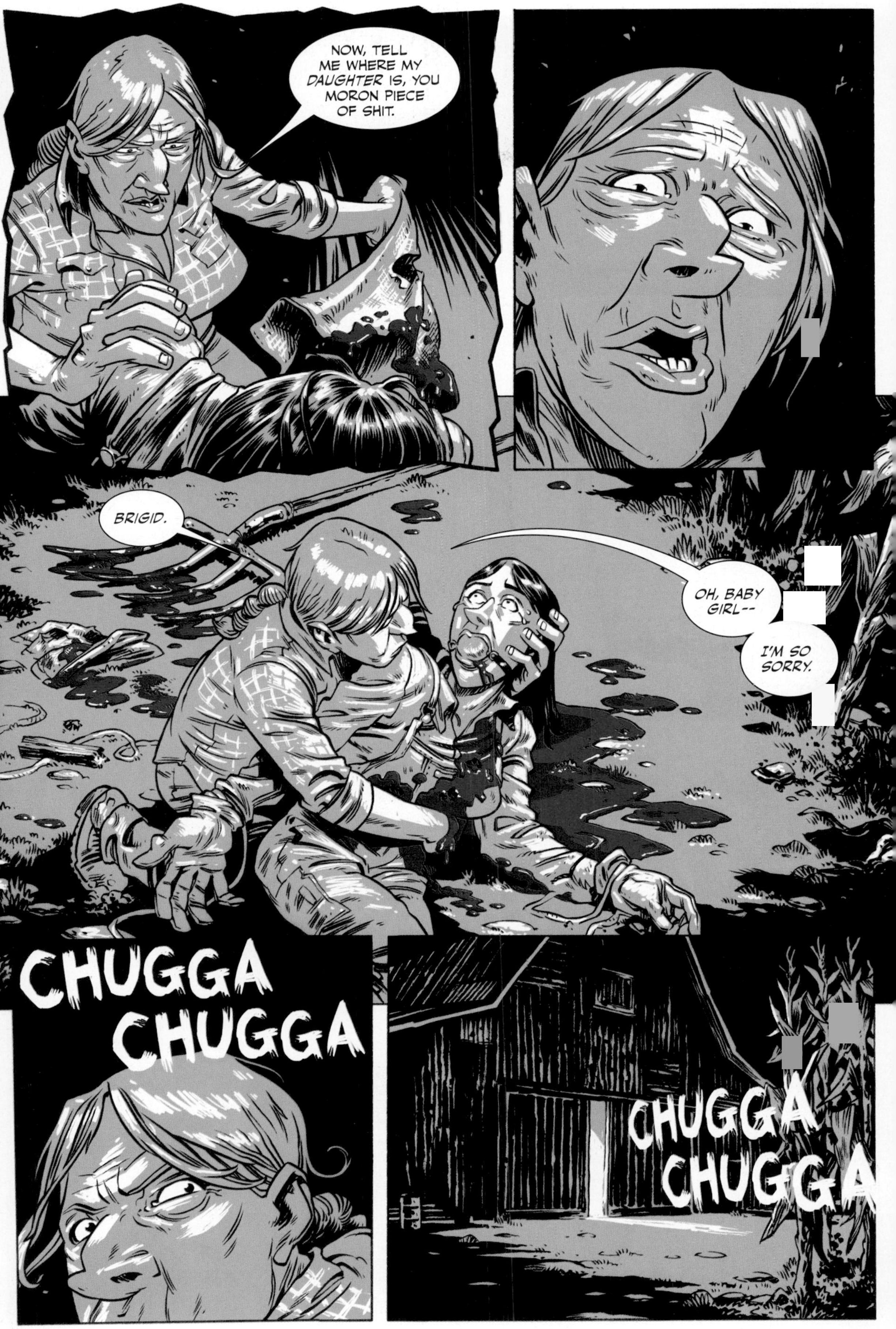
NOW, TELL ME WHERE MY *DAUGHTER* IS, YOU MORON PIECE OF SHIT.
BRIGID.
OH, BABY GIRL--
I'M SO SORRY.
CHUGGA CHUGGA
CHUGGA CHUGGA

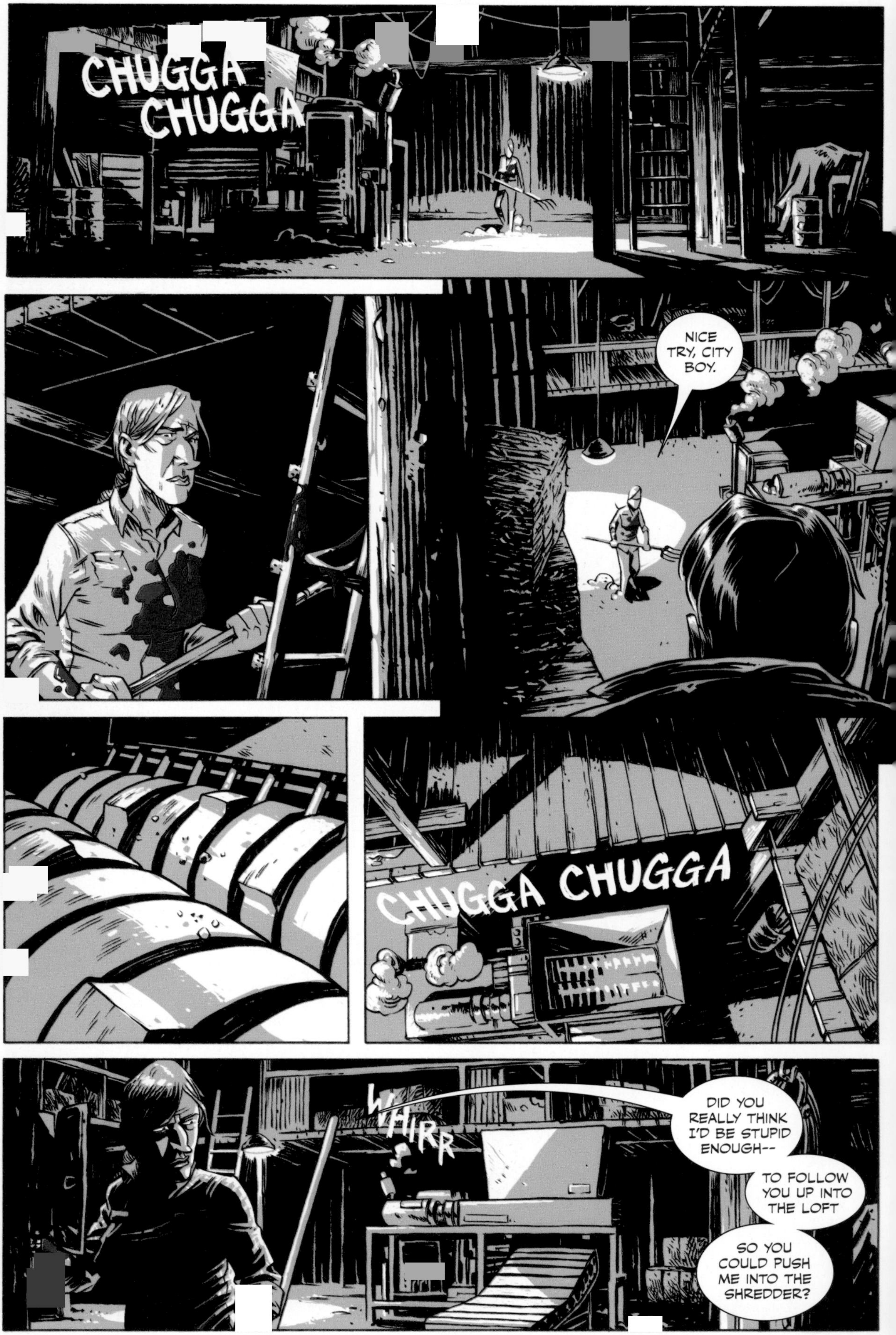
CHUGGA CHUGGA
NICE TRY, CITY BOY.
CHUGGA CHUGGA
WHIRR
DID YOU REALLY THINK I'D BE STUPID ENOUGH--
TO FOLLOW YOU UP INTO THE LOFT
SO YOU COULD PUSH ME INTO THE SHREDDER?

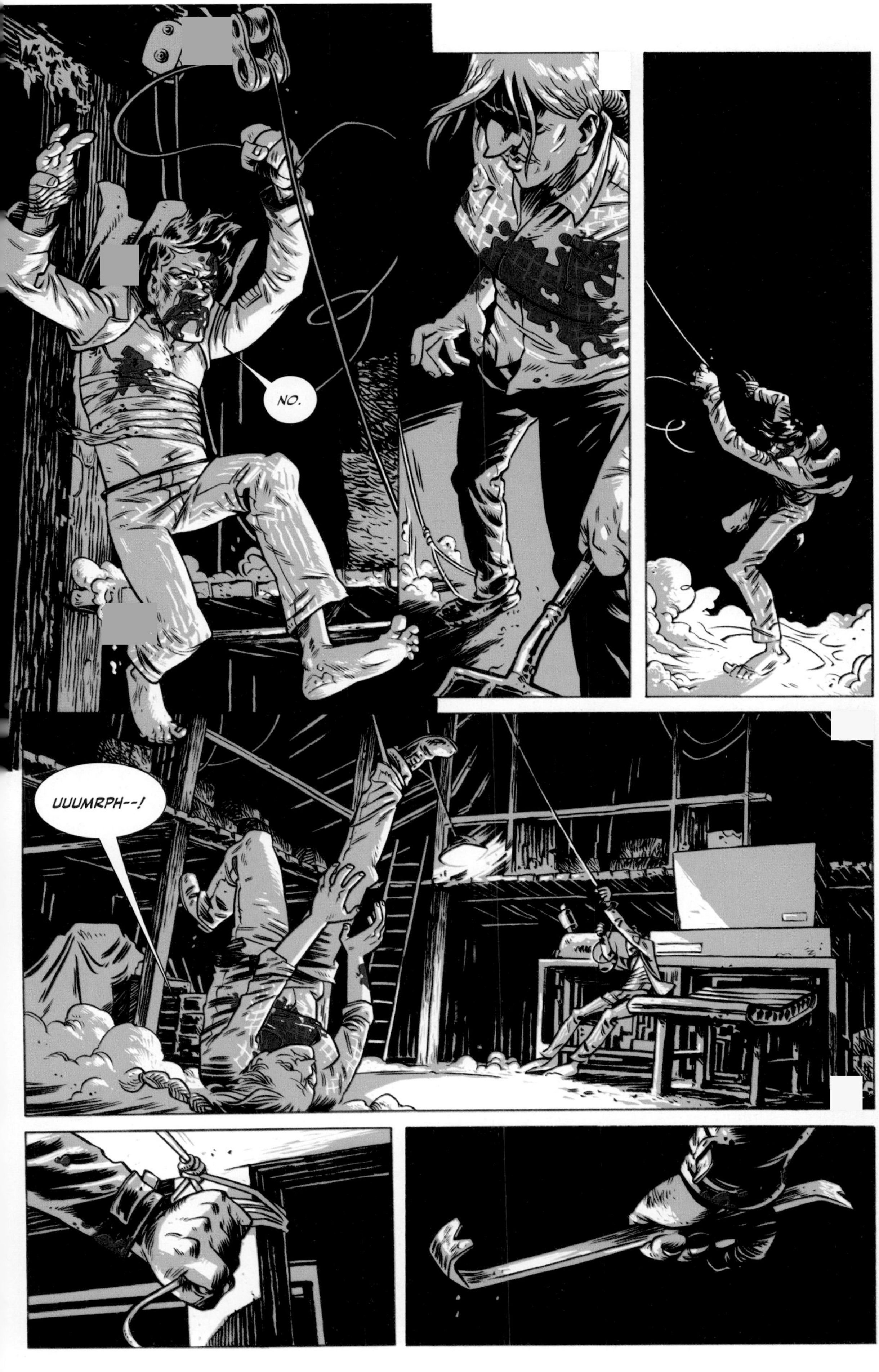
NO.
UUUMRPH--!

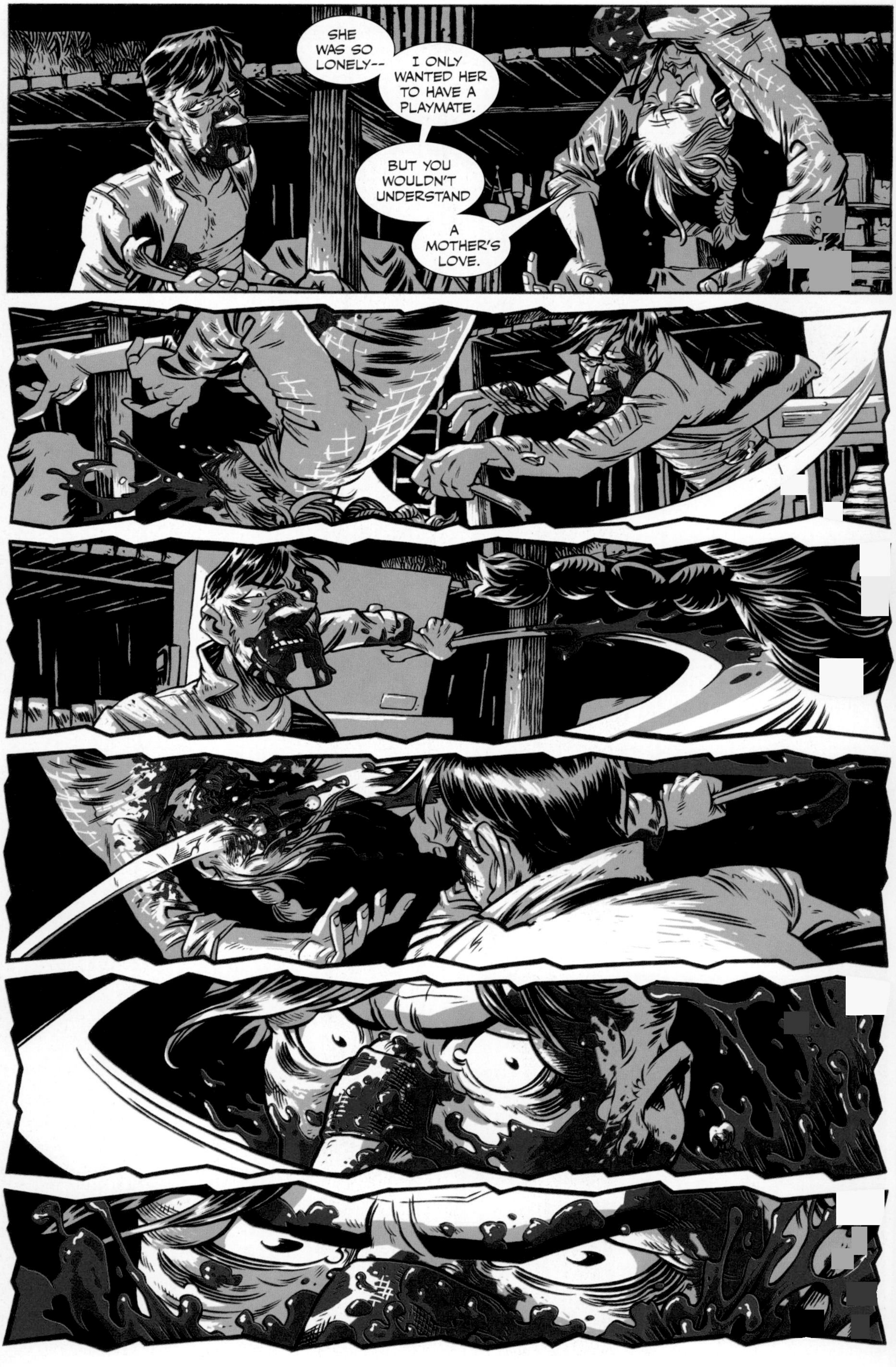
SHE WAS SO LONELY--
I ONLY WANTED HER TO HAVE A PLAYMATE.
BUT YOU WOULDN'T UNDERSTAND
A MOTHER'S LOVE.

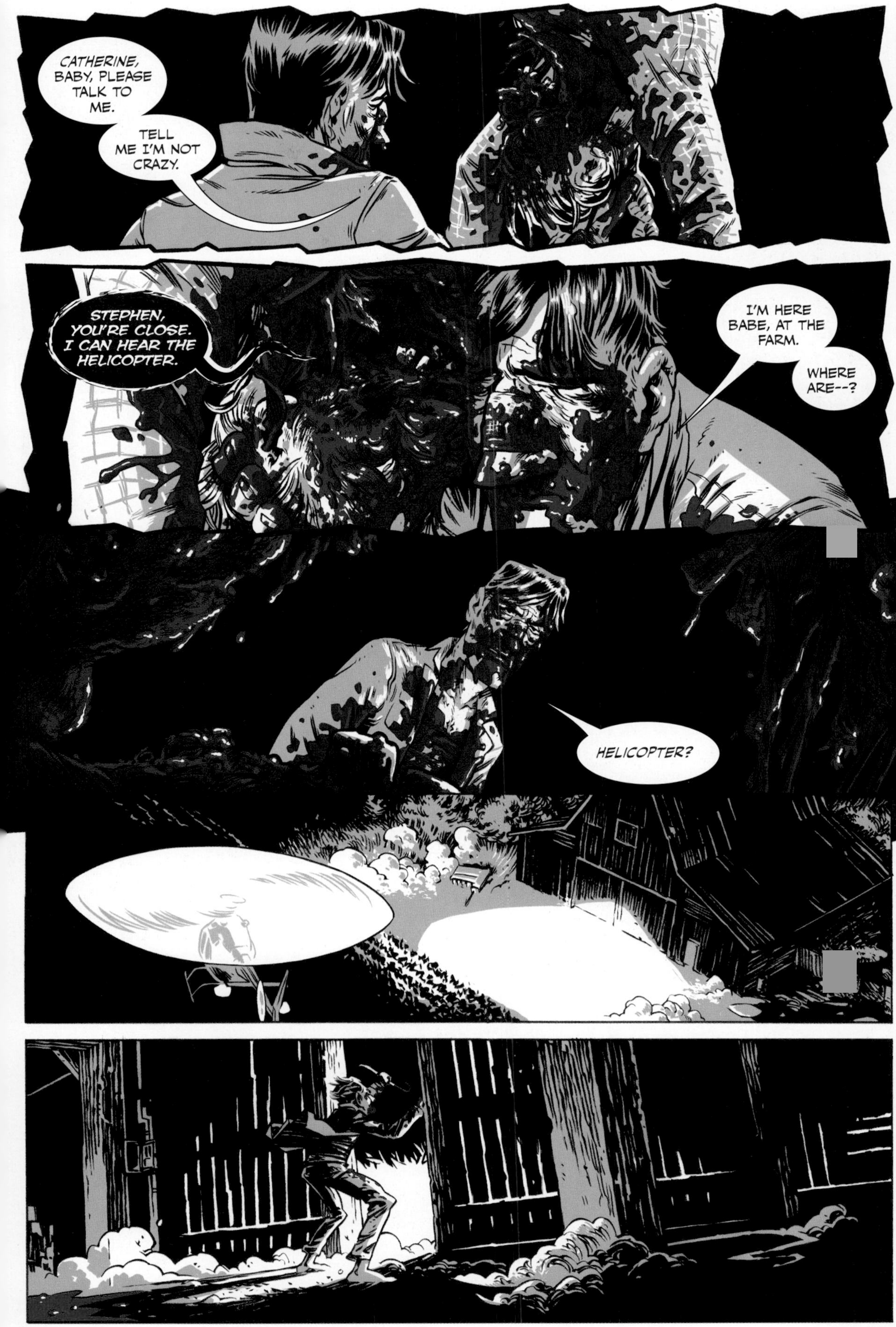
CATHERINE, BABY, PLEASE TALK TO ME.
TELL ME I'M NOT CRAZY.
STEPHEN, YOU'RE CLOSE. I CAN HEAR THE HELICOPTER.
I'M HERE BABE, AT THE FARM.
WHERE ARE--?
HELICOPTER?

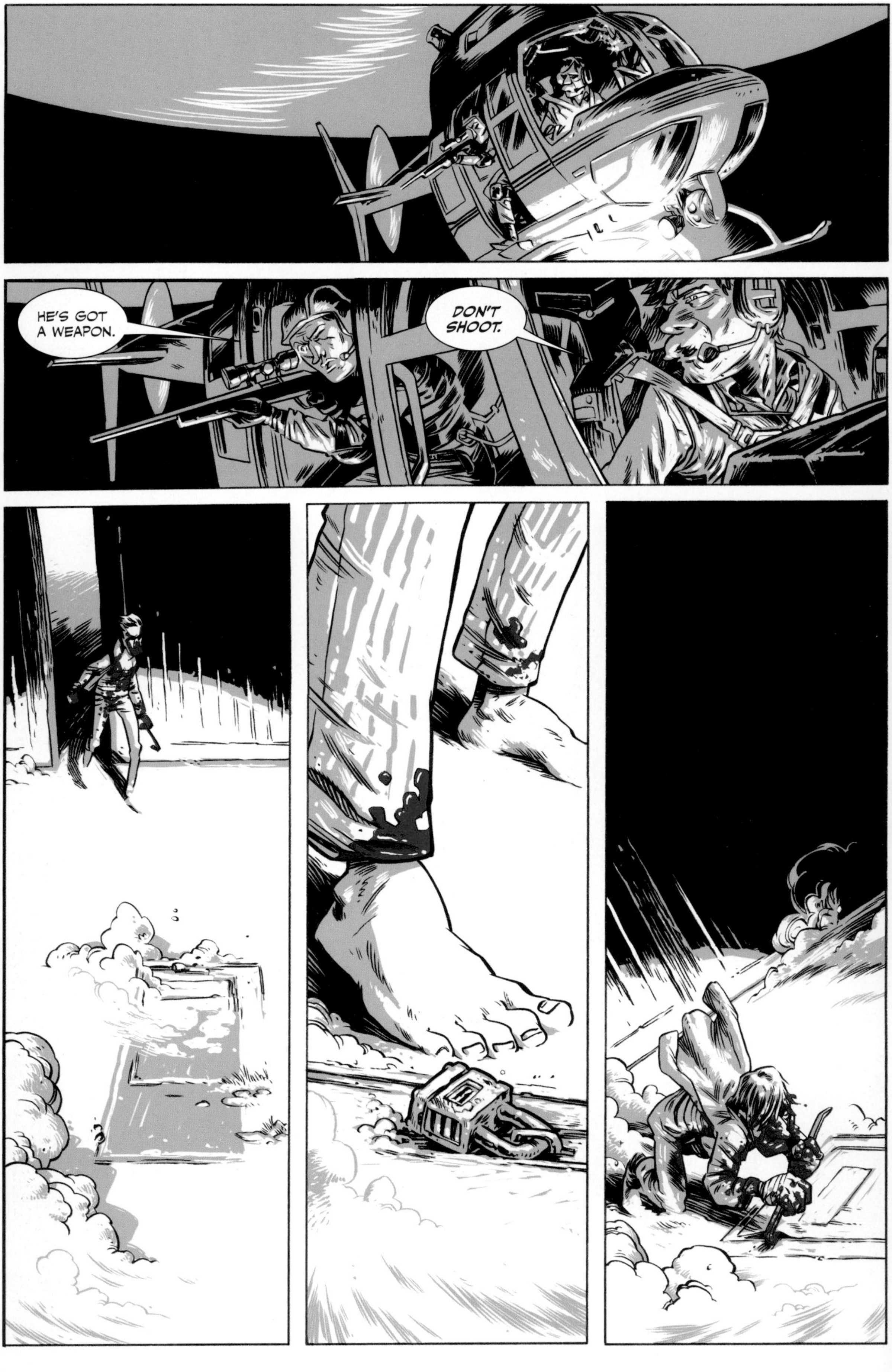
HE'S GOT A WEAPON.
DON'T SHOOT.

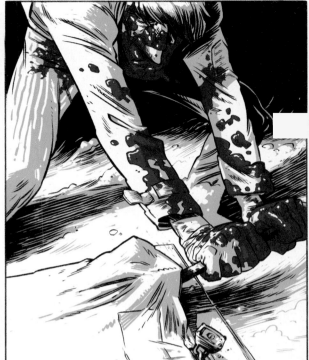

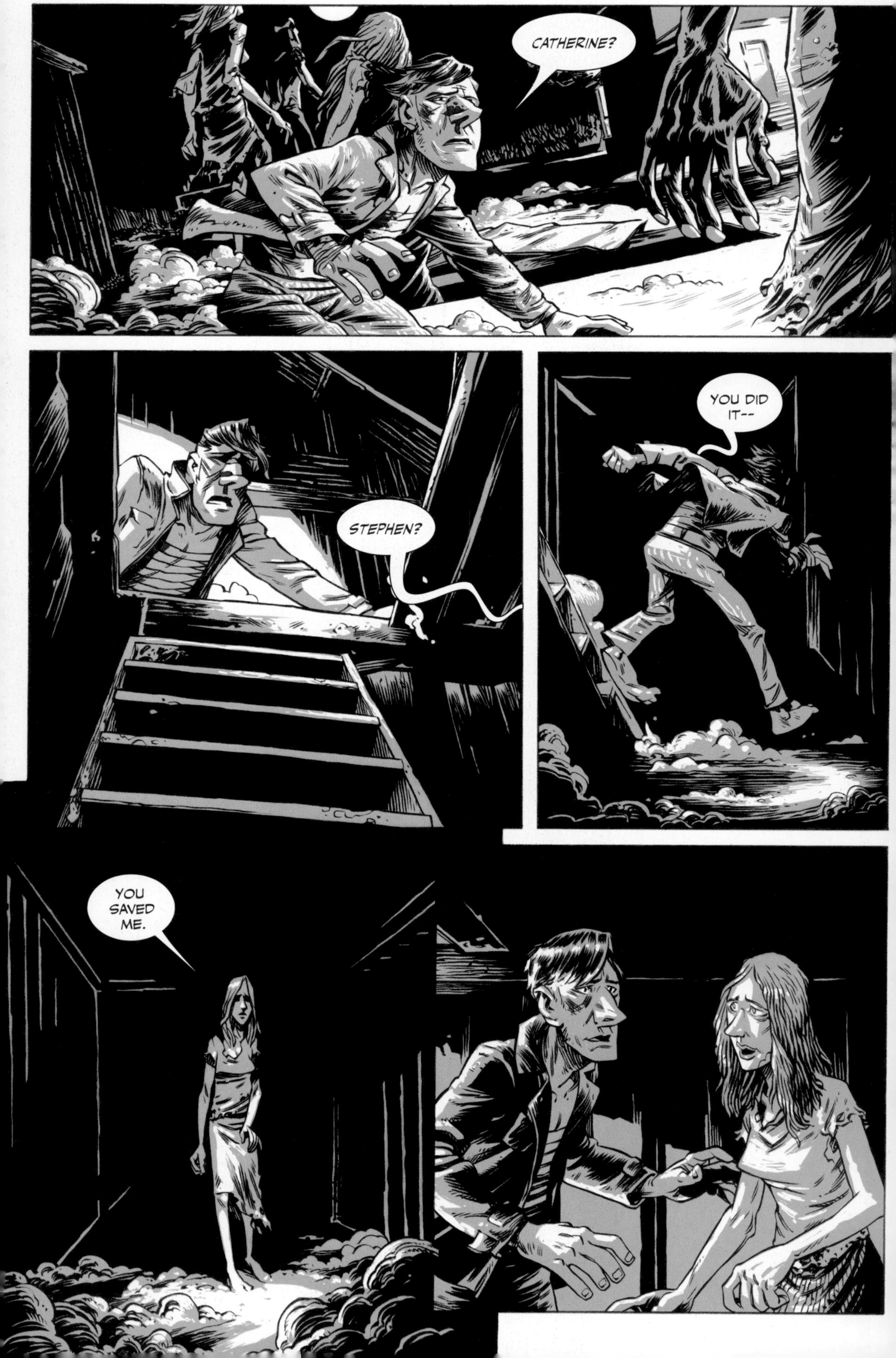
CATHERINE?
STEPHEN?
YOU DID IT--
YOU SAVED ME.

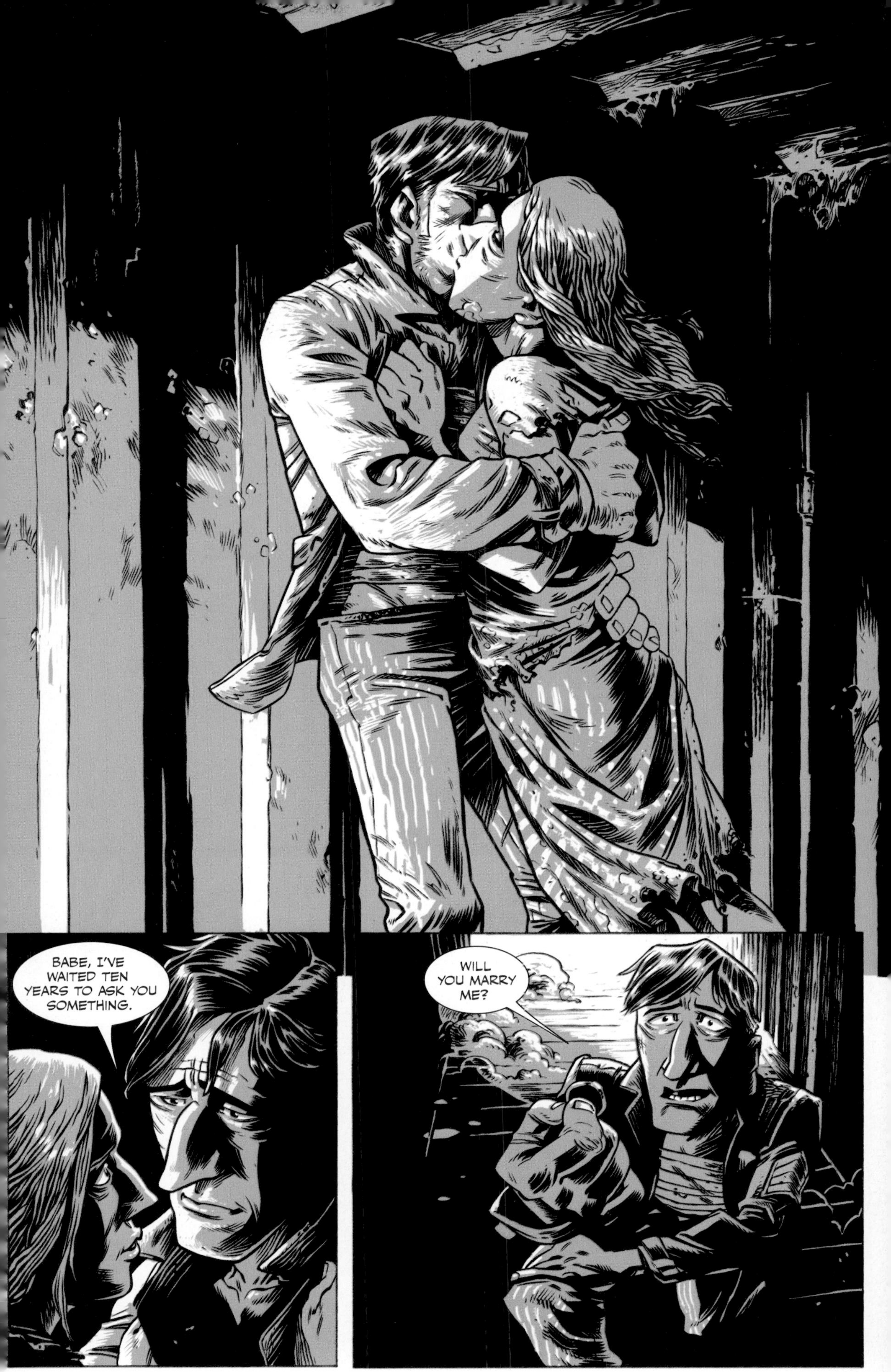
BABE, I'VE WAITED TEN YEARS TO ASK YOU SOMETHING.
WILL YOU MARRY ME?

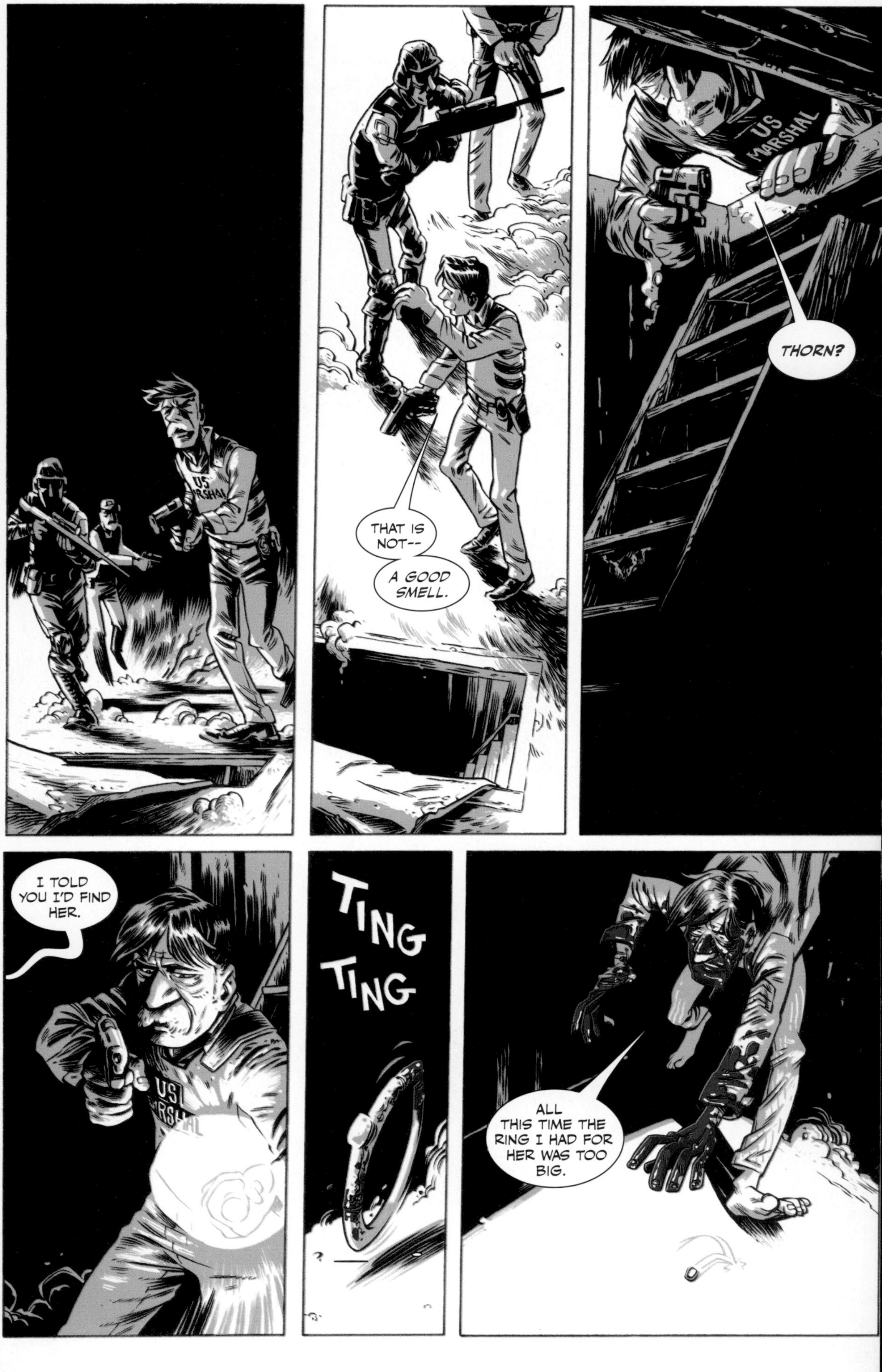
US MARSHAL
THAT IS NOT--
A GOOD SMELL.
US MARSHAL
THORN?
I TOLD YOU I'D FIND HER.
TING TING
ALL THIS TIME THE RING I HAD FOR HER WAS TOO BIG.

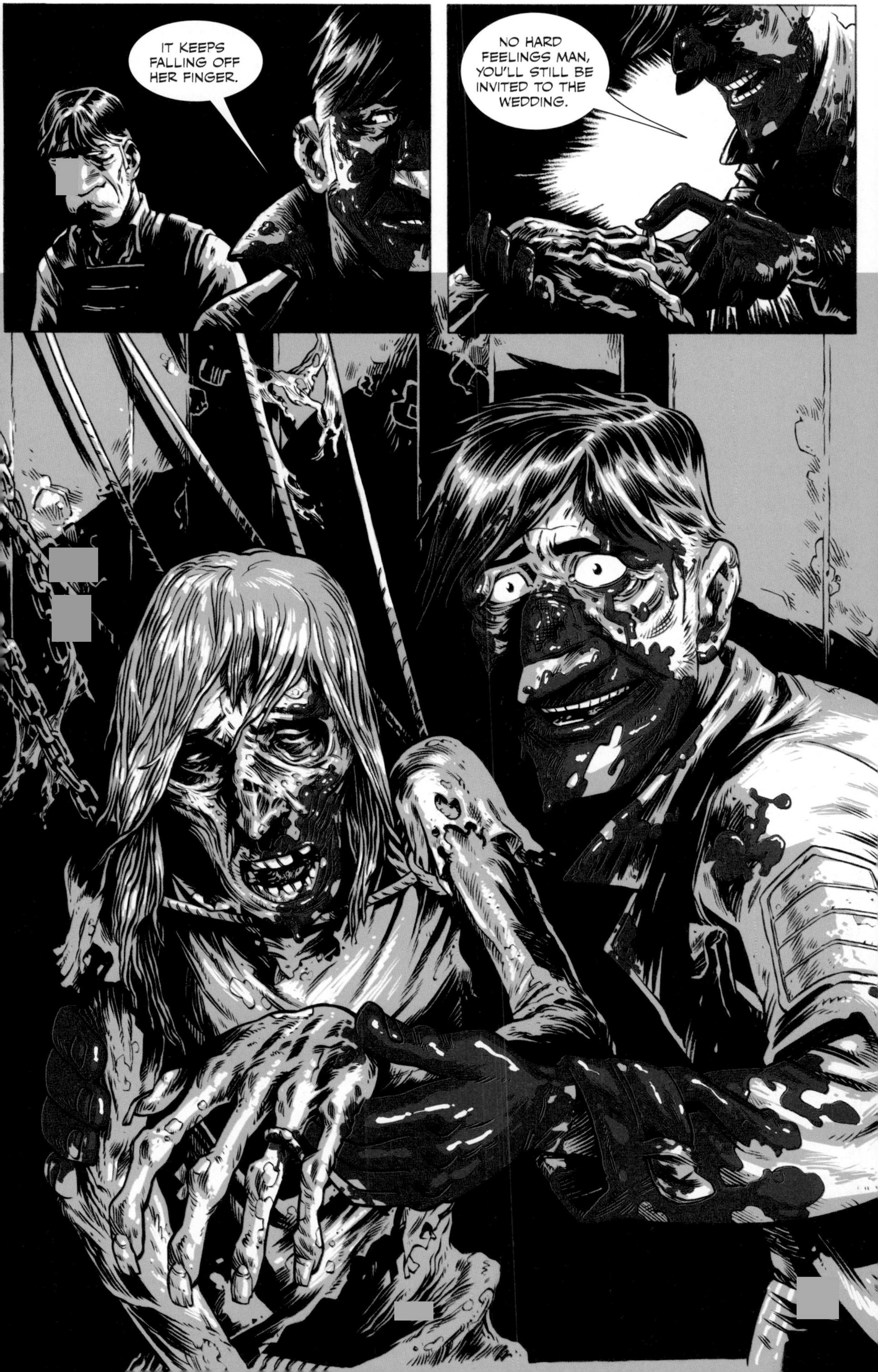
IT KEEPS FALLING OFF HER FINGER.
NO HARD FEELINGS MAN, YOU'LL STILL BE INVITED TO THE WEDDING.

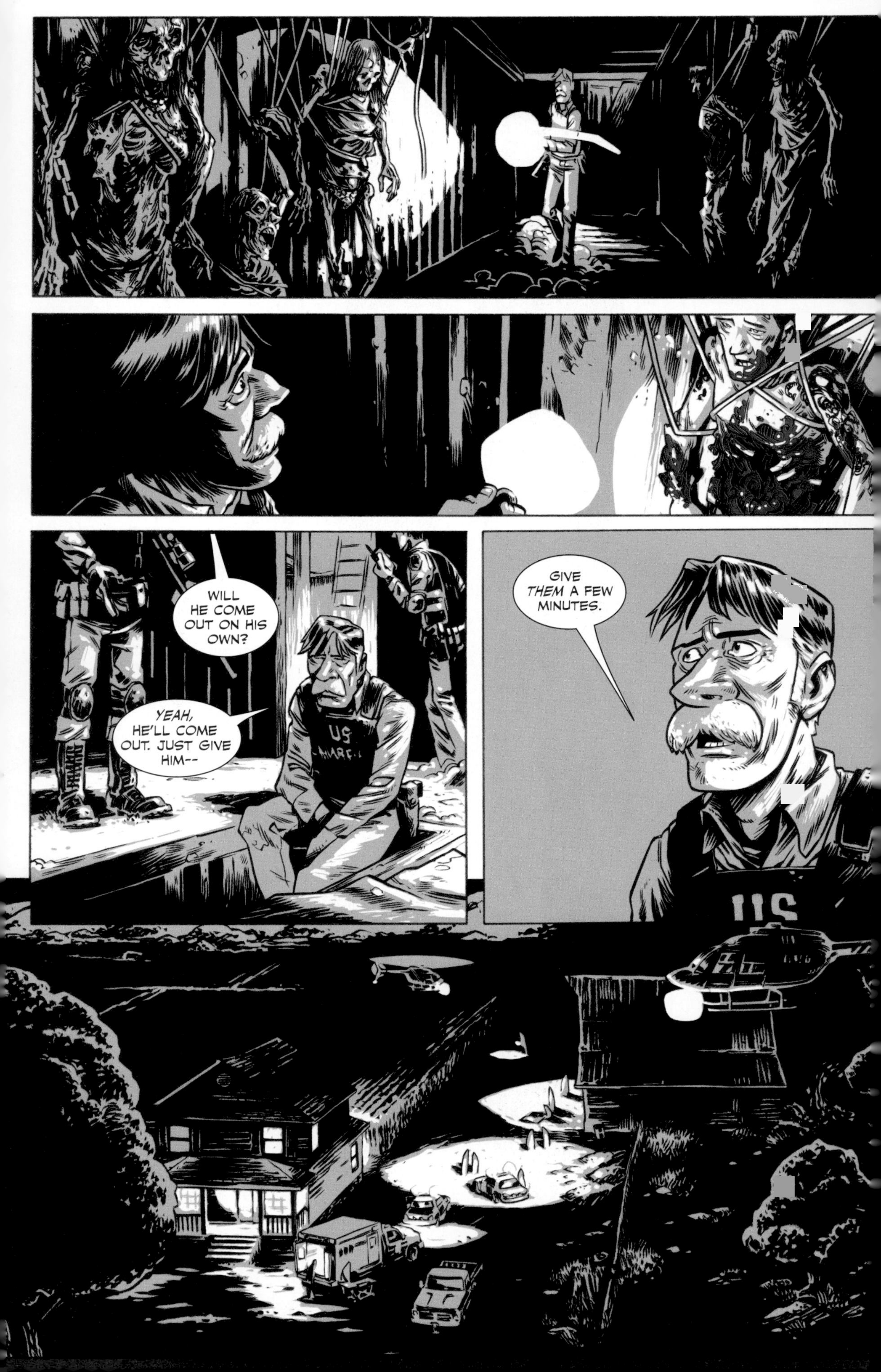
WILL HE COME OUT ON HIS OWN?
YEAH, HE'LL COME OUT. JUST GIVE HIM--
GIVE THEM A FEW MINUTES.

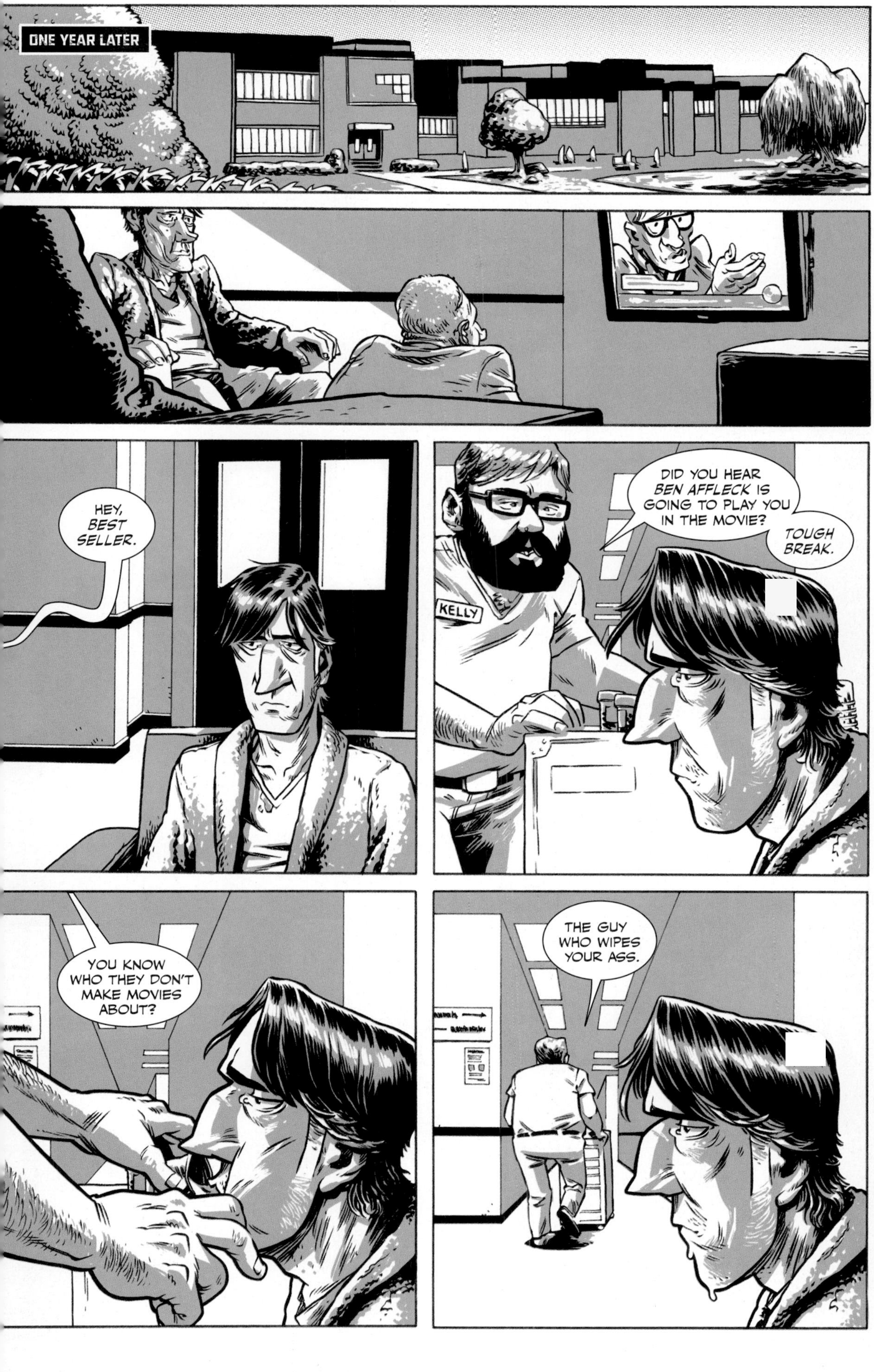

ONE YEAR LATER
HEY, BEST SELLER.
DID YOU HEAR BEN AFFLECK IS GOING TO PLAY YOU IN THE MOVIE?
TOUGH BREAK.
KELLY
YOU KNOW WHO THEY DON'T MAKE MOVIES ABOUT?
THE GUY WHO WIPES YOUR ASS.

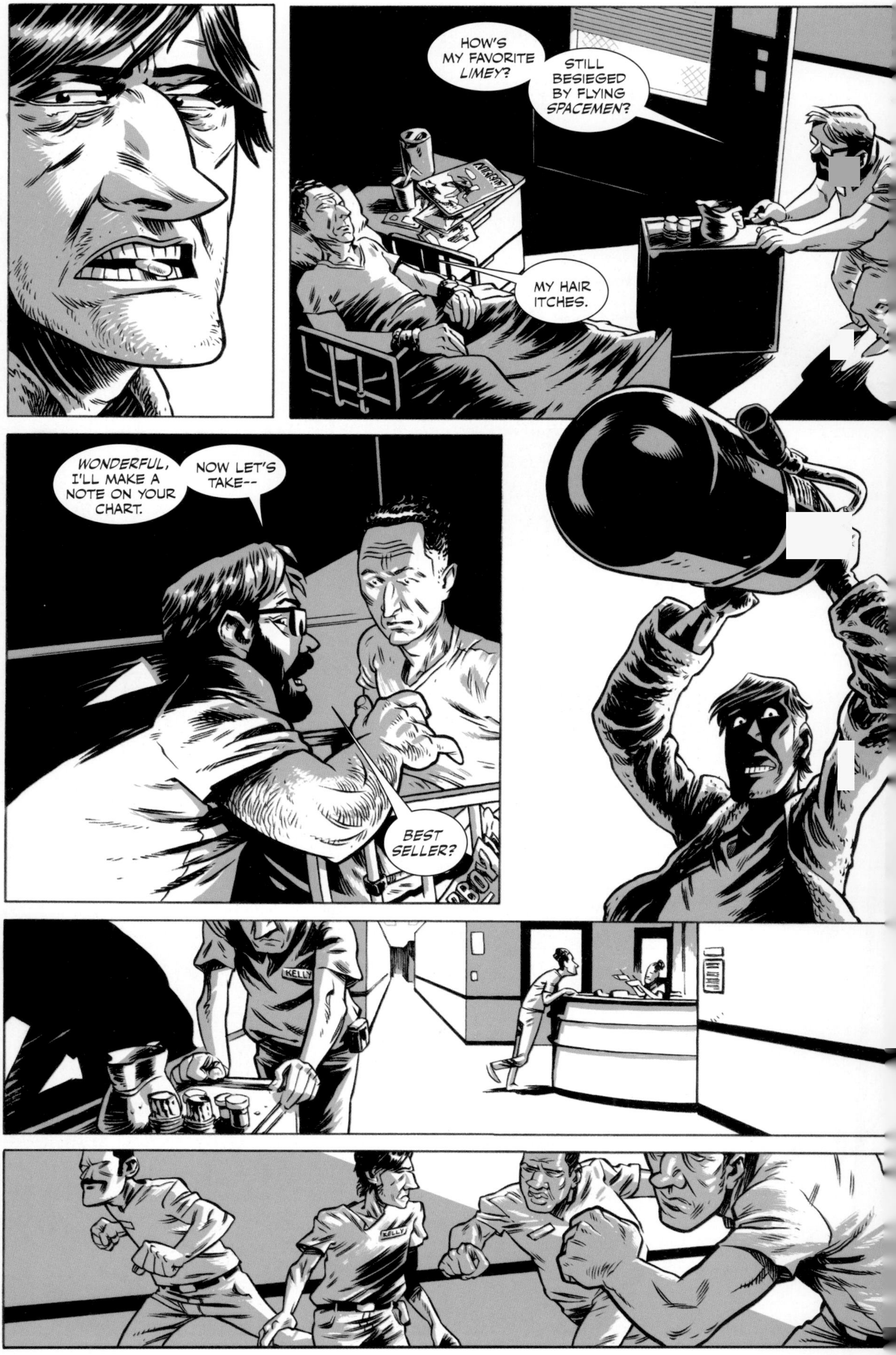
HOW'S MY FAVORITE *LIMEY?*
STILL BESIEGED BY FLYING *SPACEMEN?*
MY HAIR ITCHES.
WONDERFUL, I'LL MAKE A NOTE ON YOUR CHART.
NOW LET'S TAKE--
BEST SELLER?
KELLY

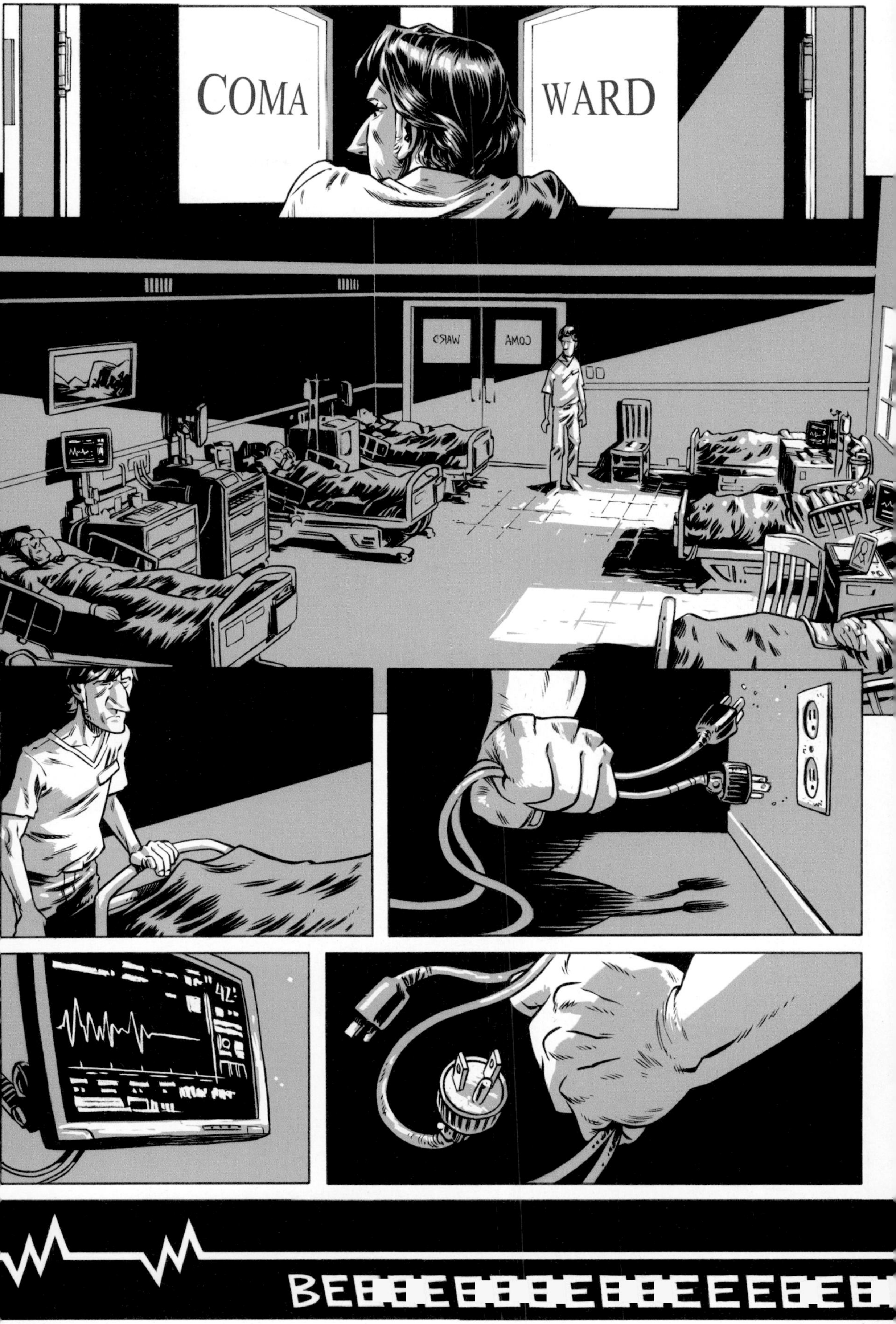
COMA
WARD
COMA
WARD
42
BEEEEEEEEEEEEEEEEE

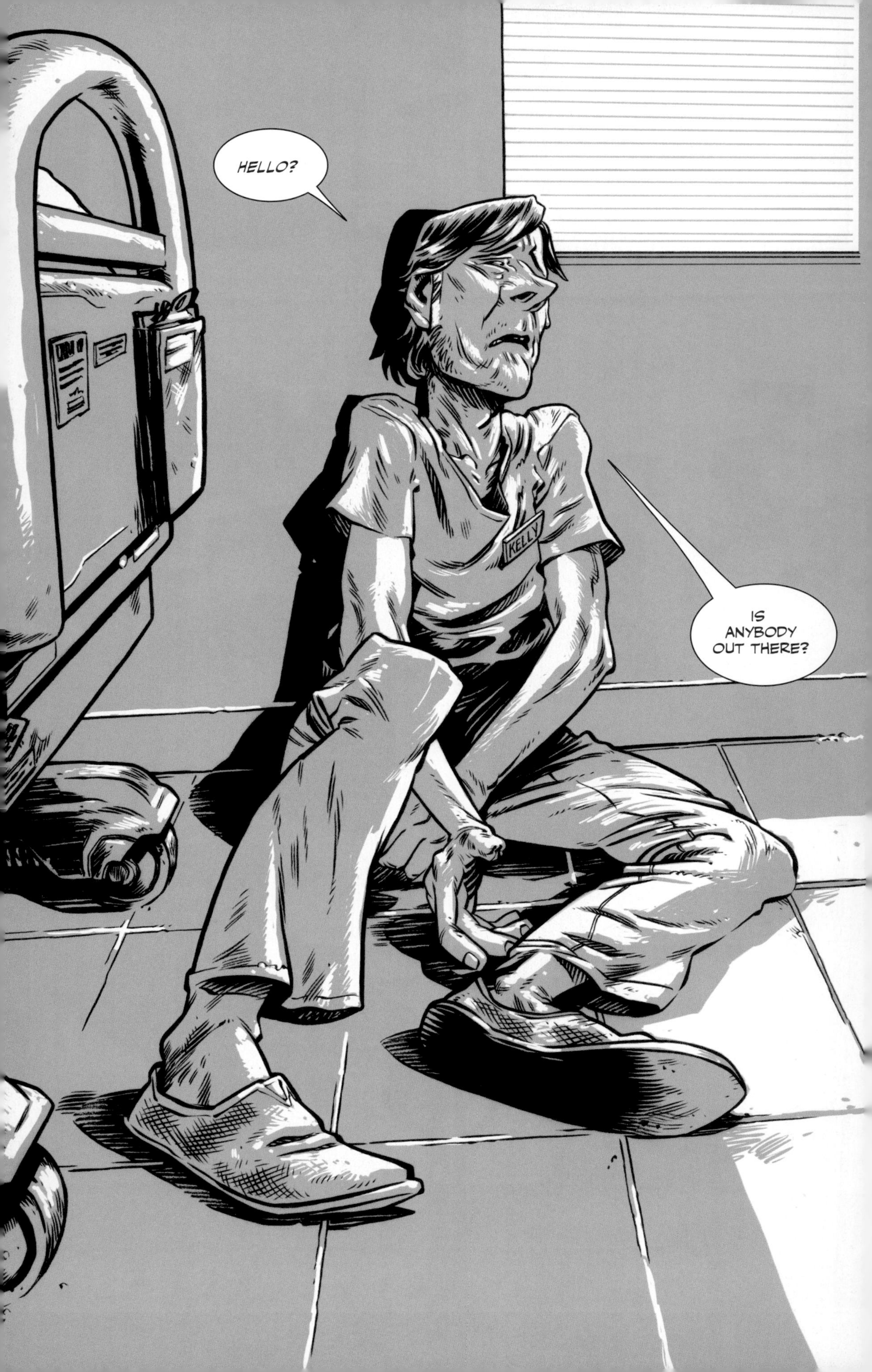
HELLO?
KELLY
IS ANYBODY OUT THERE?

The future hangs by a thread.

It was Christmas Eve of 2001 and I had recently signed my divorce papers. My childhood friend Stephenie suggested that, what with her girlfriend back on the East Coast, we might spend the holidays together. She spontaneously suggested we leave San Francisco and spend the day exploring the more rural North Bay area across the Golden Gate Bridge.

We hadn't made it a mile from her Potrero Hill apartment before her Saturn got a flat tire. Having no idea how to change a tire myself, I hovered uselessly while she rolled up her sleeves and put the spare tire on. Insisting our adventure could be salvaged, she called her girlfriend Allison and asked to borrow her pride and joy, a 62 Ford Ranchero. Allison loaned us the car, warning us that the gas gauge was unreliable.

To be on the safe side, we filled the tank and kept a fuzzy approximation of mileage and assumed consumption as we explored the less-populated other world across the bay. In a tiny town we stopped at a charming inn for dinner. We toasted to our long friendship and the future ahead. As we left the inn we passed a pair of sheriff's deputies on their way in for dinner.

Back in the car, we drove out into the night and had just started up a dark and curvy road when the car shuddered and died; we had critically underestimated the car's fuel efficiency. We let the car roll off the road and onto the shoulder. In near complete darkness, without cell reception, we weighed the options of abandoning the car and walking the two miles back to the inn or waiting for another car to pass. I joked that it reminded me of the opening scene of *An American Werewolf in London*.

Not long after, the lights of a large truck came up the hill behind us. Stephenie waved the driver down as he passed us. He was in his late forties, with dark, unkempt curly hair escaping from underneath his un-ironic trucker's cap. He was affable, if slightly annoyed that his holiday evening involved helping two stranded city kids. He offered to tow us to a gas station a few miles down the road, but first we had to get the car out of the shoulder we had let it slide back into.

He tied a length of rope between his back bumper and our front; he was concerned we might tear the bumper off of the Ranchero so it was suggested that I push while he gently pulled it onto the street. Once that was safely accomplished, he would stop, we would all get into his truck and continue on to the gas station.

As I strained to push the car off the road's shoulder his truck seemed to gently hover in place until it suddenly began to move, taking the car with it. Success! I stumbled forward, waiting for the caravan to come to a stop, then I realized that the vehicles were picking up speed. This man, whose name we never asked, was driving away with Stephenie and leaving me behind.

I broke into a run, hopelessly trying to catch up to the pair as they disappeared up the hill. The tiny red brake lights of the Ranchero danced back and forth in the darkness as Stephenie attempted to break free of the truck's control. Finally she pulled the Ranchero's emergency brake and the rope, connecting her car to his, snapped. His truck came to a stop shortly after. She undid the emergency brake and began to roll back down the road toward me. When our paths intersected she jumped out of the car and we desperatly latched onto each other. The man stood next to his running truck, lit in silhouette and just watched us.

After what seemed like an eternity he slowly got back in his truck and drove away, leaving us wondering if he was going to come back. Staying close the edge of the road and the relative safety of the woods we made our way back to the restaurant and to the deputies we had seen earlier. We told them our story and they took us to a private filling station and gave us enough gas to get back on the road. They didn't seem too concerned with our tale and wished us a happy holiday. We made it back to San Francisco in time for me to begin throwing up. The salad I had for dinner gave me the worst food poisoning I've ever had in my life.

The Ranchero was sold years ago. Stephenie and Allison, now married, live in Seattle with their adorable son. My wife and I recently had dinner with them and as I watched Stephenie interact with her son I couldn't help but think of everything that we almost lost on that dark country road over a decade ago. And somewhere out there is a man wondering what would have happened had he used a chain instead of a rope.

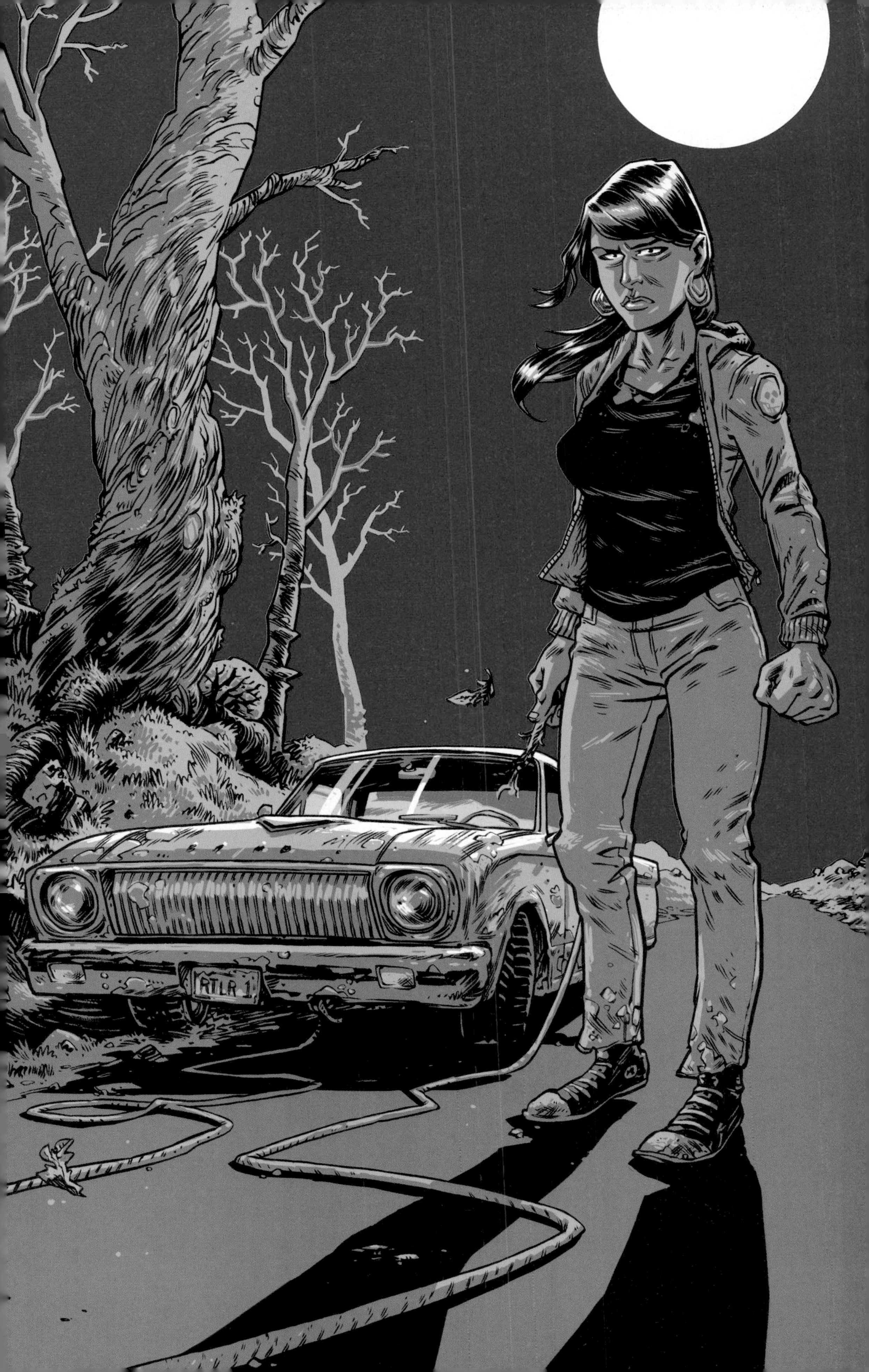
RTLR 1

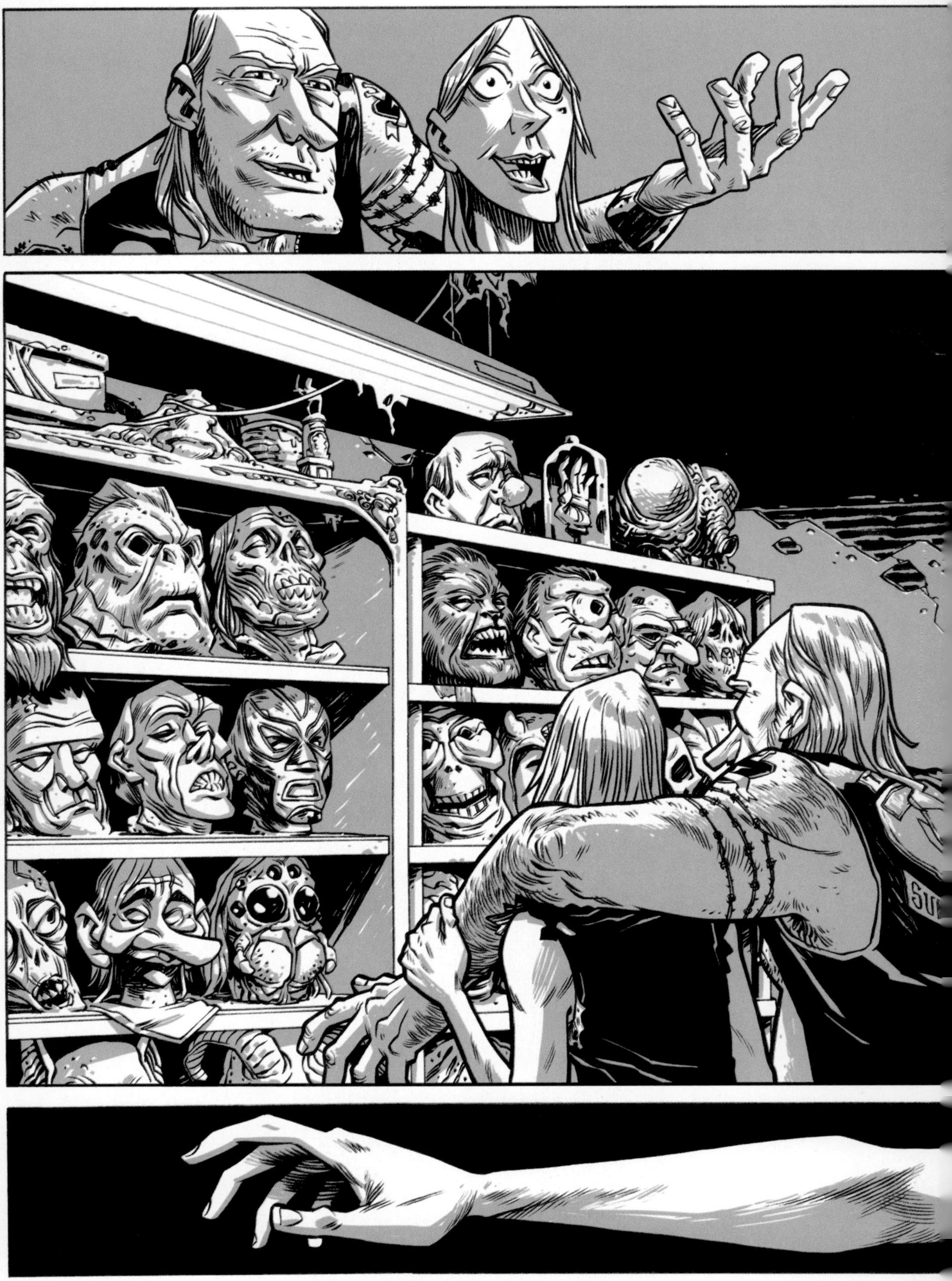

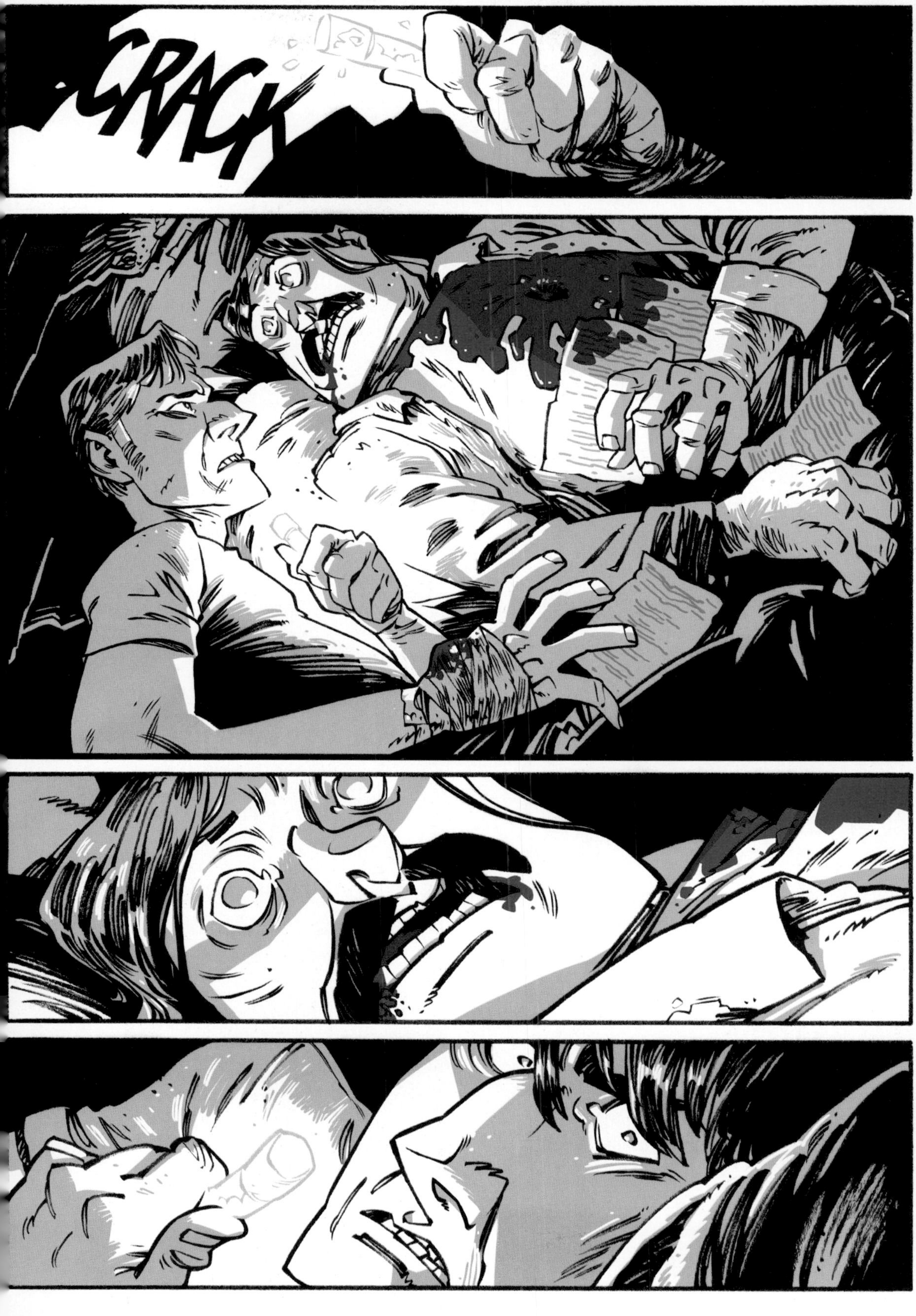
CRACK

Jason McNamara

Jason is a creative consultant and graphic novel author. He lives in Portland, Oregon with his wife, and two dogs, one of whom is so fat he keeps the house bolted down during earthquakes. Jason enjoys a stiff manhattan and wearing Michael Myers masks. He's very popular with the neighbors.

jason-mcnamara.com

@JasonMcNamara

Greg Hinkle

Greg is an artist, and co-creator of *AIRBOY* for Image Comics, living in Southern California with his wife and dog. He was last seen in rural Orange County. If found, approach with caution. Greg responds well to loud prog rock and assorted hard candies.

hinklehaus.com

@greg_hinkle

Joel Enos

JOEL would run the other way if someone tried to help him on the road, no matter how nice they seemed. He's a timid redhead who edits comics, books and manga and sometimes writes short stories that other people think are scary, though it's usually a surprise to him.

joelenos.com

@joelenos

SPECIAL THANKS to Todd Hellings, Stephenie Landry, Phoenix McNamara, Shay Lorseyedi, The Isotope Comic Lounge and everyone who supported the Rattler Kickstarter.